PELICAN BOO

Pelican Library of Business a
Advisory Editor: T.

MANAGEMENT DEC

THE ROLE OF FOl

James Morrell is Chairman of a firm of eco...
forecasting specialists and has spent most of his working car...
in business forecasting. Born in 1923, he was educated at Christ's
Hospital and, after war service in the R.A.F., at Ruskin College
and Wadham College, Oxford, where he graduated in philosophy, politics and economics. After working for Ford on project
analysis, he joined a leading firm of stockbrokers as an investment analyst, and spent ten years in the City before forming his
own company. Since 1960 he has headed a team of forecasters
drawn from different firms in industry and commerce, and the
firm's monthly service *Framework Forecasts* is widely circulated
in business and government circles. Economic Editor of *Management Today*, he writes and lectures widely on various business
subjects, is responsible for the *Sunday Telegraph* 'Business Forecast' and is adviser to a number of leading industrial companies,
stockbrokers and merchant banks. He is the author of *Business
Forecasting for Finance and Industry*, and *The Economic Background to Investment*, a study guide for the Society of Investment
Analysts (pending publication), and is Visiting Professor in Business Finance at the University of Bradford.

MANAGEMENT DECISIONS AND THE ROLE OF FORECASTING

Edited by James Morrell

PENGUIN BOOKS

Penguin Books Ltd, Harmondsworth, Middlesex, England
Penguin Books Inc., 7110 Ambassador Road, Baltimore, Maryland 21207, U.S.A.
Penguin Books Australia Ltd, Ringwood, Victoria, Australia

—

First published 1972

—

—

Made and printed in Great Britain
by Richard Clay (The Chaucer Press), Ltd,
Bungay, Suffolk
Set in Monotype Times

Contents

CONTENTS

List of Charts

List of Tables

Foreword

The object of this book is to present the lessons learned from professional experience by members of a team of forecasters. The authors are drawn from the group of economists who collaborate with James Morrell & Associates Ltd to produce the regular monthly forecasts of the British economy, year by year for five years ahead, under the title *Framework Forecasts*. From these overall forecasts specific industrial and company forecasts are constructed.

The problems encountered have a general application for all forecasters, and since every decision in life rests upon a forecast, it will be seen that the subject has a wide application. Some of the subjects treated have a specialist rather than a general interest, and these have been included to give some idea of the subject as a whole.

There are two particular aspects of forecasting which need to be stressed and which come to the fore in nearly every chapter. The first is that very few series of historical figures can be taken without question as an exact reflection of the truth. Secondly, a high degree of judgement is required in all forecasting work and in the interpretation of the forecasts. Although the book describes a system of forecasting and a scientific approach to the subject, it is still the case that the use of algebraic relationships can give a spurious impression of exactness and reliability. The problems of forecasting lie mainly in these two areas: the need for more exact measurement and the need for sound judgement and common sense.

February 1971   James Morrell

Acknowledgements

The contributors to this book are drawn from a team of forecasters who collaborate to construct regular forecasts of the economy as a whole, and of industrial sectors. The experience of the team has been built up over more than ten years, and the systems and methods outlined in the following chapters owe a great deal to the patient efforts and research of the various members through the 1960s.

In compiling this work I am indebted to the members of the team, a number of whom are not represented among the authors. The responsibility for the editorial viewpoint, however, and for any flaws in argument or presentation, must rest with me.

My particular thanks are due to Margaret Nickolls for the painstaking typing of text and tables, to Yvonne Laugharne for the charts and to Roger Brookhouse for assistance with reading and correction.

J. M.

CHAPTER 1

The Role of Forecasting in Business

BY JAMES MORRELL

Every decision rests upon a forecast. Pharaoh's decision to stock-pile wheat was taken because of a forecast that seven fat years would be followed by seven lean years. The Bible contains many instances of prophesies which were handsomely fulfilled. History, on the other hand, provides us with countless examples of forecasts which went well wide of the mark. The waves did not roll back for King Canute.

DECISIONS NEED FORECASTS

We know from everyday experience that many of the forecasts we are obliged to make will prove mistaken. Yet this does not invalidate the case for basing decisions upon forecasts. Forecasting is a dangerous, though necessary, business. Significant failures, such as the inability to meet the 4% target growth rate set in the National Plan, tend to blur the discussion of the role of forecasts. Similarly, the use of profit forecasts in takeover battles has tended to discredit the use of forecasts in certain situations. Nevertheless, the fact remains that just as we make a tentative weather forecast in deciding what to wear out of doors, so we are obliged to formulate forecasts of some kind or other as a means of determining a future course of action.

Big decisions require big forecasts. Since it is known just how uncertain the future can be, where a great deal hangs upon a decision, then it will be prudent to gather information and construct alternative estimates of differing possibilities, using differing hypotheses.

OBJECT OF FORECASTING

The object of forecasting may be summarized as:

'to minimize uncertainty and to identify and evaluate risk'.

Since decisions are based on forecasts, the object of the forecaster must be to help the decision-taker to adopt the best solution. Faced with doubts about the future and a number of unknown factors the decision-taker requires as much information about the future as is possible. In other words he needs to have his doubts and uncertainties reduced.

Because of the varying degrees of uncertainty he will also need to know how much risk attaches to alternative decisions. This too is a function of forecasting, and the forecaster will need to identify those factors which are more uncertain than others and also to point out the consequences of a mistaken forecast. The more uncertain the prediction, the greater the risk entailed in any decision based on such a set of forecasts.

The essential fact to keep in mind is that all decisions, however minor, are about the future and rest upon a view of the future. For these reasons, the problem of forecasting needs to be approached in as scientific a manner as possible. Precise techniques need to be adopted. Yet it is as well at the outset to keep in mind the imprecise nature of many of the subjects to be forecast. Not only is our knowledge of the future extremely limited and uncertain, but our knowledge of the past is – to say the least – imprecise. There are few dependable sets of statistics describing the past and the margin of error in many of the series in common use is so wide as to invalidate many forms of statistical analysis. Savings data is a notable case in point and we do not know what the true trend in personal savings is in Britain.

Thus, for the present at any rate, forecasting must continue to be regarded very much as an art and not a science. Subjective judgement will be called into play at many stages in the construction of a view of the future. For this reason, it is essential for the forecaster, in whatever field, to have some sense of history and of time.

Yet, the fact that forecasting is an art rather than a science does not mean that scientific methods should not be employed. Uncertainty must be tackled in as scientific a manner as is possible. If uncertainty is to be minimized and risk adequately evaluated, then a disciplined approach is essential.

There is a wide range of business management problems connected with, or dependent upon, forecasting. For example, no business plan is feasible without a set of forecasts outlining the environment in which the business is expected to operate. Neither is a budget feasible without forecasts and in both these fields, forecasts of sales, of each component of costs, of resource requirements and of prices, are essential. Project development hinges on forecasts. The exploitation of research must rest on forecasts. It will be seen, therefore, that a large part of management activity calls for research work and forecasting work of one kind or another.

SYSTEMATIC FORECASTING

Throughout life each man is his own forecaster. So it tends to be in business. Yet the instances where it will be necessary to set down the forecasts in a systematic fashion are increasing. This is not to say that detailed and lengthy forecasts have to be supplied for every decision and every problem. It is as well to keep in mind that forecasting is an exacting task which will absorb a considerable proportion of management time. Sophisticated forecasts must be constructed only where the forecasts will make a distinct contribution towards the problem in hand. In other words, there should be a return on a piece of forecasting as with any other form of investment in managerial time. Sledgehammers must not be used to crack nuts.

The role of forecasting in the firm is to direct attention towards alternative courses of action and to bring out the degree of certainty or uncertainty attached to the various alternatives. Only in this way is it possible to identify the risks entailed. Once this has been done, techniques are available which enable us to measure the various risks. Decisions can then be based upon well-founded risk analysis.

It is sometimes overlooked that a common body of forecasting will serve a number of purposes within the firm. The large corporation, organized in separate divisions, may well find that each division needs to forecast some similar, common subjects. In this kind of organization forecasting may be regarded as a function conducted for the business as a whole. A set of forecasts for the entire business, in which the parts are consistent with the sum, should be agreed centrally and then made available for specialist departments within the firm. Ideally, therefore, forecasting effort should be directed centrally and come under the control of the chief executive's office.

LONG-TERM VIEW

The forecasting function falls into two main parts. The planner is required to map out the course of the business over a number of years. His starting point is a set of objectives. These may be expressed either as a target level of earnings per share, a target return on capital or a target sales figure. The objectives may well be set for a horizon year, perhaps five years ahead. Forecasting to meet these requirements entails a careful study of previous trends and the analysis of the markets in which the business is likely to operate. Certain assumptions will be required about society at large, such as changing tastes and fashions, changes in the level of purchasing power and changes in population structures. Changes in working practices will need to be analysed and allowances made for changing technology.

These considerations can be judged only against a long time scale. In general the first attempt to construct a forecast along these lines will involve the identification of underlying trends and the estimation of the likely trend level to be attained at the end of the forecast period. Yet this can only be a beginning in the forecasting work, for, in many instances, straight-line trend projections will be quite inadequate for planning purposes.

CYCLICAL VIEW

For example, in a cyclical industry, if a forecast is made starting from the top of one business cycle and the trend is correctly forecast to the top of the next business cycle, a plan based on such a forecast could have disastrous results. The fact that the cycle begins to move downwards at the outset of the plan period means that there will be a shortfall of profits and cash flow in the early years of the period. Thus, the cash resources will not be available to meet the planned investment in new productive resources. This is illustrated in Chart 1.

Chart 1

A PROFIT FORECAST

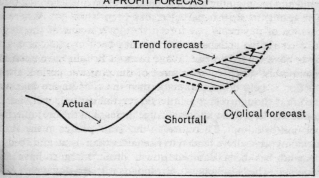

In a cyclical business, therefore, it is necessary to construct a forecast for the plan period year by year. In practice the great majority of businesses have some kind of cyclical experience. When profits are plotted out year by year over a ten-year period a cyclical pattern becomes apparent and it is quite exceptional for a business not to display such characteristics. Even a rapidly growing and successful business still shows signs of a cyclical fluctuation about its strongly rising trend. It is not only those industries most dependent upon credit conditions which display cyclical patterns. House-building, motor vehicles and other consumer durables are subject to sharp swings in demand owing to changes in the availability of bank credit and hire-purchase finance. Capital goods industries are subject to sharp cyclical fluctuations in demand as a result of fluctuations in profits in general. Investment, by and large, is financed from profits and swings in profitability inevitably lead to swings in the pattern of investment spending.

CYCLICAL CAUSES

The swings in profitability are due, for the most part, to economic policies aimed at minimizing unemployment on the one hand and maintaining a proper balance of payments on the other. The result, in British parlance, has been 'stop–go'. Where the balance of payments has forced the government of the day to take restrictive action, production has been checked and wage costs have tended to rise. Wage rates in Britain have risen at a remarkably steady rate for most of the post-war period. If production is held down and static then the chances are that wage incomes, though rising a little slower than usual, will rise fast enough to lead to an above-average increase in the cost of labour per unit of output. Therefore, in the 'stop' phases in the British economy, costs have tended to rise faster than usual and, because demand has been damped down, profit margins have been squeezed. The 'stop' phase corresponds with the down part of the profit cycle.

From this simple analysis, it will be seen that cyclical experience is not limited to those industries such as the capital goods suppliers, the building industry and the durable goods trades. For these reasons forecasting needs to be carried through on a year-by-year basis for the purposes of planning. In some instances much more detailed forecasting will be required for short periods. Sales and marketing strategies may need to be adapted to rapidly changing conditions. Successful stock control will depend upon having forecasts on a quarter-to-quarter, or even a month-to-month, basis. So that, within the framework of year-to-year forecasts, most businesses will find it useful to construct quarter-by-quarter forecasts for a year or so ahead.

MAJOR TRENDS AND CERTAINTIES

In most cases, when the analyst is confronted with the need to forecast for some years to come, the range of possibilities appears bewildering. This need not be so, provided two rules are kept in view. In the first place, major trends change only gradually. Thus, any proposition which shows a sharp change in trend must be regarded as suspect. Secondly, the first step in the forecast must be to seek for certainties. There will inevitably be a number of major factors for the forecast period which can be regarded as near certainties. These certainties will exclude certain other possibilities and permutations. For example, the decimalization of the British currency was a certainty for several years. Similarly, metrication was a certainty, since both these changes were subject to legislation and a future conversion date laid down. In another field, the supply of labour in Britain can be regarded as a near certainty. Since the potential labour force for the next few years is already born and in existence, we can measure with a high degree of accuracy the available supply of male and female labour for the forecast period. Likewise, we can assert with confidence what the age structure of the population will be and this will have some bearing on marketing for the plan period. In addition, the structure of the population will largely determine the level of spending on such things as the educational services, the health services and other social services.

It is also possible to make realistic assumptions about the pace of change in such things as taxation and legislative matters. There is only a limited amount of change which can be brought about in any one year or period of years in the tax system. Not only are there limitations on parliamentary time, but there are also severe limitations imposed by the physical ability of the administrative machine to accommodate major changes. Thus, it would be unwise to postulate a whole range of major tax changes within the life of a single parliament. A social security tax, a wealth tax, a change to value-added taxation, a reform of income tax and surtax would be impossible to accommodate within the time span of a few years. One major change in the tax system every two years would appear to be the utmost limit of reform. The prospective changes outlined in the Green Papers accompanying the 1971 Budget were exceptional.

SIGNIFICANT FACTORS

When the certainties have been set down for the forecast period, the scope for change in the things that matter to the business can be seen in a clearer perspective. Forecasting effort needs to be concentrated on those subjects which are of real importance to the business. A sensitivity analysis of different aspects of the environment would reveal large areas which are a matter of indifference to the individual business. That is to say, there will be a number of areas where a greater or lesser rate of change will have no measurable impact upon the individual firm. On the other hand, there may be one or two areas where even a small rate of change could have a critical bearing on the business. These are subjects to be identified and to be studied in depth.

INFORMATION

Forecasting for the business is impossible unless the business has established a clear system of recording information about its own history and experience. Most businesses contain a wealth of useful statistical material in their records. However, a majority of these have failed to marshal this information in a usable form. The forecaster must have full access to sales records, organized product by product, and in time intervals which facilitate comparison with external industrial and national yardsticks. The forecaster must also have access to cost data which all too often are kept a closely guarded secret.

This kind of background information is essential if an analysis is to be made relating the experience of the business to the outside world. The cyclical experience of the business can only be linked to some external indicator provided full information is available and for frequent time periods. Special factors need to be recorded, such as the distortion of deliveries due to a strike, or a change of model on the part of a competitor. Problems due to the start-up of a new plant or distortions due to special advertising campaigns all need to be recorded exactly, so that the business history can be explained and related to more general experience.

KEY RELATIONSHIPS

The forecaster will be concerned to calculate and establish some kind of relationship between the business and the outside world and to find a leading indicator. For many firms business profits are a leading indicator for future demand. There is an

Chart 2

PROFITS AND INVESTMENT

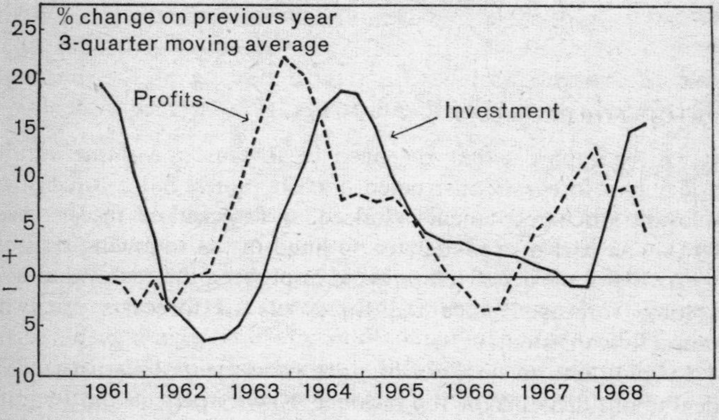

almost exact time-lag of one year between changes in company cash flow and private spending on plant and machinery (see Chart 2). In broad terms this time-lag between profit and investment is an invaluable warning tool, provided that changes in profits can be adequately detected. This is the kind of relationship we need to establish in order to refine short-term forecasts for the individual business.

FORECASTS IN CASH VALUES

The previous example illustrates another facet of business forecasting, namely the dependence of demand and production on cash. Every spending decision is dependent upon the availability of cash. This is as true for business as for the individual customer, or indeed for the government. In a sense, therefore, all forecasting problems in business should first be looked at from the cash end of the telescope.

Volume forecasts, such as the number of tons of steel of a particular grade required for shipbuilding, will depend upon a forecast of shipbuilding tonnage. This, however, will depend upon the capacity of the shipping industry to order new ships, and this may depend upon the growth in international trade and in spending. Thus, in the final analysis an income consideration underlies the volume forecast and the analysis will need to begin from a forecast of the final user's spending power.

PRICE FORECASTS

It will be apparent that the need to forecast a volume entails not only a forecast constructed in cash values, but a forecast of relevant price movements. Indeed, a forecast of prices – preferably as part of a model, as outlined in the following chapter – provides a means of refining and improving the cash value and volume forecasts, since the three sets of forecasts must be mutually consistent.

In addition, an analysis of price movements tells us a great deal about demand for the product. Newspaper sales in Britain, for example, are virtually static, yet the industry has succeeded in pushing its prices up faster than average prices. The evidence suggests that the demand for newspapers is relatively static and inelastic; that is to say, it is not particularly sensitive to price changes, although price increases do tend to reduce sales to a small extent. By comparing the price behaviour of a product with the average price movements in the economy over the same period, a useful piece of information about both past and future demand can be obtained.

FINANCIAL FORECASTS

Forecasting has a vital role in the evaluation of a business, whether for purposes of acquisition or merger, or for comparison of one firm with another, or for evaluating another firm's future demand and capacity to pay a particular contract price. The study of operating ratios, which are in the main financial ratios, for a particular business is essential to the task of forecasting future profits and rates of profitability.

In addition, the evaluation of a business for the purpose of security analysis is based upon the same methods of financial forecasting as used for acquisition analysis. In this respect the industrial analyst and the financial analyst have a common objective and a need for a common discipline. In both cases the consequences of a wrong decision can be extremely costly and the underlying forecast is therefore of the greatest importance.

THE USES OF FORECASTS

To sum up, the role of the forecast in business is to inform decision taking at various levels and functions. The major business areas where forecasts are indispensable are:

a) environmental analysis;
b) sales and pricing;
c) planning;
d) budgeting and costs;
e) project analysis;
f) research and development;
g) acquisition and mergers;
h) inter-firm comparison; and
i) security analysis.

Different aspects of the business forecasting problem are discussed in detail in subsequent chapters.

CHAPTER 2

Forecasting the National Economy and the Business Cycle

BY JAMES MORRELL

At first sight most businesses are unable to see any clear-cut relationship between their own activities and the economy at large. There is no obvious connection between changes in the Gross Domestic Product and the sales and output of the individual firm. To many businessmen the Gross Domestic Product is an abstraction, and the firm may be indifferent to whether G.D.P. grows at 2 or 3% per annum.

Yet the very actions of the authorities which contribute to changes in the Domestic Product will inevitably produce changes of consequence for the operating environment of the individual firm. The business, therefore, has a definite interest in attempting to identify the factors at work in the world at large which induce governments to make changes in economic policy. To maintain a consistent view of the outside world is by no means easy. It entails close and intelligent study of a wide range of political and economic data. Moreover, this is an unending process since events as they unfold have consequences for future action.

Relatively few firms have the resources of skilled staff to deploy on these broad environmental studies. Although growing numbers of businesses are now engaged in forward planning for a number of years ahead, most planning units have to rely on outside forecasts in order to inform the firm of the likely changes in the economic climate through the plan period. Since these forecasts may need to be accepted at face value, it is as well to have an understanding of the methods employed in large-scale forecasting, and the degree of reliability which can be placed on such forecasts. In this chapter the problem of forecasting will be examined and a forecasting model, in regular use over a number of years, will be explained in some detail.

THE MEASUREMENT OF NATIONAL PRODUCT

In order to understand forecasting techniques, it is necessary to analyse the construction of the national income accounts. The product of the economy can be measured in three ways. First, by summing all the incomes of the community; second, by summing all the spending of the community; and thirdly, by summing the value of the output.

By definition the three measures of product must be equal. This is because all income is either spent or saved; and savings are also spent in one way or another by the body which uses the savings. Thus the total of spending on both goods and services for current consumption, and on capital investment in fixed assets and stocks, must be equal to total income.

Chart 3

NATIONAL PRODUCT FLOWS

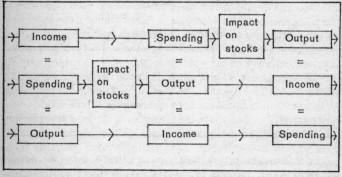

Similarly, output gives rise to income, either in the form of wages and salaries or of profits. Profits are as much a form of income as wages and salaries and are either distributed in the form of interest and dividends, or else retained as business savings. The fact remains, however, that output has a revenue value which is equal to the income it generates. Therefore, output must also

29

equal incomes; and, for purposes of measurement and estimation of the National Product and National Income,

$$incomes = spending = output$$

This sequence is illustrated in Chart 3. Here it will be seen that at each point of time income, spending and output are equal. It will also be seen that income leads to spending and spending generates output. The chart also illustrates the role of stocks, since spending will first affect the level of stocks held in the retailers' hands, and changes at the retail level will result in new orders through wholesalers to factories, and this in turn will generate orders for new production.

Chart 4

NATIONAL PRODUCT GROWTH SPIRAL

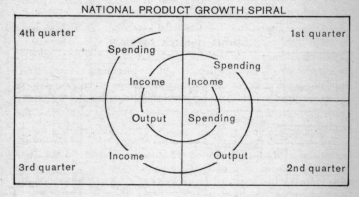

The sequence is further illustrated in Chart 4, using the simple assumption (for purposes of illustration only) that there are time-lags of roughly three months between changes in income and changes in spending, and subsequently intervals of three months between changes in spending and changes in output. It will be seen that the sequence can be thought of as a spiral. In a growing economy, the cycle of cause and effect, moving through incomes to spending to output, will result in incomes at the second round being higher than in the first round. Although it is difficult to

30

illustrate the process diagramatically, the chart of the spiral could be enlarged to show three simultaneous spirals with the income, spending and output factors being equal at each point in time, as was shown in Chart 3.

It is essential to understand the workings of the economy as set out in this form. It then becomes apparent how complex the relationships have become in a mature economy. Moreover, at this point it is as well to consider the difficulties of measurement. If there was perfect knowledge of all the transactions in the economy at all points of time, then the three estimates described above would invariably be equal. In practice this is not the case, and the problems of estimation and reconciliation of inconsistent data are discussed in Chapter 3. The first stage in forecasting, therefore, has to be the construction of a consistent set of estimates of data for the past. This is a problem which has received far too little analytical attention in all countries. It is regrettable to find that considerable research resources are devoted to exploring relationships between the economic sectors instead of giving priority to the improvement of the statistical raw material. Analysts tend to be dazzled by figures and frequently overlook the poor quality of the statistics they manipulate. In many cases fine research is unjustified because of the crudeness of the available data.

The National Income Accounts show estimates of the broad measures of product broken down into considerable detail. The forecaster then has to marshal the statistics in such a way as to draw out the sequences of cause and effect and to trace changes throughout the whole system.

THE RECENT PAST

The second problem is to estimate what has been happening in the economy in the recent past. Most official statistics are published initially on a provisional basis and are frequently subject to considerable revision in subsequent months, or even years. The tentative estimates must be converted into firm estimates for the purposes of analysis. In addition the official statistics will be published in arrears. In the U.K., for example, estimates for industrial production are published three months after the month in question. National Income Accounts are issued more than one quarter in arrears, and the same is true of balance of payments statistics. The National Income Accounts as a whole are published annually in a Blue Book and this appears in September, that is nine months from the end of the latest year covered in the accounts. Thus it will be apparent that the forecaster has, in a sense, just as important a task in estimating or forecasting what has happened in the recent months since the last available statistics appeared. To cover this problem as wide a range of indicators should be used as is available. Retail sales, bank clearings, weather statistics, foreign exchange-rate movements, monthly trade figures, unemployment statistics, all have a useful part to play in the construction of a consistent view of what has been happening in the recent past.

CHANGES IN GOVERNMENT POLICY

It is as well at this stage to differentiate between the requirements of forecasting for business and those for the government sector. In Britain the Treasury forecasts three times a year for the ensuing year and a half. These forecasts are constructed on the basis of 'no change in government policy'. The purpose of such forecasts is to highlight the changes in policy which may be necessary in order to bring about the desired economic results. In business, however, the forecaster has the problem of deciding which way the cat will jump in terms of government policy changes. It is of little use for the business forecaster to present the decision-taker with a set of forecasts based on an assumption of no changes in official policy. The object of the business forecast is to construct a picture of the economic environment as it is likely to unfold. He therefore has the task of imagining how the officials in government circles will interpret the evidence of the economy which they find, and to construct a view as to the policy recommendations the officials will present to the Ministers concerned. Some view has to be taken on both the timing and scope of policy changes. These must then be built into the business forecasting system, and the figuring will then proceed from these assumptions.

In the forecasting system described below, the assumptions are discussed in committee and agreed between a number of forecasters. It is necessary to anticipate budgetary changes and also changes in credit control and monetary policy. The question of timing will be crucial so far as the individual firm is concerned; the more so since the business cycle is largely determined by changes in government policy. The firm will need to phase its development programmes, its level of stocks, staffing policy and sales strategy, to accord with the changing environment of the business cycle as depicted in the policy assumptions.

Nearly all major changes in economic management in the U.K. in the post-war period have stemmed from developments in the balance of payments, both of Britain and the rest of the sterling area. Following a balance of payments crisis there have been important changes in both taxation and monetary policy. These crises have been all too frequent, and have occurred in the post-war period in 1947, 1949, 1951, 1955, 1957, 1961, 1964, 1965, 1966, 1967 and 1968. Although the crises have been of varying magnitudes, on some occasions the resultant economic policy has been severe in its effects. Since such changes have invariably been designed to reduce home spending and demand, and to cut back on imports, the various policy measures have had important consequences for sectors of industry.

Thus, for example, the motor industry has a marked interest in forecasting developments arising from the balance of payments, since it has been singled out for adverse treatment through changes in purchase tax, motor taxation and credit controls. Industry will have an interest in forecasting such movements so as to alter production schedules and to control the level of inventories. The household appliance industries have a similar interest, and the hire-purchase industry has a need to forecast changes in credit regulations. The construction industry too is particularly sensitive to changes in the supply of credit, and has been strongly affected by changes in monetary policy. The capital goods industries have also suffered from the fluctuations in the investment cycle, and since, as was illustrated in the previous chapter, private fixed investment is related to company cash flow, changes in government policies which tend to exacerbate the business cycle have a corresponding cyclical effect on the demand for capital goods.

POLITICAL FACTORS

In reaching agreement on the assumptions to be used for the changes in policy underlying the forecasts, it will be essential to pay close attention to politics. Not only is it necessary to appreciate the motivation of the major political parties, but it is also important to have some feel for the characteristics of the main personalities. The character of the Prime Minister or the Chancellor of the Exchequer and their individual political ambitions can be important factors in determining policy. The same will be true of other economies, for in the British case events in the United States and leading customer and supplier countries will have an important bearing upon developments at home. The timing of a U.S. recession and recovery and the timing of changes in U.S. government policy have, on occasions, a critical importance for the management of the British economy. Thus there is a need for a worldwide appraisal of political trends.

It is also important to have some understanding of the constitutional factors in the major countries. It is as well to know what the President of the United States is *able* to do, and the extent to which he depends upon the support and sanction of Congress. In Britain it is necessary to take into account the parliamentary system, and to be aware of the limitations which the parliamentary timetable imposes on the government of the day. For example, the annual finance bill pre-empts a high proportion of the available annual parliamentary time, and it is always wise to remember that Parliament is unable to complete more than a limited amount of important new legislation each year.

The value of committee work in agreeing the political and economic assumptions is that the different viewpoints garnered from varying corners of the economy can be reconciled and harmonized. There are difficult questions, such as whether or not Britain will become a member of the E.E.C., which are more safely dealt with in committee. The question of probability and timing of change can be handled with greater confidence when a number of informed opinions are brought to bear. A further advantage of the committee system is that political prejudices can be more conveniently disposed of in 'knockabout' discussion between a group of analysts, and the risks entailed through accepting the opinion of a single forecaster will be avoided.

THE FORECASTING CYCLE

A diagrammatic outline of the forecasting cycle is shown in Chart 5. It will be seen that the starting point for the forecasting cycle is shown centrally at the top of the chart, and is in fact the preceding forecast. In the system under review the forecasts are reconstructed at monthly intervals, and because of the short lapse of time between forecasts the previous forecast is used as the starting point for the next cycle. The assumptions, both about the world economy and British policy, are then applied to the previous forecasts and the statistical analysis begins at this point.

Some reference has been made to the question of adjusting the official statistics and filling in the gaps in recent knowledge, and it is as well to consider a number of the statistical pitfalls. A great deal of time is necessarily spent on testing the validity of statistics and a general conclusion is that preference should always be given to monetary statistics and in their raw unprocessed state.

Price indices are in themselves artificial concepts and approximations. An adjustment from a set of figures expressed in current values to constant prices, via a price index, means that a potential source of error will have been admitted. It will be seen in con-

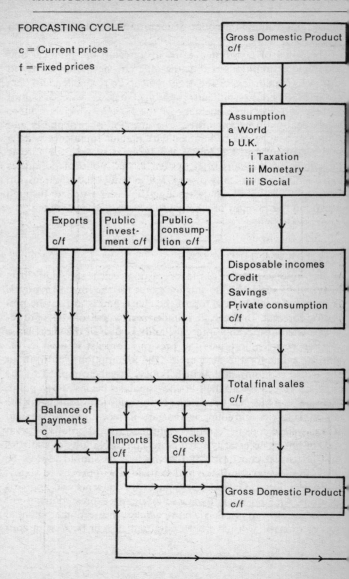

FORCASTING CYCLE

c = Current prices

f = Fixed prices

Gross Domestic Product
c/f

Assumption
a World
b U.K.
    i Taxation
    ii Monetary
    iii Social

Exports
c/f

Public invest-ment c/f

Public consump-tion c/f

Disposable incomes
Credit
Savings
Private consumption
c/f

Total final sales
c/f

Balance of payments
c

Imports
c/f

Stocks
c/f

Gross Domestic Product
c/f

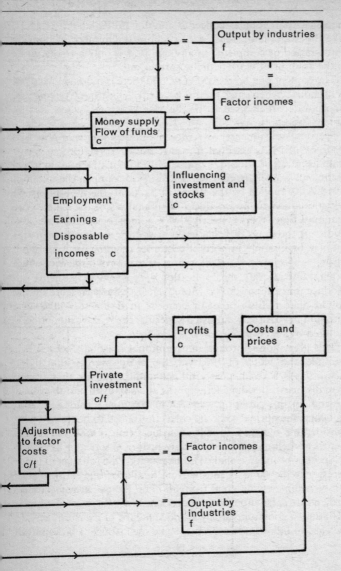

sequence that volume concepts contain potential dangers. To take the example of house construction, the number of housing units started or completed in any one year is only a rough guide to the amount of work actually carried out.

The content of a house will vary, and there is more value added to a house when such items as central heating systems are incorporated than used to be the case years ago when heating systems were a rarity.

Seasonal adjustments too represent another source of potential error. Whilst it is essential to use seasonal corrections to arrive at an estimate of a trend, extreme caution must be used in interpreting all seasonally adjusted figures. For example, the seasonal corrections applied by the Board of Trade to the monthly trade statistics are virtually worthless in an analysis of the state of the economy. Since there is nearly always some special factor tending to distort the flows of trade, such as a dock strike either in this country or in some important customer country, or a shipping strike, or special once-for-all import or export of large items such as ships and aircraft, the application of seasonal adjustments can produce misleading results. Moreover, if there is pressure on the pound there is little point or comfort in trying to analyse the situation in seasonally adjusted series. In the real world action is dictated by real events.

This also shows through in exceptional seasonal factors. For example, the winter of 1963 was the most severe within living memory. As a result nearly all economic data for that period were distorted. Building activity was at a standstill and the repercussions of this situation were felt in very many trades. In consequence, the normal seasonal corrections need to be treated with considerable reserve and it is always as well to look for special factors and climatic changes in any historical series of figures.

Another problem is that of homogeneity. One ton of coal is not necessarily the same as another ton. Similarly, one form of steel can be completely different from another. Houses are of different sizes, as are cars, and in nearly every instance there are problems of finding a common yardstick and standard of measurement. In the case of labour, for example, some means has to be found of comparing part-time workers with full-time workers. How does an hour of overtime work compare with an hour of normal time? Can a woman worker be compared with a man? It will be obvious therefore that many arbitrary assumptions have to be made in compiling background records on which the forecasts have to be constructed.

It is as well at this juncture to be warned about the temptation to use figures in such a way as to create the impression of fine degrees of accuracy. The good forecaster will adopt an attitude of extreme scepticism to the material which he has to handle. It must be remembered that with our present state of knowledge we are dealing with crude approximations about the economic world. The fact that forecasts are completed in neatly rounded tables to consistent totals, and with detail figures shown down to the smallest changes, may be necessary for the completion of the exercise, but in presenting such forecasts it should be understood that this does not necessarily imply a high degree of confidence. It follows that much of the value of highly sophisticated models is lost in the unreliability of the data. Such econometric exercises must be regarded principally as learning tools. One of their most valuable by-products is to indicate where more statistical research and information is required.

LONG-TERM TRENDS

Before embarking upon the detail of the forecasts, some set of assumptions has to be established about the underlying long-term trends in the economy. Keeping in mind the forecaster's golden rule that major trends change only gradually, the task can be simplified to this extent. There are three factors on which it is important to have a clearly defined view. These are the trends in labour productivity, the determination of the price level and the balance of payments constraint. Since the size of the working population can be forecast with some degree of accuracy, an analysis of the trend in output per man will give a guide to the likely and plausible limits to the growth of total output for the economy. Labour productivity will depend in large measure upon the stock of productive capital per worker. Therefore, unless there is a dramatic change in the rate of new capital formation, the underlying productivity trend will change only gradually. The questions of labour productivity, incomes, costs, prices and balance of payments are discussed separately in subsequent chapters. But in all cases some basic trends are discernible which can be used to write into the overall structure of the forecasts.

CURRENT AND CONSTANT PRICES

Returning to the diagram of the forecasting cycle, flowing from the assumptions made on both the world background and changes in British government policy, the impact of these factors can be traced to the various strands of spending and demand. It will be seen from the diagram that the whole work is conducted, so far as possible, in both current and constant prices. Since spending proceeds from incomes and money, it is logical to begin the analysis from the starting point of cash available to the various sectors of the economy. All spending depends upon the availability of cash and credit. Therefore, considerable importance attaches to constructing the initial forecasts in the prices of the day. At some stage in the analysis it is possible to construct estimates of cost changes, and from the cost changes estimates of price changes. Given a forecast of prices it is then possible to deflate the current price estimates and to reconstruct the forecasts in constant prices. Thus a second set of forecasts is obtained in volume terms, and an additional means of reconciliation is available.

INCOMES AND SPENDING

It will be seen from the starting point at the top of the flow diagram of the forecasting cycle that Gross Domestic Product is

equated with output by industries and also factor incomes.
Factor incomes for the whole economy are illustrated in Table 1.

Table 1

Incomes

£ thousand million

	1964	1965	1966	1967	1968	1969	1970
Employment incomes	19·67	21·19	22·74	23·72	25·41	27·30	30·23
Public-sector profits	1·02	1·09	1·14	1·23	1·46	1·57	1·60
Company profits	4·60	4·77	4·45	4·67	5·08	5·08	5·18
Other income*	4·03	4·36	4·69	5·04	5·32	5·65	6·00
Stock appreciation	−0·30	−0·34	−0·32	−0·19	−0·64	−0·86	−0·98
TOTAL	29·02	31·07	32·70	34·47	36·63	38·74	42·02

* Rent and self-employment

The major item is income from employment. Two profit totals
are shown both for the public sector and the company sector.
Profits in these definitions are before deducting depreciation and
tax. The remaining components of income are interest and incomes from self-employment, such as farming, shopkeeping and
professional services.

In order to reconcile the total incomes of the economy
measured in this way with total spending, the element of stock
appreciation which arises from increases in prices of stocks and
work in progress is deducted from factor incomes. In the model
under review, the discrepancies between the total estimate for
factor incomes and the estimate for total spending are reconciled.
In practice the two sets of forecasts are compiled separately at this
stage, and the differences in forecast totals are analysed and corrected. It will be evident, however, that there must be some
degree of common ground between the two measures. Employment incomes, for example, will be a major factor in personal
income, which in turn will determine a large part of consumer
spending.

The spending estimates are constructed in two groups. The

41

major breakdown of the expenditure estimates is shown in Table 2. Three of the items do not depend upon the model as a

Table 2

Expenditure on the Gross Domestic Product

Current prices

% change on previous year

	1964	1965	1966	1967	1968	1969	1970
Exports	+5·2	+7·0	+6·9	+2·1	+21·6	+11·3	+8·6
Investment	+19·1	+8·0	+6·2	+7·9	+7·9	+2·9	+6·4
Public consumption	+6·4	+9·6	+8·8	+10·7	+6·3	+5·3	+8·7
Private consumption	+6·9	+6·7	+5·8	+4·6	+7·4	+6·4	+9·0
Change in stocks £000 m.	0·67	0·46	0·28	0·20	0·23	0·40	0·38
Less: Imports	+12·8	+1·9	+3·8	+6·8	+19·4	+5·0	+8·1
Less: Adjustments *	+12·9	+12·2	+14·3	+3·2	+16·3	+16·0	+8·5
TOTAL	+8·2	+7·1	+5·2	+5·4	+6·3	+5·8	+8·5

* Less: taxes on expenditure, plus: subsidies

whole, but are exogenous. That is to say they are not derived from automatic relationships from other parts of the estimates. These are exports, which will clearly depend upon forecasts of the world background; public investment, which will be determined by government decision; and public authorities' current expenditure, which will also be determined by political decision.

The items depending upon other parts of the model are referred to as 'endogenous' items. In the expenditure table consumers' spending, stockbuilding, imports and the adjustment for taxes and subsidies are all derived from other relationships within the model.

Exports

The level of exports depends primarily on conditions in those countries to which Britain sells. Roughly 85% of British exports are in the form of manufactures and Britain accounts for roughly 11% of world trade in manufactures. A good guide to the trend of exports is obtained by studying the relationship between British export totals and world exports of manufactures.

Britain has a declining share of world trade, and fluctuations in this trend are taken into account as the pattern of British exports changes. A check on the export forecasts is also obtained by examining the import forecasts made by Britain's major customers. Such a check has been possible only in recent years, but is a useful cross-reference to other forms of export forecasting.

Capacity to export is also affected by pressures on the home market. When home demand is rising rapidly, delivery dates tend to lengthen; in the past this has led to some loss in export competitiveness. In the natural order of things exporting is more costly than selling on the home market; therefore, exports are particularly sensitive to cost development between competing countries. Unit labour costs and economic forecasts for the U.S.A., Germany, France, Italy and Japan give a guide to the competitive pressures that British goods are likely to meet in other markets.

The export forecast, therefore, is largely determined by events outside the control of the British authorities, although the forecast will be influenced by estimates of pressures on home resources and resultant cost forecasts.

Investment

Investment spending is considered under two broad headings:

1) Private sector, and
2) Public sector.

Private-sector investment is particularly sensitive to changes in business cash flow. Therefore the forecast of company profits derived in another part of the model is a leading indicator for forecasting changes in private business investment.

Investment in housing is considered separately. The private-sector housing programme is strongly subject to liquidity considerations, the flow of funds to the building societies and the rate of interest being important factors determining changes in housebuilding activity.

In the public sector, investment spending is influenced by changes in government policy. For example, when the balance of payments is critical and home demand has to be repressed, some sectors of government spending are also repressed. Housebuilding is affected, regardless of the fact that it has a strong political priority. Other forms of public-sector investment, including investment by nationalized industries and local authorities, come under the same influences.

Information on the public investment programme is given by the authorities from time to time and this is the prime source for forecasting public-sector investment. A check is made on changes in the programme by studying the history of the expansion and contraction of programmes in the past. A cutback in public-sector investment has never been sustained for more than about two years. Given the cyclical nature of the economy this is a useful guide in anticipating changes in the timing of programmes in the future.

Public Authorities' Current Account Spending

Government current spending can also be thought of as determined outside the model. Although governments are subject to the overall restraints imposed by the general situation, they are at least masters in their own house. The private sector responds to changes imposed on it by government policy. The government makes both the policy and the responses, so far as its own spending activities are concerned. In this, governments are subject to democratic pressures and we can gauge the limits within which government spending policies can move.

The major items of public-sector current spending are:

1) Defence,
2) Education, and
3) Health

Defence spending has accounted for a declining share of both government spending and the national product, and this trend is likely to continue in the 1970s. Both education and health spending are closely influenced by population factors. The number of young people determines the number of school and university places required. The number of old people has a great influence upon the requirements of the National Health Service. Spending on these items has been on a strongly rising trend, and, although economies have been made, the structure of the population ensures that a growing requirement for education will continue for the foreseeable future.

First estimates of these three externally determined sectors – exports, investment and government spending – give some guidance to prospective changes in the level of output and spending. This sub-total is then used to correct the preliminary estimates from the previous forecast of output and incomes.

Personal Incomes and Spending

Personal incomes comprise wages and salaries, receipts of rent, interest and dividends, pensions and allowances, and profits of private and non-corporate businesses. The last item includes sole traders, such as farmers and shopkeepers, and also professional incomes of lawyers, stockbrokers, accountants and so on. By far the most important element is wages and salaries.

A set of relationships linking changes in output with changes in employment is used to construct estimates of changes in wage rates. On past experience (1970 excepted) a relationship can be established between the level of unemployment and the rate of change in wages. The higher the level of unemployment the lower the rate of wage increases, and vice versa. This relationship is discussed in greater detail in a later chapter. Thus, from the estimate of output, an estimate of the community's income from employment is derived. This is the first requirement in making estimates of total personal incomes and consumers' spending.

Gross incomes are adjusted for income tax, surtax and National Insurance contributions. The resultant figure is total disposable income. This figure, however, does not represent consumers' total spending capacity. Incomes are supplemented by credit derived from bank advances, hire purchase and so on.

By adding the net changes in credit to incomes an estimate is obtained of total disposable funds available to the consumer. Adjustments are now made for savings. Personal savings are extremely difficult to gauge. The estimates in the National Income Accounts are derived as a residual – the difference between estimates of incomes and spending. Some elements of savings can be measured, including National Savings, unit trust investment, building society investment, pension fund contributions and life assurance. But a large area of savings, notably stock market transactions, is not yet covered by official statistics. Estimated savings are deducted from total disposable funds to arrive at the forecast of consumers' spending.

Stocks

At this juncture the four main components of spending have been forecast. The sum of these forecasts for exports, investment, government spending and consumers' spending is referred to as 'total final sales'. A total of transactions measured in this way gives an indication of the requirements of the economy for stocks of goods throughout the productive and distributive system.

Changing levels of production and distribution require different levels of stocks. These are held at various points within the economic community. In the first place, producers hold stocks in the form of raw materials and work in progress. Secondly, stocks of finished goods are held by manufacturers, wholesalers and retailers. In addition, stocks are held by consumers. Generally, little account is taken of the consumers' level of stockholding and it is assumed that once the consumer has bought goods from the shops those goods are consumed. However, when consumers anticipate a strong rise in selling prices, a motive exists for stock-piling in the home. On these occasions the future levels of purchases are affected and due account is taken of any such tendency in constructing the forecasts of both consumer spending and stock movements.

The various holders of stocks are affected in different ways at different times. Thus, in a sudden upsurge of activity a manufacturer's stocks are run down. His attempts to rebuild stocks may well be frustrated by the continued demands of his customers. Therefore, manufacturers may achieve a build-up of stocks only when demand for finished products begins to moderate.

Monetary policy and interest rates are also an important influence on stockholding. High interest rates are a weapon capable of deterring the build-up of stocks. By raising the cost of holding stocks, an incentive is created to run at a lower level of stockholding and in this way the pressure on productive resources can be reduced.

Imports

Stocks of raw materials inevitably contain a high proportion of imports. It is necessary, therefore, to complete the estimate of changes in stocks in order to derive part of the forecast for imports.

The forecast of imports is broken down into two main components. There is a clear relationship between stock changes and imports on the one hand, and changes in the level of total final sales and imports on the other. In the first case, the relationship is basically a volume concept. Certain items of production require definite volumes of raw materials. A given production of cigarettes requires a given tonnage of imports of tobacco. Similarly, where demand for imports of other consumer goods does not vary to any great extent and is, therefore, inelastic, as in the case of certain foodstuffs, then a volume relationship appears to be highly relevant. Nevertheless, it must not be overlooked that even where these kinds of imports are concerned, there is a cash consideration underlying every transaction. The relationships between the money values of total final sales and of stock changes and the level of imports in current prices must also be established. Imports are then forecast under the main heading of food, raw materials, semi-manufactures (which are, in the main, materials for industry), manufactures and fuel.

Total Home Demand

The model can now be thought of in terms of demand. The total level of home demand has been established and this requires certain levels of output. Most of this output will be provided by the home economy and allowance has been made for that part which will be supplied by imports. The import forecast is deducted from the estimates of total final sales plus stocks (the sum of which is known as total final expenditure). The resultant total is the Gross Domestic Product measured in market prices.

One more adjustment is required before the forecasting cycle of spending is completed. In order to get corresponding estimates of Gross Domestic Product by output and incomes, as well as by spending, the effects of indirect taxes and subsidies are removed from the expenditure forecasts. This entails forecasting excise duties, purchase tax and so on, as well as subsidies. The resultant total is the Gross Domestic Product in terms of factor costs. Once this adjustment has been made, a direct comparison is possible between the estimates of Gross Domestic Product by spending and those made from incomes and from output.

A forecast has now been derived in the form of a set of spending accounts. This is reconciled with the refined income analysis, incorporating detailed profit forecasts. To arrive at these, however, it will have been necessary to construct cost and price forecasts.

Costs and Prices

From the preliminary estimates of wage incomes and output, estimates are made of the forecasts for unit labour costs. These are a major determinant of total production costs and future price developments. The forecasts of prices, when considered with the forecasts of costs, give some indication of the probable developments of profit margins.

It is, of course, necessary to take into account the forecast of import prices in estimating changes in total costs. Imports are considered later in the forecasting cycle, but assumptions about import prices, derived from the forecast levels of world production and demand for commodities, are brought into the cost estimate at this stage. Price forecasts are made for the U.K. economy at this juncture and the method is outlined in Chapter 7.

DETAILED FORECASTS AND RECONCILIATION

Up to this point the model has been constructed along macroeconomic lines. That is to say, the exercise has been carried through by examining the economy in the broadest possible terms. An alternative approach would be to construct the forecasts of the separate parts of the economy in some detail and then to add the pieces together and construct a total. In practice it has been found that the best results have been obtained by forecasting the grand total first, breaking down the total into the appropriate sub-totals and then reconciling the parts so that they fit within the agreed totals.

When the first estimate of the Gross Domestic Product has been completed and revised to remove inconsistencies, estimates can be constructed in greater detail. The estimates of consumer spending and capital spending are broken down into component parts and a reconciled forecast of production by industries is prepared.

The construction of the estimates for both incomes and spending in current prices is subject to a further cross-check once the spending estimates have been deflated to allow for price increases. The expenditure table is re-forecast in constant 1963 prices. Further inconsistencies can be detected at this stage and appropriate adjustments made in both the current and constant price estimates. Imports and stockbuilding, for example, will both depend upon volume considerations as much as price factors.

At the end of the sequence of reconciliations, the final total for Gross Domestic Product in both current and constant prices is shown once again in the diagram at the foot of the cycle with the three measures of incomes, spending and output as equal. But from the estimates important features will have emerged about the balance of payments. Both the export and import factors together with the cost and price estimates will throw new light upon Britain's balance of payments prospects, and this potential situation can be checked against the original assumptions and further adjustments made in the forecasts. In practice if the re-forecasting is undertaken sufficiently frequently, then the message from the forecasts about changes in balance of payments outlook will not differ greatly from one forecast to the next.

PROFITS AND THE STOCK MARKET

One important aspect of the forecasting cycle is the sequence in which cost and price forecasts are used to construct estimates of company profits and cash flow. Not only are these forecasts used as leading indicators for company investment spending; they are also employed as a means of gauging total corporate income, including income from abroad, and earnings per share. The company sector accounts constructed in this way provide a profile of possible stock market movements, although this cannot be given any degree of precision unless interest rate movements are taken into consideration.

It is necessary, therefore, to deduce from the assumptions about fiscal and monetary policy how the money movements are likely to influence interest rates and security prices. When the profit forecast is combined with the interest rate forecast, the probable resultant changes in market levels will contain some kind of implication for the state of business confidence and this in turn will throw more light on the investment spending forecast. The question of forecasting profits, interest rates and market factors is discussed in subsequent chapters.

Another facet of the market forecast is its significance for the personal sector. A large rise in equity prices will give rise to capital gains. The proceeds of capital gains will be used in part to finance an element of consumer spending. Conversely, at a later stage, the above-average rise in share prices and in associated dividend incomes will give rise to increased tax bills. A year or so later, therefore, extra tax liabilities will tend to exert a dampening influence on this sector of personal spending and consumption. Details of the forecasts of this nature have an important role in verifying and reconciling the forecasts as a whole and give added emphasis to the identification of important turning points.

IDENTIFYING TURNING POINTS

What will emerge from forecasts constructed in this way is a picture of the changes of the economy through time, with one period influencing the next. In the forecasting system under review the forecasts run for five years ahead. In general a rough forecast is made for the horizon year for some items in order to establish an overall trend position. But the forecasts are approached by moving forward from the recent past quarter by quarter and year by year throughout the forecast period. In this way a clear view of the prospective business cycle is obtained. By starting from the agreed political assumptions and by incorporating the appropriate time-lags in relationships between the factors and sectors, a distinct cyclical movement will be apparent for a large number of the items forecast. Within this framework certain turning points begin to be visible and the forecaster will start to identify potential turning points signalling changes in direction.

It will be apparent from what has been said about the unreliability of certain of the background data that extreme caution must be used in interpreting some of the forecasts. However, it will be evident from the way in which this kind of forecasting model is constructed that the numerous cross-checks applied should result in a higher degree of consistency than would be supposed by examining the degrees of error in the background statistics. For most forecasting purposes, the object is not to attain a degree of precision of plus or minus 1 or 2%. Rather the decision-taker wants a clear guidance on the risks involved. He will want to know whether the estimates will be valid within ranges of, say, plus or minus 5 or 10%. Of greater importance he will need to know more about turning points. If the sector with which the business is concerned is about to turn downwards or to turn upwards, advance warning of the turning points will be invaluable.

A good system of forecasting should provide such warnings, and arising from the general system illustrated in this chapter in diagrammatic form the detail will throw up the cyclical movements of particular interest to the individual business. Much of this detail is discussed in subsequent chapters.

CHAPTER 3

The Statistical Raw Material

BY L. S. STANILAND

A major concern of the analyst and policy-maker is the reliability of the economic data available to him. What is ideally required is a precise and fully up-to-date measure of all the various facets of economic activity of importance to the community, so that reliable forecasts can be made. In this connection it is well to bear in mind that economic data is of little value unless it can be used for forecasting purposes.

Much of what follows will appear to be wholly destructive and will undermine the reader's confidence in published statistics. This is not to say that such statistics as we have cannot be used for forecasting purposes. Rather, we need to understand the weaknesses of certain sets of figures in order to set about eliminating some of the errors. This is possible only when we know how the historical data has been compiled and what can be done to 'improve' this information via reconciliation of different sets of figures. In this chapter this difficult and technical subject is explained in some detail so as to make the analyst aware of the pitfalls of unquestioning use of statistics and to suggest ways of interpreting the past with a greater degree of confidence and assurance.

THE MEASURES OF NATIONAL OUTPUT

There are a number of published measures of national output – or the Gross Domestic Product (G.D.P.). The total can be estimated by adding up all the incomes received by businesses and individuals; by adding together the expenditure made by businesses, individuals, the public authorities and overseas buyers of goods and services; or by adding together the various outputs of agriculture, mining, industry and the services performed by various trades, such as catering, insurance and distribution. In the case of expenditure, published estimates are available both at the current prices ruling and in volume terms at constant prices. The quarterly output measure of G.D.P., of which about half is accounted for by industrial production, is published only in

Table 3

Incomes and Expenditure

Factor incomes	£000 m.	*Expenditure*	£000 m.
Incomes from employment	25·3	Exports	8·6
Income from self-employment	2·8	Consumers' expenditure	27·1
Gross trading profits of companies	5·1	Public authorities' current expenditure on goods and services	7·7
Gross trading surpluses of the public sector	1·5	Gross domestic fixed capital formation	7·8
Rent	2·4	Value of physical increases in stocks and work in progress	0·2
Total domestic incomes	37·0	Total final expenditure	51·4
Less: Stock appreciation	−0·6	*Less:* Imports	9·0
		Less: Factor cost adjustment	6·1
TOTAL	36·4	TOTAL	36·3

constant prices, while the incomes estimate is obviously presented only in current prices. Most of the forecasting work described here is concerned with Gross Domestic Product rather than Gross National Product, the difference being that the latter includes net property income from abroad.

The breakdown of incomes and spending at current prices in 1968 (as shown in the 1969 National Income and Expenditure Blue Book) is shown in Table 3.

NEED FOR RECONCILIATION

As Table 3 shows, the different measures of G.D.P. do not necessarily agree. The difference between the two current prices estimates was about £130 million, or about 0·4% of G.D.P. In some years it has been less and others appreciably more. The 1966 Blue Book estimate for 1965 showed a difference of £330 million – or over 1% of G.D.P. – and the difference in estimate has not been reduced much since then.

The difference between the factor incomes and current price expenditure data is referred to as the 'residual error'. This is not to imply that either measure of the national income is the

Chart 6
NATIONAL INCOME AND EXPENDITURE

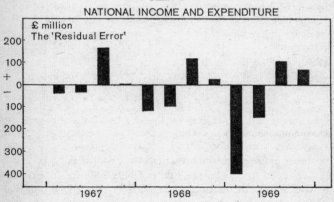

more correct. It is simply the unexplained difference between two measures purporting to be opposite sides of the same coin. Chart 6 shows the extent of the errors during three earlier years. The differences can be in either direction, but are usually negative in the first two quarters of the year and positive in the second two. In fact, over a period of years there has been a tendency towards a substantial minus in the first quarter of the year, although not of the dimensions of the near £400 million (or over 4% of G.D.P.) recorded in the first quarter of 1969. According to the official

Sources and Methods book,[1] which is published by the Central Statistical Office and describes in great detail the way in which the national income accounts are compiled, differences in estimates of personal savings suggest that a large part of the residual error can be attributed to the personal sector.

The year on year changes in published quarterly expenditure and factor incomes in 1968 and 1969 are shown in Table 4. The

Table 4

Divergencies in Spending and Incomes

		Expenditure (% change on year earlier)	Factor incomes (% change on year earlier)
1968	i	+5·4	+6·3
	ii	+4·1	+4·7
	iii	+5·9	+6·6
	iv	+7·8	+7·3
1969	i	+2·7	+5·8
	ii	+5·5	+5·8
	iii	+4·6	+4·8
	iv	+5·9	+5·7

(The reader may be forgiven for thinking that the first quarter 1969 expenditure change is in error.)

problem of divergent movements in the statistics is, of course, not confined to current price data. Chart 7 shows differences in quarterly movements over three years in the official seasonally adjusted constant price indices of expenditure and output. In the fourth quarter of 1967 the expenditure figures showed a fall of $\frac{1}{2}$% while the output data recorded a rise of nearly $1\frac{1}{2}$%. In the following quarter expenditure rose by 3%, but output by only half as much. Again, in the fourth quarter of 1968, expenditure rose nearly $1\frac{1}{2}$% more than output, but in the following quarter fell by over 2% more than output. Taking the two quarters together in both cases produces much smaller divergencies, suggesting that timing and seasonal adjustment factors were at

1. *National Accounts Statistics: Sources and Methods*, H.M.S.O., 1968.

work. Whatever the reasons (which will be considered later) it is clear that the Chancellor of the Exchequer is faced with an unenviable task in endeavouring to guide the economy by finger-tip

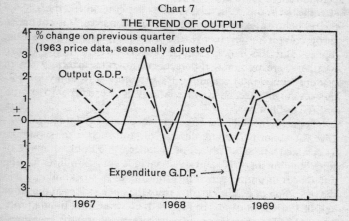

Chart 7
THE TREND OF OUTPUT

control methods. He cannot even be sure of the extent to which the economy moved in the past!

REASONS FOR DIFFERENCES IN ESTIMATES

An understanding of the problems associated with the individual series is essential to any understanding of the differences between the various measures of G.D.P. Ideally, work done, expenditure on the goods and services so produced and the incomes from these activities should coincide. In practice, timing differences can arise between payments and work done, particularly where production is a lengthy process, as in the case of capital equipment. For example, a difficulty arose in the fourth quarter of 1968 and the first quarter of 1969 as a result of the ending of the 5% temporary increases in investment grants for plant and machinery and ships. Payments were accelerated into the fourth quarter of 1968 and payments in the following quarter were depressed.

Also, a corresponding increase in output of capital goods almost certainly took place in the final quarter of 1968. The question is whether an adjustment needs to be made to the recorded expenditure figures, and, if so, how much? Where adjustments are sizeable, as in this case, it is probably better to amend the original figures before attempting to apportion differences. It is not necessarily correct simply to average the two quarters' expenditure figures. But the major problem arises when it is not known whether there are timing differences or not. One arbitrary way of dealing with capital spending, for example, is to apply a three-quarter moving average to the quarterly figures in order to smooth out the oscillations.

Of course, the published figures may already make some allowance for abnormal timing differences, and such cases should be ascertained where possible. For instance, Blue Book estimates of stockbuilding in 1967 and 1968 include an allowance for the differences in timing between the estimates of stockbuilding and the recording of exports arising from the dock strikes in the latter half of 1967. It must not be assumed, however, that timing problems only affect the correspondence between alternative measures. They could also distort one measure in isolation. For example, if progress payments for capital spending are being recorded as capital expenditure, while the resulting work done is also being recorded in the producers' work in progress, this will result in double counting in the total expenditure measure of G.D.P.

In the case of industrial production, the monthly index differs in timing from other quarterly estimates of national output and incomes. The monthly production figures allow for variations in the number of working days, while other data is based on calendar quarters. A further problem here is that part of output is, in fact, deliveries, not actual production, so that movements into or out of producers' stocks can distort the output measure. For example, the production index for the fourth quarter of 1969 shows an increase of under a half per cent on the previous quarter, and total output (including services) of under one per cent. By contrast, the expenditure measure shows an increase of over 2% in the same quarter. No doubt a part of the difference can be accounted for by the marked build-up of manufacturers' stocks in the fourth quarter of 1969 – largely finished goods included in the expenditure figures.

A number of other problems arise in the measurement of output. As with expenditure at constant prices, an important proportion of output is obtained by deflating current price sales data. This involves problems of price indices. In this connection it is almost impossible to allow fully for quality changes which should properly be added to the quantity of output and not be incorporated in the price index. For instance, where extra processing is involved in the manufacture of an article (e.g. the application of additional coats of paint), this amounts to additional value added in real terms. In any case, price indices cannot be used for every conceivable quality, size or type of product. Moreover, a significant proportion of output (e.g. school-teaching) is measured from employment statistics and hence assumes no change in individual productivity. Thus, if fewer teachers are employed the statistics suggest that educational output goes down.

The re-basing of the index of industrial production on to a 1963 = 100 basis showed some significant discrepancies compared with the 1958 = 100 basis. 'Weights' (the proportionate contribution of each industry to total national output) were reduced for industries such as mining and quarrying and metal manufacture, and increased for industries such as chemicals and gas, electricity and water. At the same time, certain revisions were made to indicators of output. The effect was to show a growth in industrial output of nearly 20% between 1963 and 1968 as compared with only 17% on the previous 1958 basis – a difference of $\frac{1}{2}$% per annum compound. Of course, as consumers we were not one whit better off as a result of this revision – the goods had been produced regardless of the method of measurement of output. But it did mean that the growth of productivity – one of the two major constraints to economic growth – had been that much higher than originally indicated.

Above all, in endeavouring to understand why the different measures diverge, it is well to appreciate that the figures are far from precise, and in certain cases a good deal of estimation is required. This is particularly so, for example, in the case of stocks, where estimates of changes in the value of stocks have to be further subdivided between the value of the physical change in stocks (which represents the creation of real resources, and hence a part of G.D.P.), and the change in value due merely to changes in prices. The latter, referred to as 'stock appreciation', forms part of business profits, but has no part in G.D.P. (the output of real resources), and has to be deducted from total domestic incomes to arrive at the factor incomes measure of G.D.P.

REVISIONS TO PUBLISHED STATISTICS

An equal or even larger problem is the constant revision to published data. In consequence, the forecaster has first of all to forecast what the historical data will eventually look like. Revisions to past data are more extensive than might be imagined. Chart 8 shows subsequent amendments to National Income and

Chart 8

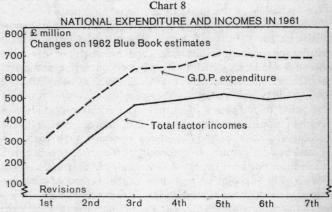

NATIONAL EXPENDITURE AND INCOMES IN 1961

Expenditure data for the year 1961 as first published in the 1962 Blue Book. It is true that the bulk of the revision took place in the first three years, but revisions have since continued in a relatively modest way in subsequent editions of the Blue Book. On the expenditure side, the cumulative revision shown is almost £700 million, or nearly 3% of the first Blue Book estimate. Nearly a half of the revision was made in the first following year and over 90% within the first three years. For factor incomes the picture was fairly similar, but the first revision accounted for only about 30% of the cumulative change over the succeeding seven years. Later, the degree of revision was rather smaller than for expenditure.

Unfortunately for the analyst, the extent of the revision is not constant, and, worse still, it is not always in the same direction. In the case of expenditure, subsequent amendments to the first Blue Book publication were as in Table 5. Initial revisions

Table 5

Cumulative Revisions to the Spending Estimates

(Expenditure Estimates of G.D.P.)

Data (years)	1st		2nd		3rd		1969 Blue Book	
	£m	%	£m	%	£m	%	£m	%
1959	+162	(0·8)	+221	(1·1)	+230	(1·1)	+495	(2·4)
1960	+ 56	(0·3)	+111	(0·5)	+268	(1·2)	+426	(1·9)
1961	+320	(1·4)	+490	(2·1)	+639	(2·7)	+695	(3·0)
1962	+303	(1·2)	+505	(2·1)	+541	(2·2)	+650	(2·6)
1963	+457	(1·7)	+478	(1·8)	+568	(2·2)	+667	(2·5)
1964	+141	(0·5)	+317	(1·1)	+395	(1·4)	+491	(1·7)
1965	+259	(0·9)	+409	(1·3)	+464	(1·5)	+464	(1·5)
1966	+309	(1·8)	+463	(1·4)	–	–	+463	(1·6)
1967	+504	(1·5)	–	–	–	–	+504	(1·5)
Mean	+279	(1·0)	+374	(1·4)	+444	(1·8)	–	–

to Blue Book estimates have, therefore, fluctuated between 0·3% and 1·7%; second-year revisions between 0·5% and 2·1%; and third-year revisions between 1·1% and 2·7%. It may well be that the range of ultimate revisions will be rather less. The highest cumulative Blue Book revision so far published is 3·0% (or £695 million) in respect of 1961.

For total factor incomes, the corresponding Blue Book revisions are given in Table 6. First revisions have thus ranged

Table 6

Cumulative Revisions to Income Estimates
(Factor Incomes Estimates of G.D.P.)

Data (years)	1st		2nd		3rd		1969 Blue Book	
	£m	%	£m	%	£m	%	£m	%
1959	+54	(0·3)	+45	(0·2)	+46	(0·2)	+173	(0·8)
1960	+9	nil	+131	(0·6)	+159	(0·7)	+331	(1·5)
1961	+153	(0·6)	+322	(1·4)	+478	(2·0)	+517	(2·2)
1962	+319	(1·3)	+440	(1·8)	+413	(1·7)	+469	(1·9)
1963	+186	(0·7)	+227	(1·1)	+354	(1·3)	+435	(1·7)
1964	+167	(0·6)	+184	(0·6)	+223	(0·8)	+327	(1·1)
1965	+205	(0·7)	+361	(1·2)	+425	(1·4)	+425	(1·4)
1966	+259	(0·8)	+412	(1·3)	–	–	+412	(1·3)
1967	+318	(0·9)	–	–	–	–	+318	(0·9)
Mean	+186	(0·7)	+272	(1·0)	+300	(1·2)	–	–

between virtually nil and 1·3% of the first Blue Book estimate; second revisions from 0·2% to 1·8%; and third revisions from 0·2% to 2·0%. The highest cumulative revision so far published in this case is 2·2% (or £517 million) in respect of 1961.

The revisions from first publication of the quarterly national incomes data in *Economic Trends*, as distinct from the annual data referred¦ to above, can be much larger, as Table 7 shows. In fact, some of these alterations will have already been incorporated in the annual data first published in the Blue Book revisions. For example, the first Blue Book revision in respect of 1967 G.D.P. expenditure was as much as £504 million, and subsequent revisions in the next two years amounted to no more than £43 million. It can be seen that, in forecasting future revisions to recent data, guidance based solely on annual Blue Book revisions is not enough. This is particularly evident in the case of the 1968 factor incomes estimates, where revisions to the second and third quarter were downwards, while for the year as a whole the total revision was upwards. This particular experience has engendered a greater amount of uncertainty than hitherto in the reconciliation process.

Table 7

Revisions to 1967 and 1968 Quarterly Data*

£ million

		Expenditure	Factor incomes
1967	i	+240	+73
	ii	+121	+164
	iii	+214	+150
	iv	+245	+241
		+820	+628
1968	i	+283	+86
	ii	+127	−79
	iii	+167	−48
	iv	+231	+264
		+808	+223

* Change between first publication and data in July 1970 *Economic Trends*.

While revisions to overall series may be relatively small in certain cases, they often mask considerably larger discrepancies in the constituent parts. For example, the revised index of industrial production for the food, drink and tobacco industry, where changes in the series were made, showed an increase between 1963 and 1968 of 15% compared with 10% on the previous basis. In chemicals a very respectable increase of 32% became an impressive 40%, and the ratio to total industrial production growth improved from 1·78:1 to 1·86:1. For vehicles (including aircraft and railway rolling stock) the ratio moved up from 0·56:1 to 0·84:1.

In the case of the construction industry, a component of the industrial production index, the *Monthly Digest of Statistics* for August 1969 showed a 5½% fall in output between the final quarter of 1968 and the first quarter of 1969. The July 1970 issue by contrast showed a decline over the same period of only 3%. This same issue also shows a remarkable change in quarterly movements compared with only the previous month's issue for gas, water and electricity output – undoubtedly the result of revised seasonal adjustments. This is illustrated in Table 8.

Table 8

Gas, Electricity and Water Output
(*Monthly Digest of Statistics*)

(*1963 = 100*)
Seasonally adjusted

		June 1970	July 1970
1968	i	129·7	127·6
	ii	124·6	125·1
	iii	128·4	129·2
	iv	129·1	131·0
		128·2	128·2
1969	i	142·6	139·8
	ii	132·7	133·7
	iii	130·9	132·4
	iv	137·0	138·9
		136·2	136·2
1970	i	148·9	145·6

Chart 9 shows the first revisions to Blue Book estimates of consumer spending and personal incomes, both of which account for the greater part of the relevant G.D.P. estimates for expenditure and incomes. The extent of the first revision to the spending data has varied considerably, from approaching 2% in respect of 1963 data, to a negligible proportion in the case of 1967 spending. The figures, however, do suggest that the position in respect of first revisions has not deteriorated over time. In the light of the enormous revision in respect of 1966 data, the same

Chart 9

CONSUMER SPENDING AND PERSONAL INCOMES

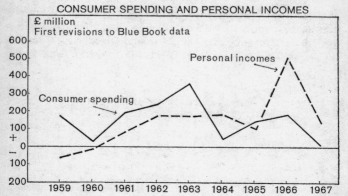

cannot be said of personal incomes. The first annual revision here was no less than £510 million, or 1·6% of the 1967 Blue Book estimate. However, since the adjustment to factor incomes in total was less than this, part of the error in personal incomes must have been compensated by changes elsewhere.

A more detailed analysis of overall changes in Gross National Product and factor incomes is shown in Table 9, for the years 1963, 1964 and 1965. The table shows a number of areas where major changes have taken place. The changes for each sub-component in the three years are not directly comparable, for in the 1969 Blue Book the data for 1965 incorporates only three revisions, while there have been five years' revisions to the 1963 figures. Even so, the large revisions in respect of rent and stocks stand out.

The size of the revisions to the stock estimates are truly alarming and throw considerable doubt on the validity of using this

Table 9

Revisions to First Blue Book Estimates of Expenditure
(as published in 1969 Blue Book)

	For 1963		For 1964		For 1965	
	£m.		£m.		£m.	
Consumer expenditure	+462	+2·3%	+159	+0·7%	+157	+0·7%
Public authority current expenditure on goods and services	+77	+1·5%	+101	+1·9%	+157	+2·7%
Gross fixed capital formation	+83	+1·7%	+52	+0·9%	+51	+0·8%
Physical increase in stocks	+84	+62·2%	+128	+24·3%	+18	+4·5%
Exports and property income from abroad	+41	+0·6%	+99	+1·3%	+46	+0·6%
Less:						
Imports and property income paid abroad	+43	+0·6%	+68	+0·9%	+54	+0·7%
Other	+22	+0·6%	+8	+0·2%	−25	−0·6%
G.N.P. (factor cost)	+682	+2·6%	+463	+1·6%	+400	+1·5%
Income from employment	+119	+0·7%	+126	+0·6%	+296	+1·4%
Income from self-employment	−5	−0·2%	+5	+0·2%	+24	+1·0%
Gross trading profits	+120	+3·0%	+55	+1·2%	−56	−1·2%
Rent	+173	+12·4%	+120	+7·6%	+132	+7·6%
Gross trading profits and surpluses of public sector	+15	+1·7%	+8	+0·8%	−2	−0·1%
Total domestic incomes	+422	+1·6%	+314	+1·1%	+394	+1·3%
of which stock appreciation	−13	−6·3%	−13	−4·1%	−31	−8·5%

kind of data for analysis and forecasting. Yet there is a crude method of dealing with the problem, for reconciliation of the tables and forecasts as a whole will tend to pull a dubious individual item such as the stock estimate roughly into perspective. It should be clear from this piece of statistical inquiry that there is a real need for much more intensive research on the part of the official statisticians into methods of collection of information and more accurate accounting methods and measurements so far as stocks and inventories are concerned.

The revisions to rent are more surprising. Since roughly half the housing in the country is owned by local authorities, it might be assumed that this large element of the rent total would be known with complete accuracy. Yet this is not the case. So far as private housing is concerned, owner-occupiers are regarded as paying a notional rent. The estimate for this element rests on an arbitrary calculation and the total estimate remains suspect, and to this extent is highly unsatisfactory. The analyst would be better served if the detailed components of the official rent estimate were to be made available.

The data in Table 9 shows only a small proportional adjustment to the consumer spending data for 1964 and 1965, and an above average adjustment in those two years for public authority current expenditure on goods and services. In fact in the 1969 Blue Book there was a switch of expenditure on school meals, milk and welfare foods (provided free or at subsidized prices) from consumers' expenditure to public authority current spending. Had this not been so, the adjustment to the 1965 public spending data would probably have been nearer 0·5% than the 2·7% shown in the accounts, without the underlying data being any more correct.

This and the extent of changes in other sub-categories over several years can be seen from the analysis in Table 10 in respect of 1964. Recent changes in merchandise exports highlight some of the difficulties in interpreting the data. During 1969, unrecorded exports to the tune of £130 million were uncovered in respect of 1968 – equivalent to about 2% of total exports of goods in that year. This illustrates the extent to which the official statisticians are in the hands of the people involved in supplying the basic data. (In fact this discovery did nothing to improve the overall balance of payments position, since it merely implied a corresponding reduction in the value of unrecorded transactions.)

Table 10

Subsequent Revisions to Data for 1964
Blue Book Years

£ million

Data year 1964	1966	1967	1968	1969
Consumers' spending	+46	+158	+243	+159
Public authority current spending	−34	−12	−16	+101
Gross fixed capital formation	+26	+54	+58	+52
Stocks	+90	+123	+113	+128
Exports	+41	+59	+71	+99
Imports	+22	+49	+58	+68
Taxes and subsidies	−5	+12	+8	+8
G.N.P.	+152	+321	+403	+463
Employment incomes	−41	+40	+85	+126
Self-employment	+56	+15	−11	+5
Gross trading profits	+129	+99	+70	+55
Public sector surplus	+5	+8	+8	+8
Rent	+35	+49	+96	+120
Total domestic incomes	+184	+211	+248	+314
of which stock appreciation	+17	+27	+25	−13

The classic case of subsequent revision, however, relates to the 1958 savings estimate. The annual revisions are given in Table 11. Revisions to data for later years have been on a smaller, though still sizeable, scale. The explanation of the original errors and drastic revisions lies in the method of savings estimation. Incomes and spending are estimated separately. What is not spent is, by definition, saved. Any underestimate of spending will result in an over-estimate of savings and, in general, this has been the basic tendency over the years.

It would, in fact, seem pointless to attempt to forecast revisions to savings independently with any reasonable degree of accuracy.

Table 11

Personal Incomes and Savings in 1958

Blue Book year	Personal income £m.	Savings £m.	Savings ratio %
1959	18,928	1,341	7·1
1960	18,817	1,115	5·9
1961	18,618	831	4·5
1962	18,554	743	4·0
1963	18,575	774	4·2
1964	18,538	680	3·7
1965	18,659	677	3·6
1966	18,632	658	3·5
1967	18,600	605	3·3
1968	18,587	616	3·3
1969	18,524	616	3·3

While revisions in earlier years were generally downwards, they have been upwards in more recent years. Moreover, in the case of the 1965 estimate as published in 1966, the first revision was a *reduction* of £166 million, or minus 13%. By the third revision, however, the original estimate had *increased* by £115 million, or 6%.

To be of maximum use to the forecaster, the reconciliation process should also allow for differing revisions to the individual sub-items making up the component series. A mere reconciliation of overall measures of G.D.P. is of value, for example, in assessing labour productivity trends, but the industrial fore-caster in particular has generally to consider smaller constituent parts of G.D.P. with as much care as the total. The real difficulty, however, is in judging the individual adjustments to make. As the following breakdown of 1966 consumer spending shows, a pro-rata adjustment to all of the various spending components is inappropriate.

Table 12
Consumers' Expenditure in 1965
Blue Book years

	(current prices)			(1958 prices)		
	1966	1968		1966	1968	
	Total	change		Total	change	
	£m.	£m.	%	£m.	£m.	%
Food	5,112	−7	−0·1	4,474	−4	−0·1
Alcoholic drink	1,417	−2	−0·1	1,170	−3	−0·2
Tobacco	1,428	nil	nil	1,012	+30	+3·0
Housing	2,479	+67	+2·7	1,769	−10	−0·6
of which rent, rates and water	2,010	+83	+4·1	1,370	+6	+0·4
Fuel and light	1,097	−10	−0·9	951	−11	−1·2
Clothing	2,034	+35	+1·7	1,833	+22	+1·2
Durable goods	1,829	+63	+3·4	1,942	+56	+2·9
of which furniture	510	+55	+7·8	420	+46	+11·0
Running costs of motor vehicles	917	+11	+1·2	764	+9	+1·2
Travel	728	+8	+1·1	554	+16	+2·8
Other	5,667	+93	+1·6	4,815	+32	+0·7
TOTAL	22,708	+248	+1·1	19,284	+137	+0·7

The problem is also well illustrated by the fixed capital expenditure figures for 1965. As has been shown in Table 9 the total of the amendments to the fixed capital formation estimates between the 1966 and 1969 Blue Book resulted in an increase at current prices of £51 million, or 0·8%. But the bulk of the adjustment was in private-sector non-housing investment on the one side and public-sector housing on the other (see Table 13), suggesting that this is where most forecast revisions to capital spending estimates should be concentrated. The fact that private-sector housing figures have not been revised, whereas public-sector housing figures have been substantially changed, is highly suspicious;

Table 13

Cumulative Revisions in 1965 Capital Spending
Blue Book years

	(current prices) 1967		1968		(1958 prices) 1967		1968	
	£m.	% change	£m.	% change	£m.	% change	£m.	% change
Private sector								
1. Housing	nil	nil	nil	nil	nil	nil	nil	nil
2. Non-housing	+62	+2·3	+76	+2·8	+70	+2·8	+75	+3·0
Public sector								
1. Housing	nil	nil	−3	−0·5	−8	−1·6	−11	−2·2
2. Non-housing	+5	+0·2	+6	+0·3	−24	−1·3	−17	−0·9
TOTAL	+67	+1·1	+79	+1·3	+38	+0·7	+47	+0·8

for the flow of statistics ought, in theory, to be subject to a higher degree of surveillance in the public than the private sector.

REASONS FOR REVISIONS TO STATISTICS

Revisions to statistics are made for a variety of reasons. It may be as a result of chance (as in the case of the unrecorded exports referred to earlier) or later information; and different methods of calculation may lead to changes in the seasonal adjustments. Classification changes will also entail revisions, as in the case of expenditure on school meals, milk and welfare foods, and, in addition, changes have resulted from a re-basing of data.

Revisions may also be expected where provisional figures have been based on incomplete returns or inquiries. In the case of manufacturing industry capital spending, the figures are firstly obtained on a voluntary basis from a sample of larger companies, accounting for about two-thirds of spending by this sector. Subsequently, a simple annual census, based on a larger sample, is carried out. It is not until the full census inquiries, taken at about five-year intervals, have been completed that comprehensive data is obtained for the whole industry. Similarly, early estimates of spending by the distributive and service sectors are also obtained from sample returns. With stocks and work in progress too, the quarterly inquiries are not fully comprehensive, with the result that the estimates for the latest year published are less reliable than those for earlier years.

In the case of wages and salaries, while almost complete data can be obtained from P.A.Y.E. or other returns in respect of the previous financial year, the greater part of the latest calendar year given in the National Income Blue Book has to be estimated on a quarterly basis. These quarterly estimates are then subsequently revised when P.A.Y.E. returns of pay and tax for the financial year become available.

Past Blue Books give other interesting examples of revisions such as the upward revision of rent, rates and water charges, in the light of information on the total number of owner-occupied houses derived from the Sample Census of Population for 1966. Other revisions have resulted from the introduction of new or fresh inquiries (e.g. Board of Trade monthly inquiries in the motor trades, the Family Expenditure Surveys and Census of Distribution). Elsewhere, for example, a revision to estimates of spending on tobacco at constant prices resulted from a revaluation of the main types of cigarettes separately; while in the field of personal incomes, employers' National Insurance contributions have been revised upwards in the light of the Government Actuary's third survey of occupational pension schemes in 1967. In sum, therefore, the scope for revision is wide.

THE RECENT PAST

The reason for reconciling past data lies chiefly in establishing relationships between various economic sectors. It is also of importance in establishing trends, although it is arguable whether past trends in isolation tell us anything at all about the current position. In any case, the available data is already out of date before the public has access to it. There is a delay of at least three months before a quarter's national income data is available. Retail trade figures relate usually to the previous but one month, but in any case the coverage, which is based on samples, is incomplete. The trade and unemployment figures are the most up-to-date indicators, but again are only a partial guide and also need careful interpretation. Another commonly used indicator, the index of industrial production, can be positively misleading.

One central problem to all short-term statistics is the accuracy of seasonal adjustment. This is most important, since, in general, trends cannot be satisfactorily determined from unadjusted data, although many people use statistics in this way. Year on year percentage changes can be misleading without knowledge of the underlying trend in the preceding year. On the other hand, unadjusted data is likely to be more accurate than seasonally adjusted data. Seasonal movements change over time and random changes may be impossible to eliminate satisfactorily. In practice it may be as well to look at the statistics in both ways when endeavouring to establish trends. The trade figures are very difficult to comprehend on a seasonally adjusted basis, and a three or six months' moving average of the unadjusted figures may be found to be the most useful method to adopt.

The dangers of underlying seasonal adjustment can be readily appreciated in the case of the unemployment series. Since unemployment is important both politically and as one of the most up-to-date indicators of economic trends, it is most important to measure the trend correctly. Past figures showed a tendency for the trend to rise up to the middle of the year and then to fall in the latter part of the year. New adjustments have led to a more shallow movement for past years. Table 14 shows the

Table 14

Unemployment
Thousands (seasonally adjusted)

	1967		1968		1969	
	Old	Revised	Old	Revised	Old	Revised
January	454	453	520	547	506	532
February	454	461	503	547	487	529
March	467	474	509	539	504	534
April	495	491	535	541	519	525
May	505	508	545	540	518	515
June	524	520	569	541	543	517
July	543	532	580	544	577	541
August	559	542	585	553	585	553
September	563	541	575	543	580	548
October	541	532	551	539	555	543
November	536	535	529	531	536	538
December	538	540	520	525	545	550

seasonally adjusted monthly data for the past three years on both the old and new bases.

As a guide to the pressure of demand in the labour market (and hence to prospective wage pressures and supply bottlenecks), it is also necessary to take account of the level of vacancies. In practice, a most useful way of using the data is to deduct vacancies from the seasonally adjusted unemployment data after having applied a three months' moving average to both series, to smooth out errors in seasonal adjustment and random fluctuations. Even so, because of the time-lags between changes in production and employment, the most up-to-date unemployment figures are still only a guide to national output some three months previously. There are, of course, other short-term indicators such as wage rates and bank statistics, but the sad fact is that estimates of the most recent past have in most respects to be forecasts.

RECONCILIATION

The annual output data appears to have been revised to a lesser extent than the constant price expenditure measures. Table 15 shows this in the indices relating to 1961 data.

It may be argued that, because of this relative stability, the output measure is the more reliable. This does not follow. The smaller extent of revision may be solely due to less new informa-

Table 15

Expenditure and Output
(*1958 = 100*)

Blue Book years

	1962	1963	1964	1965	1966	1967	1968
Expenditure	110·1	111·3	112·6	112·7	112·7	112·7	112·7
Output	112·1	111·8	112·0	112·1	112·1	112·1	112·1

tion becoming available in a given period. In fact, as we have seen when the base is changed, previous errors in industrial production then become evident. In any case, we have to deal with quarterly data as well. On balance, therefore, since both seasonal and price factors are abstractions, it is preferable to start the reconciliation process with the two current priced measures – incomes and expenditure – making any preliminary amendments and forecast revisions to each series. Greater revisions will be allowed for the latest quarters. Then, for want of a more precise procedure, the mean of the revised totals can be used and the difference allocated between the various sectors and sub-sectors.

If all estimates were equally reliable, this would be easy, but as we have seen, certain data is subject to more revision than others. The official *Sources and Methods* book grades the reliability of annual estimates in three categories, A, B and C. The highest grading is accorded to income from employment, consumers' expenditure, trading surpluses of public corporations, public authorities' current expenditure, exports and imports of goods and services, and taxes on expenditure and subsidies. At the bottom end of the reliability grading, implying a reliability of only plus or minus more than 10%, lie stocks and net property income from abroad.

As an example of how published statistics can be 'corrected', the data included in the April 1970 *Economic Trends* for 1967, 1968 and 1969 have been altered by the figures shown in Table 16.

Table 16

Major Adjustments Applied to the Official Statistics
£ million

Current prices	1967		1968		1969	
	Basic 3rd yr	Actual	Basic 2nd yr	Actual	Basic 1st yr	Actual
Income from employment	+50	+99	+125	+106	+225	+191
Private consumption	+75	+43	+200	+210	+375	+410
Total incomes	+75	+148	+200	+165	+350	+248
Total spending	+100	+41	+250	+211	+525	+595

The 'basic' adjustments have been calculated from the pattern of revisions over the past ten years. The 'actual' revisions applied have been arrived at by applying the 'basic' revision and splitting the difference between the official estimates of income and spending in current prices. Although this may appear to be a rough and ready method, it appears to give more satisfactory results and provides a framework for reconciling component parts of the historical data.

The final stage in this method of approach is to adjust the published output data to the reconciled totals. In this case, the annual indices for agriculture, mining, manufacturing, gas, electricity and water are considered to be the most reliable. Lesser reliability is accorded to the construction and service sectors.

With the addition of estimates of the most up-to-date position, the forecaster is thus ready to set about his primary task. But in choosing his forecasting methods, he would do well to bear in mind that the achievement of a unique and correct calculation of the historical quarterly and annual figures is out of the question. It is essential, therefore, to apply commonsense methods to produce sensible data and to construct the ensuing forecasts with a sufficient appreciation of the limitations of the statistical raw material. The forecast can be no better than the underlying statistical analysis. The accuracy of the analysis will depend upon the veracity of the historical data, and the ultimate forecasting edifice must not be greater than the statistical foundations will stand.

CHAPTER 4

Forecasting Assumptions – The Importance of the Balance of Payments and Future Government Policy

BY D. F. V. ASHBY

IMPORTANCE OF ASSUMPTIONS IN FORECASTING

All forecasts are based on assumptions. Whether these are explicitly expressed or only implied, both the maker and the user of the forecast must have a clear understanding of the assumptions on which the forecasts are based. The establishment of assumptions is of the greatest importance in forecasting, and depending upon the nature of the problem may require considerable research. Within the areas of the firm's own competence, assumptions are often established quickly and with little argument. If it knows its markets well, the firm can make realistic assumptions about the behaviour of its competitors, such as when they will launch new products, or how they will react to other new products. It will also be able to make reasonable assumptions about consumers' reactions to price and tax changes, and probably about changes in production technology.

However, when the forecasters and planners turn to external changes affecting the general economic environment in which the firm and industry operates, there are added difficulties in making and agreeing assumptions. How can the business forecaster know what to assume about government tax policy, or credit availability? Major decisions in these fields have in the past been largely influenced by balance of payments considerations. The evidence suggests this will continue to be the case and for this reason the forecaster must study the balance of payments in order to determine his assumptions about future government policy, and hence the effects upon the firm.

FIRM ASSUMPTIONS

The starting point for constructing the economic forecast must be an examination of what is already known about the future. Although there is always an element of doubt whether abnormal factors will intervene, it is reasonable to expect that government policy changes already announced for a few years ahead will be implemented.

A case in point is the raising of the school-leaving age in 1973, which was announced in January 1969, and which both major political parties accepted. This will have a measurable effect on the supply of labour in that year, and therefore on the physical limits to the output of the economy. It will also affect consumer spending. For particular types of products where teenagers account for a substantial portion of the demand (e.g. pop records) the reduction in spending power could be significant. Other examples are decimalization of the currency (announced several years in advance), metrication, issue of Special Drawing Rights by the International Monetary Fund, and tariff cuts agreed as part of the 'Kennedy Round'.

On a longer time scale, future changes in the age structure of the population are calculated by the Government Actuary, and are available as forecasting aids so far as certain market factors are concerned. Future government spending on pensions, health services and education will be determined by population factors. The size of the potential labour force can be estimated and its implications for the growth of the economy can be allowed for in the forecasts.

Similarly, the introduction of Special Drawing Rights (S.D.R.s) under the aegis of the I.M.F. in January 1970 provided another certain benchmark for future years. When agreement was reached on the S.D.R. scheme, it was decided to issue $3,000 million-worth in each of 1970, 1971 and 1972. These issues could be taken as certain, and doubtless when the scheme is extended a similar programme of annual issues will be agreed, giving the forecaster at least one firm reference point for his forecast of world trade – a highly important factor from the British point of view.

Another reference point for forecasting world trade, and also import and export prices, is the programme of tariff cuts agreed in 1967 as a result of the 'Kennedy Round' of tariff negotiations. The first of these cuts was made by the U.K. on 1 July 1968 and additional cuts were scheduled until 1 January 1972. Similarly, if and when British entry to the E.E.C. has been negotiated, a fairly precise programme of tariff and other changes will be known for several years ahead. While one may legitimately question whether some parts of such a programme will be effected on time (for example, there may be doubts as to whether the value-added tax will come into force on schedule), it will be reasonable to use most of the programme as a firm set of assumptions about the future.

ASSESSING OTHER ASSUMPTIONS

Apart from using these 'known facts' about the future as the basis for firm assumptions, the business forecaster must also make assumptions about future developments which are not already 'programmed'. Entry to the E.E.C. provides an excellent example of the problem of handling uncertainty. When, and if, the date and conditions of entry have been decided, then there will be a well-defined timetable that can be used as the basis for firm assumptions. But until these firm dates are known, the forecaster has the problems of deciding:

a) whether or not the U.K. will join;
b) the most likely joining date.

Once he has decided the answer to question (a), he can then look at the chances of joining year by year through the period for which he is forecasting. Taking account of the administrative and political problems involved, he will decide which year is the most likely date for entry. For example, he may assess the chances of joining within a year or two as negligible, but rising sharply to a peak in, say, 1973 and then falling away rapidly so that if Britain has not joined by 1976 she may not join at all.

In this example, the forecaster has selected 1973 as the most probable date, and will therefore assume, for forecasting purposes, that this is the effective date of entry. It is important at this point to distinguish carefully between forecasting and planning. While it was reasonable for the forecaster to base his forecasts on the assumption that 1973 was the year of entry, it would *not* have been reasonable for the planner to gear all his plans to a single entry date. The forecaster's range of possibilities may have shown that although 1973 was the most likely date, in two other years the chances were almost as great. If the business conducting this exercise expected to be affected substantially by E.E.C. entry, it should have prepared contingency plans for entry in each of the other years where the chances of entry were regarded as high.

SETTING THE CONSTRAINTS

Assuming that the forecaster has set his assumptions for the forecast period, the next stage is to examine the constraints which limit the operation of the economy. If he is not familiar with the capabilities of the economy and of the related administrative machinery, the forecaster may produce an economic prediction which is absurd. There are limits to what the economy can do and to what the political system will allow.

The constraints within which the economy operates will be discussed under three headings: Physical, Administrative and Political.

PHYSICAL CONSTRAINTS

It is obvious that there is an upper limit to what the economy can physically produce. There is a certain supply of labour in the economy, working with a given stock of equipment. Theoretically, one might argue that the maximum capacity of the economy would be the total population working all the time, using all the equipment available. But only part of the population is available for work. Old-age pensioners and children do not form part of the regular labour supply. It would be possible to increase the labour supply by immigration, but in the United Kingdom this possibility has been virtually excluded by political decision.

Future changes in the age structure of the British population have already been referred to. Population growth is relatively slow in this country and amounts to less than 1% per annum. As the proportion of old and young non-working people in the population is rising, it will be seen that the prospective growth rate of the working population is very low indeed. This is in marked contrast to the United States, where the working population is growing at around 2% a year, and where the maximum productive potential of the economy is increasing correspondingly faster than in Britain.

Another drag on the growth of productive potential is the continuation of the movement towards shorter working hours and longer holidays. Although the actual working week is not shrinking as fast as the official working week, because of overtime working, the likelihood is for the number of hours actually worked each week to continue to decline. Nor is there any reason to expect the trend towards longer holidays to slow down; a few years ago the norm was two weeks a year, now it is three, and in ten years' time it will probably be four.

With a virtually static labour force and the total number of hours actually worked equally sluggish, it will be possible to raise output only if labour productivity rises. 'Productivity' is in some ways an ambiguous concept because, although it is true that greater efficiency can lead to higher output, it is also true that in years when demand is strong, and is allowed to push output up rapidly, higher productivity results from demand expansion. There are elements of both cause and effect in the concept.

Nevertheless, there is considerable evidence that, from the causal point of view, the level of productivity is associated with the stock of capital equipment per worker.[1] It is also generally

[1] See *Why Growth Rates Differ: Post-war Experience in Nine Western Countries*, by Edward F. Denison, Brookings Institution, 1967.

accepted that the capital/worker ratio is low in this country, and that this is one of the reasons why Britain's economic performance has been so much weaker than that of most other industrial nations.

Since the end of the war, the proportion of the economy's output devoted to investment in capital has risen fairly steadily, and the amount of investment in manufacturing industry in relation to the working population has risen quite sharply. The result of this up-grading of the worker, in terms of the amount of equipment available, has been a slowly rising trend in productivity. In the five years 1965–9 output per man-hour rose at an average rate of 3·2% a year, compared with an average of 2·8% per annum in the previous five years. However, it would be unrealistic to expect any dramatic upturn in the productivity trend in the next five years, and this therefore sets an upper limit to the growth rate of the economy.

ADMINISTRATIVE CONSTRAINTS

Much was written at the end of the 1960s about the administrative burden borne by the Inland Revenue as a result of earlier tax changes. In consequence the potential to change the tax system, and thus to influence the economy, was restricted. This form of administrative constraint also applies to other areas of government policy. It takes time to develop new policies and even more time to work out the detailed procedure for setting new policies in motion. No matter how efficient a political party may be at planning changes while it is in opposition, it cannot immediately implement its programme on taking office, even if the economic circumstances are appropriate.

POLITICAL CONSTRAINTS

Similarly, although it may be physically possible for the economy to move beyond these limits, the government of the day may not be prepared to initiate some forms of development, either because of conflict with the ruling party's political philosophy or because such moves may be judged to be unacceptable to the nation as a whole. The most obvious examples of these constraints are those that are political in the narrow sense, that is those which conflict with the philosophy of the party in power. The differences between the major parties have diminished to the point at which many observers cannot distinguish between them. It may also be argued that in recent years the force of economic events has compelled governments to accept policies which are repugnant to them. There is some truth in this argument, but there are still differences in emphasis which play a part in giving a distinctive shape or colour to the overall policy.

In Britain there are differences in emphasis between the parties in the areas of unemployment, income distribution and government intervention. One party may be prepared to tolerate a higher level of unemployment than the other, so that it will persevere longer with policies that raise unemployment levels. Similar distinctions may apply in other areas. Yet, even though one party may be prepared to go further than the other on these issues, there is a point beyond which neither party would go because the nation at large would not condone the consequences. Even on issues where there are no doctrinal differences between the parties, public opinion sets certain limits which the policy-maker cannot escape.

Inflation is a good example. When the Conservative administration took office in 1970, it was effectively prevented from implementing policies that would have aggravated the inflationary situation. It was impolitic for the government to eliminate agricultural subsidies immediately, since this would have raised food prices, pushed up the cost of living and so given another impetus to wage inflation.

The effects of past experience on these constraints can be very important. In Germany, as a result of the unpleasant experiences of hyper-inflation in the 1920s, tolerance of inflation is much lower than in the U.K., although there are signs that this tolerance is now rising.

THE BALANCE OF PAYMENTS

The most important of the constraints affecting economic policy in recent years has been the balance of payments. Successive governments have found that this has been the overriding consideration in shaping policy.

It is important to establish why the balance of payments is a constraint. Chart 10 shows how above-average rises in the

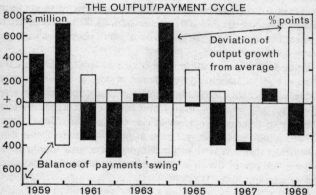

Chart 10

THE OUTPUT/PAYMENT CYCLE

output of the economy during the past ten years have been associated with adverse swings in the current account of the balance of payments. These swings might have been tolerable if they had been compensated by opposite movements on private capital account, if devaluation had been accepted as a policy choice or if the U.K. had had enough reserves to buy time in which to correct the imbalance. The fact remains, however, that the U.K. has inadequate reserves to meet the requirement of an international currency. For this reason Britain cannot sustain a balance of payments deficit and is compelled to react quickly to adverse movements.

It is sometimes argued that the balance of payments is an artificial constraint. If the British economy were allowed to expand rapidly and without interruption for several years the resultant improvement in productivity and unit costs might transform its competitive position *vis-à-vis* the rest of the world. It was this philosophy that inspired the unsuccessful 'dash for freedom' in 1963/4. Other Chancellors have been less adventurous than Mr Maudling on that occasion.

An additional reason why the government is still obliged to aim for a continuing balance of payments surplus on current account is the existence of a large volume of international debt. Both before and after the 1967 devaluation Britain borrowed extensively abroad to meet the payments deficits of those years. Part of those debts, initially more than £3,000 million, is still outstanding and for this reason a continuing payments surplus is required for some years.

Because of the overriding importance of the U.K. balance of payments in influencing government policy, it is vital for the business forecaster to analyse the payments factors correctly. However, this remains one of the most difficult parts of the economy to forecast. An error of one fifth of a percentage point in forecasting the economy's growth rate is negligible, but if the error arose through underestimating exports, this would represent a difference of over £80 million on the balance of payments current account at 1970 prices.

THE WORLD BACKGROUND

The logical sequence the forecaster must follow in preparing a balance of payments forecast is to begin with the world background. Before constructing forecasts of British exports the forecaster must assess prospects in the main export markets and the general trading environment. To construct a forecast of world trade in manufactured goods, it is necessary first to prepare a forecast of world industrial production. In practice, this means preparing forecasts of total output and industrial production for the main industrialized countries of North America, Western Europe and Japan.

To convert this into a forecast of the volume of world trade in manufactures requires assumptions about tariff changes expected during the period (previous examples being the 'Kennedy Round', the formation of the E.E.C. and E.F.T.A.), and about the supply of international liquidity available to finance this flow of trade.

Although there is no clear evidence to suggest that tightening international liquidity or the exchange rate disturbances of the late 1960s seriously impeded the growth of world trade during that period, it is important to form a view about liquidity and exchange rates as part of the world trade forecast (and, at a later stage, in forecasting U.K. exports). This is another illustration of the circular nature of the forecasting process, because two of the most important components of world liquidity are U.S. dollars and sterling held by other countries as part of their international reserves. The rate at which new liquid reserves are created depends, therefore, partly upon the size of the balance of payments deficits of the U.K. and the U.S.A., as well as on the willingness of other countries to accept dollars and sterling. But it is the U.K. balance of payments that we are trying to forecast. At this stage in the forecasting cycle, therefore, one can feed in only a very general view of the likely development of the balance of payments, adjusting it at a later stage when the probable outcome is clearer.

In assessing the U.S. balance of payments prospects attention must be focused not just on the trade balance but also on other major factors such as U.S. military spending abroad (which is related to the international political situation), the U.S. Aid programme, Wall Street stock price levels compared with those in other major stock markets, the Eurodollar market and tourist spending by Americans abroad. The other components of international liquidity must also be examined. Increases in liquidity within the International Monetary Fund system by the creation of Supplementary Drawing Rights or the enlargement of quotas are usually documented at least a year or two in advance, and it is reasonable to assume that the members of the I.M.F. will not allow the rate of new reserve creation to slacken significantly.

Additions to the stock of gold reserves are derived from newly mined gold, gold dis-hoarded by private holders and sales by the Soviet bloc. The forecast must, therefore, take into account movements in the free gold price, any anticipated changes in the role of gold in world liquidity, and economic developments in the Communist countries.

In this assessment, most weight will be given to developments in the U.S. economy, which is by far the largest in the non-Communist world and the major export market for many trading nations. This pre-eminence used to be expressed in the saying 'When America sneezes, the rest of the world catches pneumonia', because of the rapidity and severity with which U.S. recessions were reflected in the economies of other countries. The formation of the E.E.C. and the continued rapid growth of the Japanese economy have weakened the force of this analogy by reducing the relative weight of the U.S. economy, but it is still true that most attention must be given to the future developments in the U.S.

Some assessment of developments in the primary producing countries is also necessary to build up a complete picture of world trade prospects. This involves an appreciation of expected movements in commodity prices, since these determine movements in the primary producers' reserves and hence in their purchases of the industrialized nations' exports. There is typically a lag of about twelve months between a general rise in commodity prices and the spending of the reserves generated by the higher prices.

In forecasting commodity prices over the medium and long term, it is sufficient, for this exercise, to forecast the general level only, ignoring movements in particular commodities. Because of greater efficiency in the use of raw materials, increasing supplies and the substitution of synthetics for natural products, the general level of commodity prices tends to decline when the volume of world industrial production rises by less than 5% a year. Therefore, the forecast of world industrial production is brought into the forecast again at this point.

When looking at the shorter-term forecast for commodity prices, individual commodities must be examined in the light of known information about strikes, opening of new mines, stock levels, crop failures, etc.

A balance of payments forecast is measured in actual money values. Therefore, a forecast of world trade in volume terms is inadequate as background to the analysis. Price factors must be applied to the volume forecast. In the past, the average level of prices of manufactured products in world trade has risen relatively slowly, and between 1956 and 1969 prices rose at an average rate of less than 1% a year. However, this provides an excellent example of the dangers of making naïve projections of past changes forward at the same rate. The pace of price changes accelerated markedly in 1969 and 1970 as inflation spread throughout North America and Western Europe. Although it would be equally wrong to suggest that the most recent experience will be continued throughout the 1970s, it will clearly take some time for the rate of increase to fall back to previous levels.

It is also important when constructing the price forecast to look at both individual countries and exchange rates. Japanese export prices, for example, fell by 12% between 1959 and 1966, and rose by 6% from the second quarter of 1968 to the second quarter of 1970. So far as exchange rates are concerned, since international comparisons of export prices are made in dollar terms, allowance must be made for the effects of currency realignments. For example, the devaluation of sterling at the end of 1967 reduced the index of U.K. export prices of manufactures from 110 in 1967 to 104 in 1968 (1963 = 100), and since the U.K. accounts for over 10% of world trade in manufactures this helped to pull the overall index down from 107 to 106.

EXPORTS

With a forecast of world trade in manufactures, in both value and volume, it is now possible to move on to a forecast of U.K. exports of goods. Britain's share of world trade has been declining steadily, from 18·1% in 1958 to 11·2% in 1969 (in value).

The decline was slowed, but not halted, by devaluation. A forecast which suggested that the U.K. share would increase for several years would be unrealistic, as would one which suggested a much more rapid decline in share than before devaluation. The most reasonable forecast for the early 1970s would be for continuing

Table 17

Export Prices of Manufactures
(*1963 = 100*)

	World	U.K.
1958	97	93
1959	96	93
1960	98	95
1961	99	96
1962	99	98
1963	100	100
1964	101	102
1965	103	105
1966	106	110
1967	107	110
1968	106	104
1969	109	107

decline, but at a slower rate than before devaluation. However, if the price forecast, made at a later stage of the forecasting cycle, showed a more rapid rise in U.K. prices than in competitors' prices, this would justify a faster rate of decline in the U.K. share of world trade.

This approach gives a good overall guide to the expected total of U.K. exports of manufactures, which represent about 85% of Britain's total merchandise exports. The forecast must also be substantiated by a country-by-country analysis of prospects for British exports, in the light of the forecasts of industrial production already prepared for the world trade forecast. This analysis will also involve examination of separately prepared forecasts of U.K. manufacturers' costs, home selling prices and the pressure of home demand, since manufacturers are reluctant to export at a loss. Relative price movements between the U.K., her principal competitors and her main markets (including the effects of exchange rate changes) are also taken into account.

These forecasts are then weighted in accordance with the share of exports going to particular markets. Chart 11 shows how the

Chart 11

EXPORT DESTINATIONS

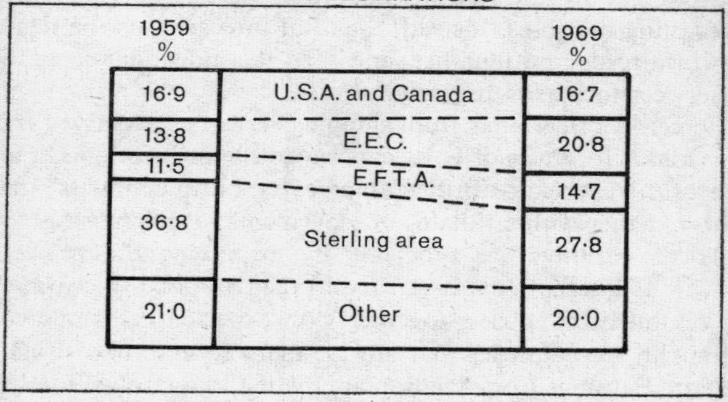

1959 %		1969 %
16·9	U.S.A. and Canada	16·7
13·8	E.E.C.	20·8
11·5	E.F.T.A.	14·7
36·8	Sterling area	27·8
21·0	Other	20·0

proportion of exports going to the relatively slow-growing markets in the overseas sterling area has declined in favour of the faster growing markets of the E.E.C. This will tend to raise the export growth rate in the future.

After the export forecast has been constructed this way round, it should also be checked by forecasting exports by main commodity groups, namely chemicals, textiles, metals, machinery and transport equipment, other manufactures and non-manufactures. For the short-term view, news of large export contracts and the state of export order books should be taken into account.

For balance of payments purposes this forecast will be in value terms, but it must also be consistent with the volume forecasts that are incorporated into a forecast of the overall volume of activity in the U.K. economy. This implies price forecasts for exports, which again must be consistent with movements in domestic costs and prices, competitors' prices and the U.K. share of world trade by value.

Services

Exports of services, which amount to over one-third of exports of goods, cannot be forecast in terms of individual markets, because no country breakdown is available. The annual balance of payments book gives a split of all items in the invisible balance, between sterling and non-sterling areas, but this is of no use for forecasting purposes. Instead, the total forecast must be related to world trade and liquidity, and then the individual categories of services forecast separately.

Forecasts of earnings from shipping services are derived from the volume forecasts of U.K. exports and imports of goods, and of world trade (since British ships carry other countries' trade too), together with estimates of movements in freight rates.

Travel earnings are predicted by examining the projected growth of international tourism and relative prices between the major tourist countries, together with expected economic conditions in the countries that are the main sources of visitors to Britain. Earnings from aviation are related to the travel forecast, passenger fares, and an estimate of the amount of trade to be carried by air.

'Other services' in the balance of payments accounts comprises a miscellaneous collection of items, embracing the insurance, banking and other financial services provided by the City, royalties, services between related companies, professional fees, contractors' overseas earnings and so on. Many of the figures are estimated and this the Central Statistical Office readily admits to being rather crude, so that the analyst cannot hope to achieve a high degree of accuracy in forecasting the total. The attempt must be made, however, because this is now the largest category of services, and its net contribution (earnings minus expenditure) to the balance of payments has increased substantially in recent years. For a long-term forecast, the recent trend can be projected, with adjustments for the likely impact of E.E.C. entry on the financial earnings. (See Table 18.)

Earnings from government services are small, and since they show no marked changes are relatively simple to estimate. These consist mainly of spending in this country by U.S. military forces, and payments by foreign governments for U.K. military services. From 1959 to 1969 this item was between £36 and £46 million a year. There is no reason to expect any marked change.

Table 18

Miscellaneous Services

£ million

	Credits	Debits	Net
1964	558	291	+267
1965	590	320	+270
1966	648	345	+303
1967	755	366	+389
1968	897	432	+465
1969	1,010	490	+520

When the forecasts of individual categories of services have been completed, the total is checked against total exports of goods, to ensure that the forecaster is not predicting a sharp change in the proportion of services to goods without adequate reason.

Volume Estimates

The concept of volume, or constant price, estimates is not easy to apply to services, where there is no physical output to measure. As with goods, a volume forecast is not needed for balance-of-payments forecasting, but it is required to complete the forecast of the economy's total output. This is a particularly difficult area to forecast. Even estimating the past is difficult, for, as the Central Statistical Office points out, 'Exports and imports of services cannot, for the most part, be accurately estimated at constant prices. From the data that are available, only rough price indices can be constructed.'[1] Therefore only a broad estimate of the price factors can be attempted.

1. *National Accounts Statistics: Sources and Methods*, H.M.S.O., 1968.

Freight rate forecasts based on the expected development of world trade and the size of the world's merchant fleet are used to deflate the current-price forecasts of earnings from shipping. For civil aviation, estimates are made of the expected changes in passenger fares, and these are used as price deflators, since passenger transport provides the bulk of revenue. As the movement of freight by air increases, this will have to be brought into the calculation. Earnings from tourism are deflated by appropriate sectors of the U.K. retail price index. For earnings from financial services, the Central Statistical Office uses various components of the retail price index to deflate the historical data; for forecasting purposes it is sufficient to use a forecast of the services component only of the U.K. retail price index.

When the volume forecasts for exports of goods and services are completed, a comparison should be made with forecasts for other components of demand in the economy, to ensure that they do not imply an output growth rate higher than the economy can sustain.

IMPORTS

Forecasting imports is in many ways a more automatic exercise than forecasting exports. There are clear relationships between changes in the levels of stocks and imports, and also between the economy's total output and imports. It is necessary, therefore, to begin the import forecast in volume terms, then to apply price factors and so arrive at the value figures for the balance of payments forecast. In preparing longer-term imports forecasts, the forecast changes in the volume of total final sales (exports, plus investment, plus public and private consumption) are multiplied by an appropriate factor to give the changes in the volume of goods and services imported into the economy. This factor is estimated from the historical evidence of the ratio between changes in output and changes in imports, with adjustments for factors such as the effects of devaluation and entry to the E.E.C.

It is used only as an average over several years, because special factors, such as the introduction of import deposits, may cause short-term fluctuations. Imports tend to rise faster than home demand and the appropriate ratio is now approximately 1·4:1.

In shorter-term forecasts the influence of changes in the levels of stocks is important, because imports are estimated to account for about half of total additions to stocks. Therefore, when forecasting imports on, say, a quarterly basis for up to two years ahead, the forecast of stockbuilding used to build up the total output forecast referred to above must be analysed for its import implications. There is a relationship between the level of production and the level of stocks required for that production. Therefore, a change in production will bring about a change in the desired level of stocks. This too will affect imports.

These methods yield an overall forecast of the volume of imports of goods and services. This is then broken down into separate forecasts for goods and services. The goods forecast is further split into its main components of food, raw materials, semi-manufactures, manufactures and fuel. Although the countries of origin of imports are detailed in the statistics (by value only) there is no special reason to forecast by geographical sources.

Import prices must also be considered, category by category. For manufactures and semi-manufactures, the determining factors are expected cost and price (including exchange rate) movements in supplier countries. For fuels, the overall balance of supply and demand must be projected, together with the changing pattern of fuel requirements as refinery capacity is built up in the U.K.

For food and raw materials, the commodity price forecasts used in predicting world trade should be applied to the particular product mix of U.K. imports. Adjustments must be made to take into account U.K. membership of international commodity agreements, such as the Commonwealth Sugar Agreement and the International Wheat Agreement, and also the fact that some imports of raw materials are brought in under contracts, which are re-negotiated only periodically. Changes in the free-market prices of many commodities are not reflected in U.K. import prices until two or three quarters later.

Most of the factors considered in forecasting the export of services are also brought into the services imports forecast. Military spending abroad (which amounts to about £275 million a year) has to be forecast in the light of government defence commitments overseas. This item in particular has had great significance for the balance of payments and strenuous efforts have been made to reduce the total and so to relieve the strain in the payments position.

TRANSFER PAYMENTS

The forecasts discussed so far have concerned payments and receipts for goods and services only. These are the items that enter not only into the balance of payments, but also into the calculation of total output and spending in the economy. To complete the forecast of the balance of payments on current account, transfer payments must also be brought into the reckoning. The three categories to be considered are:

a) interest, profits and dividends
b) government transfers, and
c) private transfers.

Interest, profits and dividends are forecast by examining expected movements in interest rates, both in the U.K. and abroad, profit forecasts for the U.K. and for major foreign countries (especially the U.S., where Britain has substantial investments), reports of major companies operating overseas and figures of foreign investment in the U.K. and British investment abroad. It is unrealistic to aim at a high degree of precision in these forecasts because the official statistics are subject to such wide margins of error. Early in 1970, for example, the Central Statistical Office announced that the net earnings of oil companies (which are included in this item) had been overstated by a total of £180 million from 1964 to 1968.

The main items of government transfers are economic grants and contributions to international organizations (such as the International Development Association), the aid programme and transfers for military purposes (e.g. contributions to N.A.T.O.). There is no credit side for this item while the debit side is not volatile and is well documented in the government's expenditure estimates.

The net outflow of private transfers has risen substantially in recent years (from £23 million in 1964 to £77 million in 1969). This is associated with homeward remittances by immigrants, and can be expected to continue to rise steadily. In the past, Irish

Table 19

Balance of Payments – Current Account

£ million

	1964	1965	1966	1967	1968	1969
Export of goods	4,486	4,817	5,182	5,122	6,273	7,061
Import of goods	5,003	5,042	5,214	5,576	6,807	7,141
Visible trade balance	−517	−225	−32	−454	−534	−80
Payments for U.S. military aircraft	−2	−12	−41	−98	−109	−61
Visible balance	−519	−237	−73	−552	−643	−141
Invisible credits	2,642	2,849	2,898	3,134	3,669	4,129
Services	1,621	1,715	1,805	2,022	2,414	2,661
Interest, profits and dividends	890	999	959	969	1,094	1,292
Transfers	131	135	134	143	161	176
Invisible debits	2,518	2,689	2,782	2,894	3,345	3,572
Services	1,706	1,788	1,840	1,904	2,132	2,303
Interest, profits and dividends	495	557	579	601	777	841
Transfers	317	344	363	389	436	428
Invisible balance	+124	+160	+116	+240	+322	+557
CURRENT BALANCE	−395	−77	+43	−312	−321	+415

workers in the U.K. accounted for substantial transfers to Ireland. More recently the build-up of workers from the Commonwealth has resulted in an increased flow of remittances back to their countries of origin.

CAPITAL FLOWS

These calculations complete the forecasts of the current account, and show how, as a trading nation, Britain is faring *vis-à-vis* the rest of the world. But for a complete appreciation of the total currency flows in the balance of payments, it is necessary to forecast investment and other capital flows.

The presentation of this part of the balance of payments statistics was changed by the Central Statistical Office in 1970. The previous classification of the accounts tried to separate long-term capital movements from short-term movements, in the belief that the former, together with the current balance, were the most relevant elements in presenting an account of the overall payments position. This classification was seen to be unrealistic because of the difficulty of separating short-term from long-term capital flows. Moreover, the operational significance of the money movement concept (which used to be shown as 'the balance of monetary movements') is far greater. What the authorities are concerned about in their watch on the foreign exchanges is the total currency flow out of or into the United Kingdom, and how this can be influenced and controlled. The new presentation of the balance of payments statistics makes sound sense, the more so since the significance of the balance of payments is to indicate likely changes in economic policy. The purpose of balance of payments forecasting is to decide what action the government will take, so the forecaster must analyse all the factors entering the authorities' assessment of the balance of payments.

However, this new arrangement has not made the forecaster's task any easier, and the monetary movements will always remain difficult to predict. The most important items are the flows of investment, changes in the amount of trade credit given and received, and changes in other countries' sterling balances held in the U.K. Between 1964 and 1969, the net investment flow swung from an outflow of £238 million to an inflow of £67 million – a change which can be attributed partly to the restrictions on British investment abroad and partly to U.S. investment

Table 20

Investment and Other Capital Flows

£ million

	1964	1965	1966	1967	1968	1969
Official long-term capital	−115	−85	−80	−57	+17	−98
Overseas investment in U.K.	+161	+242	+277	+381	+615	+684
U.K. private investment abroad	−399	−354	−303	−463	−735	−617
Eurodollar borrowing for investment abroad	+15	+9	+15	+73	+176	+70
Import credit	−1	+4	−3	+27	+67	+256
Export credit	−70	−69	−183	−185	−345	−333
Sterling balances	+50	−92	−123	−216	−377	+108
Foreign currency transactions of U.K. banks	+138	−73	−162	−47	−124	−106
Other short-term flows	−67	+110	−2	+32	−53	−16
TOTAL CAPITAL FLOW	−289	−308	−564	−455	−759	+48

in the U.K. as a base for exporting to Europe. So the forecast must involve assumptions about the continuance and effectiveness of investment restrictions, and of the scope for further foreign investment in the U.K.

Trade credit has to be split between imports and exports, to build up a meaningful forecast. The big increase in import credit in 1969 represented foreign financing of import deposits.

However, although the abolition of the deposits resulted in the unwinding of some of this borrowing, it is likely that quite a large part will remain. In forecasting both import and export credit, the forecasts of import and export values will obviously be relevant. It is also important to take into account the liquidity position in the U.K. and in the country's principal trading partners, as well as the state of confidence in sterling, since these factors will affect the desire and ability to give and take credit.

Table 21 shows how the total currency flow is made up. The

Table 21

Total Currency Flow

£ million

	1964	1965	1966	1967	1968	1969
Current balance	−395	−77	+43	−312	−319	+416
Investment and other capital flows	−289	−308	−564	−455	−759	+48
Balancing item	−11	+32	−26	+201	−81	+279
E.E.A. loss on forwards	–	–	–	−105	−251	–
TOTAL CURRENCY FLOW	−695	−353	−547	−671	−1,410	+743

'E.E.A. loss on forwards' is the losses made by the Exchange Equalisation Account in its vain attempts to support the forward sterling market before devaluation.

'balancing item' shown in the accounts is too large to ignore but impossible to predict, because it represents the errors and omissions in the official statistics. These are the currency flows which the authorities know to have taken place, but which cannot be precisely allocated within the accounts. Changes in the balancing item can reflect changing confidence in sterling. This in turn tends to influence the timing of payments for exports and imports. It has been suggested, for example, that a favourable movement of those differences in timing, or 'leads and lags', lay behind the unusually large balancing item in 1969. For forecasting purposes the balancing item is best regarded as neutral over a period of years. It is generally the case that a plus in one year is followed by a minus and this can be used as a forecasting guide.

When the forecast of the total currency flow is complete, the effects of these movements on government policy can be considered. The government's reactions will be determined by the

Table 22
Official Financing
£ million

	1964	1965	1966	1967	1968	1969
I.M.F. (drawings + repayments −)	+357	+489	+15	−339	+506	−30
Other monetary authorities (drawings + repayments −)	+216	+110	+294	+691	+790	−669
Sale of $ portfolio	–	–	+316	+204	–	–
Official reserves (drawings + repayments −)	+122	−246	−34	+115	+114	−44
TOTAL OFFICIAL FINANCING	+695	+353	+591*	+671	+1,410	−743

* The difference between this figure and the £547 million shown in Table 21 represents a gold subscription to the I.M.F.

policy options open to it. If a massive outflow of currency can easily be financed, the reaction will be different from a situation where all the financing possibilities have been exhausted. Table 22 shows how the currency outflow was financed in 1964–8 and how the inflow was disposed of in 1969.[1]

1. Allocations of Special Drawing Rights, which began in 1970, are shown in the balance of payments accounts as separate from the Total Currency Flow and from Official Financing. The effect of the allocations is to reduce the need for official financing (if the total currency flow is negative) or to increase the funds available for debt repayment or reserve building (if the currency flow is positive).

One source of financing no longer exists. In 1966 and 1967 the entire portfolio of government-owned foreign securities was sold and the proceeds transferred to the reserves. Ability to borrow from the I.M.F. is determined by the size of the U.K.'s quota, the amount already outstanding, and the extent to which other countries have borrowed sterling from the Fund. The willingness of other monetary authorities to finance the U.K. balance of payments depends on their own payments positions, the amount of debt outstanding and political factors. If the possibilities of borrowing have been exhausted and the reserves have been run down, a forecast of a large currency outflow is likely to cause a marked policy reaction, leading in the last resort to devaluation.

When the balance of payments forecast is complete, it may also be checked against payments forecasts for the U.K.'s major trading partners, to ensure a reasonable degree of consistency. However, in view of the difficulties and uncertainties referred to above in constructing a balance of payments forecast for one country, it will be apparent that a large-scale forecast for many countries, although desirable in theory, may be both hazardous and extremely costly in practice.

THE BALANCE OF PAYMENTS AND THE FIRM

This discussion of how balance of payments forecasts are prepared has been set in the context of the influence of the balance of payments on government policy. The individual firm is interested, because the changes in government policy which flow from the balance of payments forecast will affect its own operating environment. In addition, for many companies which export a large part of their output or are heavily dependent on imported raw materials and machinery, particular parts of the forecast will be directly useful in their own planning. The analyses of economic prospects in overseas countries, which are an essential part of the overall forecast for total U.K. exports, will form the basis of the company's overseas marketing plans. Forecasts of import prices, adjusted to fit the particular mix of raw materials that the company uses, can be incorporated into its overall cost forecasts and budgets.[1]

Finally, there are many firms which are neither direct exporters nor importers, and which may consider balance of payments forecasting remote and unnecessary. They are wrong, because they *are* affected indirectly by what is happening to imports and exports. They may not import directly, but many of their suppliers do. They must anticipate changes in import prices because these will eventually work through into their own costs. It is important for the manufacturer to be fully informed of his suppliers' costs, so that he is in a better position to bargain and to plan his own pricing policy. It is essential to know as much about suppliers' and customers' businesses as possible and this highlights the need to have some understanding of the balance of payments, the payments prospects and how these will affect government policy.

A general understanding of the importance of the balance of payments as an influence on government policy will assist the firm in its appraisal of its operating environment. Many important business decisions, notably the location of plant in different countries, will be influenced by balance of payments and future exchange rate considerations. For example, Britain's entry to the Common Market poses critical problems to the business decision-taker in this respect, and although the individual firm cannot be expected to carry out balance of payments studies in depth as outlined above, it will find it worthwhile to obtain some analysis of the problem so as to identify the risks involved in the investment decision.

1. Forecasts of import prices for balance of payments purposes do not allow for adjustments in tariffs. Imports are recorded c.i.f., and are then adjusted down to an f.o.b. basis for the balance of payments statistics, so tariffs are not included. When calculating the impact of import prices on the individual firm, tariffs must be added in.

CHAPTER 5

Monetary Policy, Cash Flows and Interest Rates

BY C. C. DAVIS

The successful forecasting of monetary policy, which in the final analysis signifies forecasts of the availability of funds and the rate of interest, is now widely recognized as an important factor in corporate planning and budgetary control. Such recognition stems from the fact that all economic transactions originate from and are settled through a movement of money (regardless of whether this is effected through an immediate transfer or through an extension of credit). This implies that changes in the volume of money and credit must inevitably exert some influence on the output of goods and services and/or the general level of prices.

Behind this apparently simple relationship there are a number of specific problems and complications. The phrase 'monetary policy' necessarily implies the exercise of judgement by those responsible in the Treasury and the Bank of England concerning the objectives which government economic policy should be seeking to achieve at any given point in time. Two main complications arise from this; in the first instance, monetary policy is not the only way by which the authorities are in a position to regulate the economy. Both fiscal policy and direct controls are in theory alternative methods for achieving the same objectives and, although the differences between these various courses are often overemphasized, changes in the overall level of taxation and the incidence of specific taxes always have some impact on the monetary system. Moreover, there is still a wide area over which fiscal policy in particular can be, and has been, readily substituted for the more active use of monetary measures.

THE ROLE OF MONETARY POLICY

The second, but less obvious, difficulty stems from the fact that the emphasis placed on monetary policy has never been solely determined by the extent to which other courses of action have been considered more appropriate, as, for example, on political or social grounds. Changing views on just how far monetary policy itself is capable of influencing the economy have also proved an important factor, particularly over the past decade. This is one area in which economists have long debated the pro's and con's but where, unfortunately, an inconclusive outcome remains an acute source of difficulty to practising business economists. The conclusions reached by the Committee on the Working of the Monetary System 1959 (the Radcliffe Report) have been called in question and it is of interest to note what happened in the decade following the publication of the Report.

Chart 12

U.K. INTEREST RATES

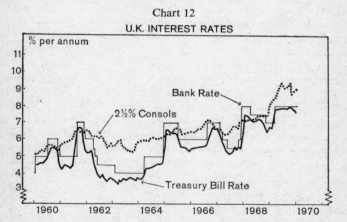

In that period Bank Rate was changed on no less than twenty-four occasions, while short-term money market rates moved within a range of 3% and 8% and long-term rates between 5½% and nearly 10% (see Chart 12). Coupled with these extreme movements were almost permanent limits and restrictions of the volume of bank lending and most other forms of credit.

The timing of the frequent changes in Bank Rate, and thus in nearly all other short-term rates, was largely determined by the recurrent crises in the U.K. balance of payments position, finally culminating in the devaluation of November 1967. Long-term interest rates, on the other hand, followed a less cyclical pattern, but showed a secular upward trend throughout the decade. This can be taken as one indication of the extent to which other factors exercised a more important influence on this sector of the money market.

Yet whereas the main practical result of the Radcliffe Report has been a policy principally geared to influencing the economy's balance of payments position, the 'monetarist school' postulates a more far-reaching policy. It is claimed that changes in the money supply are capable of influencing, quickly and with a high degree of accuracy, both the external payments and the general level of activity in the domestic economy. This can be done directly, through control over the volume of money, rather than indirectly by establishing appropriate levels of interest rates.

In support of this approach, it is an inescapable conclusion that the balance between the supply of money (defined as the community's stock of liquid assets as represented by its deposits with the banks and the cash in circulation) and the need for money (represented by the national income) does have a significant influence on the long-term rate of interest. In this context, the balance between demand and supply may conveniently be expressed in terms of the 'velocity of circulation' or the rate at which the existing stock of money has to be turned over each year to finance the distribution and movement of the national income. The general trend over nearly the whole of the post-war period of a steadily rising velocity of circulation, accompanied by a rise in the long-term rate of interest, will be immediately evident from Table 23. Despite this close relationship, it is important to point out certain special features of the period, which, while not invalidating the previous argument, do at least have some bearing on forecasts of future trends.

In the first instance, the way in which the United Kingdom

financed its war 'effort' between 1939 and 1945 had the effect of leaving the economy in an abnormally liquid position; the rapidity with which the economy returned to a less liquid state (and therefore to higher interest rates) in the period up to the early

Table 23

Velocity and the Long-term Rate of Interest

	*Income velocity of circulation**	*Long-term rate of interest†*
		%
1946	1·22	2·60
1948	1·29	3·21
1950	1·39	3·54
1952	1·66	4·23
1954	1·75	3·75
1956	2·03	4·73
1958	2·12	4·98
1960	2·70	5·42
1962	2·31	5·98
1963	2·50	5·58
1964	2·54	6·03
1965	2·56	6·42
1966	2·53	6·80
1967	2·51	6·69
1968	2·43	7·39
1969	2·49	8·89

* Gross Domestic Product at Factor Cost/Money Supply
† Yield on 2½% Consols

1950s must, therefore, be taken as representing a return to a more normal relationship. Secondly, it will be apparent that in the four-year period 1965–9 the previously close and positive relationship between changes in the velocity of circulation and the long-term rate of interest no longer held good; and that in fact, whereas the velocity of circulation declined, interest rates escalated at a far more rapid rate than at any time in the preceding twenty years.

This most recent experience highlights two secondary factors: first, that annual increases in the national income reflect not only increases in the volume of goods and services, or total real output, but also changes in the price level. Given that the volume of money outstanding at any point in time is primarily used as a 'medium of exchange' and that it is also used as a 'store of value', it follows that the repercussions on the level of interest rates of an increase in the national income in real terms is likely to be different from one which results principally from a rise in the overall price level.

Secondly, whereas it is general practice to regard annual changes in the money supply as being derived from one single source, this is an over-simplification. The elements which determine changes in the money supply are in reality derived from two main sources: the borrowing requirement of the public sector, and the volume of bank lending to the private sector. The relative importance of these two sources of money as an influence on long-term interest rates is discussed in greater detail later in this chapter. All that requires to be borne in mind at this stage is that an increase in the money supply resulting from an increase in the government's borrowing requirement need not, and does not, necessarily have the same effect on the long-term rate of interest as one resulting from a rise in bank lending to the private sector.

After making due allowance for these qualifications, it is nevertheless possible to establish a forecast of long-term interest rates in terms of a forecast of incomes and the money supply. The question of forecasting the national income has already been discussed in detail in Chapter 2 and an important conclusion is that forecasts can be made with a fair degree of confidence, since fluctuations in the growth rate of national income have not been highly significant in the past. This is one area in which major changes in trend occur only gradually.

Despite the remarkable *long-term* consistency in the post-war period of the annual growth in money incomes the rate of growth in real output and the rate of price inflation tend to fluctuate to quite a marked extent over the shorter-term business cycle. The changing importance of the inflation factor as a determinant

Table 24

Retail Prices and Interest Rates

	% change in retail price index	% change in long-term rate of interest *
1960	+1.0	+12·4
1961	+3·4	+14·4
1962	+4·3	−3·5
1963	+2·0	−6·7
1964	+3·3	+8·1
1965	+4·8	+6·5
1966	+3·9	+5·9
1967	+2·5	−1·6
1968	+4·7	+10·5
1969	+5·4	+20·2

* Yield on 2½% Consols.

of the growth in the national income must, therefore, be taken into account in forecasts of cyclical changes in long-term interest rates. It will be seen from Table 24 that during a period of rapid rise in interest rates, retail prices have also risen sharply.

CHANGES IN MONEY SUPPLY

Turning to the problem of forecasting the future rate of growth in the money supply, it will be noted (Table 25) that the net deposits of U.K. residents with the U.K. banking sector represent by far the most important item, both in absolute terms and in terms of annual changes. The currency issue (notes and coin) on the other hand is a relatively minor factor, which expands at a more or less steady rate to meet the community's additional requirements for ready cash as the value of sales rise. Since 1962 this increase has averaged just over £100 million a year, and, since there are no strong grounds for assuming any significant change in the future, forecasts of this particular component of the total money supply do not normally present any great difficulty.

Table 25

Money Supply

(Average amounts outstanding)

£ million

	Currency in circulation with public	Net deposits of U.K. residents with banking sector	Total money supply
	+	+	=
1963	2,240	8,505	10,745
1964	2,341	9,085	11,426
1965	2,517	9,648	12,165
1966	2,702	10,272	12,974
1967	2,796	10,963	13,759
1968	2,887	12,204	15,091
1969	2,954	12,790	15,744

As far as the more significant factor affecting the money supply is concerned, namely bank deposits, it can, at the outset, be readily established that a change in the central government's borrowing requirement has a certain influence on the rate of expansion from year to year. (Table 26.) The relationship is admittedly far from exact, but nevertheless represents a useful starting point on which to base short-term or medium-term forecasts of the money supply. This is because the government's borrowing requirement is outlined annually in the Budget statement, and the out-turn of both revenue and expenditure generally comes close to these Treasury estimates.

It is nonetheless important to bear in mind that the Budget estimates are based on forecasts which assume no change in fiscal policy apart from those introduced in the Budget itself. Those engaged in forecasting are thus still faced with the task of coming to at least some general conclusions concerning the probability of changes during the twelve months between Budgets.

To quote an example, it is clear that the decision to reduce and abolish the import deposit scheme during the 1970/71 fiscal year radically altered the government's financing for the period. The forecaster who aims to anticipate such changes in policy must, therefore, make some assessment of the likelihood of such an occurrence, as well as to quantify its impact.

Table 26

Government Borrowing and Money Supply

£ million

	Central government net balance	*Increase in deposits of U.K. residents with the banking sector*	*Increase in money supply*
1962	−79	381	311
1963	+148	625	697
1964	+423	388	597
1965	+597	720	915
1966	+521	470	536
1967	+1,134	1,184	1,309
1968	+755	935	987
1969	−1,116	317	463

Although policy changes of this kind have been important in the past, the basic reason that changes in the overall money supply are not directly related to the government's borrowing requirement stems from the fact that the borrowing requirement itself can be 'financed' through more than one source (see Table 27).

It will be immediately apparent that in recent years a large part of the central government's requirement has been met from borrowing overseas. The take-up of this debt by foreign institutions, which include the International Monetary Fund as well as official government agencies, has, of course, represented the counterpart to the run of balance of payments deficits incurred

Table 27

Net Acquisition of Government Debt

£ million

	By overseas sector	By U.K. banks	By other U.K. residents	Currency	Central government net balance
	+	+	+	+	=
1962	−290	+41	+240	−70	−79
1963	+111	+3	−38	+72	+148
1964	+637	−530	+107	+209	+423
1965	+114	+308	−21	+195	+597
1966	+459	+121	−124	+66	+521
1967	+494	+231	+275	+125	+1,134
1968	+1,166	−140	−321	+52	+755
1969	−688	−655	+82	+146	−1,116

by the United Kingdom during the 1960s; it therefore reflects the way in which these deficits were financed, as opposed to a drawing down of the official reserves of gold and foreign currencies.

DOMESTIC CREDIT EXPANSION

As was shown in Chapter 4, forecasts of the balance of payments position, and hence changes in the level of overseas indebtedness, are notoriously difficult. Moreover, solving this problem has not been significantly eased – as is sometimes suggested – by the introduction of a concept into U.K. monetary policy known as Domestic Credit Expansion (D.C.E.).

Changes in domestic credit comprise changes in money supply less the balance of payments. There is basically nothing new in the concept itself, which in many respects has a certain similarity to the mechanism that used to provide for a close relationship between the volume of money circulating within the internal economy and the external payments position which used to apply under the gold standard. D.C.E., unlike the money supply, is largely unaffected by receipts from external transactions, whether as a result of short-term capital flows or the balance of payments. Its main advantage, therefore, lies in making possible a more accurate assessment of domestic monetary policy, for while a change in receipts from external transactions can alter the pattern of the financing of the central government's borrowing requirement as between sources, it does not directly affect its total. D.C.E. on the other hand will be larger than the increase in the total money supply when financial transactions with the overseas section are in deficit, and smaller when such transactions are in surplus. This is illustrated in Chart 13.

Chart 13

MONEY SUPPLY AND DOMESTIC CREDIT EXPANSION

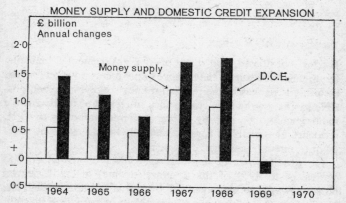

Breaking down the problem of forecasting likely changes in the money supply in this way is also useful now that the government appears to be committed to spelling out annually a figure for Domestic Credit Expansion which it holds to be appropriate. £400 million was the limit set by the Chancellor in his Letter of Intent to the International Monetary Fund for 1969/70 (a limit comfortably met), while an increase of £900 million was laid down as a less formal commitment for 1970/71. Here again, however, the mere fact that such figures are put forward does not excuse those engaged in forecasting from making their own assessment of whether they will be achieved, even if they provide a useful base for arriving at a comprehensive forecast of the future availability of credit and the level of interest rates. In addition, the limitations of the D.C.E. concept must always be borne in mind. It is only one component of the money supply equation, and in the context of the U.K. monetary system, which is strongly influenced by external pressures, the effects of changes in the receipt and payment of funds arising from overseas transactions are often no less important than domestic influences. In any event the U.K. authorities have now abandoned the attempt to apply the D.C.E. regulator and monetary management since 1970 has been accorded a less important role.

THE NATIONAL DEBT

Having considered that part of the government's financing requirement relating to the balance of payments position and the associated changes in the internal money supply, it is then possible to analyse the impact of policy in respect of the borrowing requirement to be met by selling government bonds to U.K. residents. This problem is more generally known as the management of the national debt.

The absolute size of this debt (£33,500 million in 1969 and equivalent to 89% of the national income) makes a neutral policy towards its management by the authorities impossible. Not only is there the continuing problem of refunding the debt as various gilt-edged issues reach maturity, but, as the Radcliffe Committee pointed out, the mere existence of the debt on this scale is an indispensable part of the mechanism which gives strength to the structure of the financial institutions of this country. Measures designed to change the structure of the debt have, therefore, always to take this factor into account.

The Bank of England's basic policy in managing the debt has traditionally been one of maximizing, over the long term, the holding of debt by the private sector, taken to include the whole range of financial institutions such as insurance companies and pension funds, as well as the general public. To the extent that this policy is successful, a reduction in the money supply is achieved, since payments for the purchase of government debt lead to a reduction of bank deposits by the private sector and a transfer to the Bank of England. Exactly the same result occurs when the banking system itself buys gilt-edged.

Although no exception has ever been taken to these basic objectives of Bank of England policy, there has been mounting criticism in recent years of the way in which this policy has been put into practice. This has been specifically directed at the Bank of England's contention that in the last resort maximizing 'outside' holdings of government debt depends upon the maintenance of an orderly market in which prices move gradually rather than dramatically. To achieve this the Bank of England must stand ready to intervene by buying or selling bonds on a scale sufficient to keep prices – and thus interest rates – at levels felt to be appropriate in the circumstances prevailing at the time.

It is now argued, however, that such a policy is basically wrong, and that the drastic decline in bond prices that has occurred over the past decade is a measure of this mistake. This claim, which now lies at the heart of the argument of the 'monetarist' school of economists, suggests that any prolonged intervention in the market must be self-defeating, on the grounds that once it is known that the Bank of England is supporting the market in government debt at what is regarded as an 'unnatural' level, a volume of private sales is encouraged. This must inevitably inflate the money supply, since as the Bank of England buys bonds from the public it effectively puts extra cash into private hands, thereby adding to those very pressures which dictated a decline in prices in the first instance.[1]

Past experience certainly provides a good deal of support for this diagnosis. It is nevertheless a case where diagnosis is perhaps easier than cure, for the latter implies that successful control over

1. Professor A. A. Walters has suggested that this policy is equivalent to crucifying Britain on a 'gilt-edged' cross (*Money in Boom and Slump*, I.E.A. Hobart Paper 44).

the money supply has to be effected through the sale of bonds by the government broker on a *falling* market – an operation which is manifestly impossible.

Generally, the Bank of England can now successfully sell bonds to the public only on a rising market. It is admittedly true that at any point in time there must be a given level of prices which would attract buyers of bonds, thereby contributing to the deflation of the money supply, but as yet insufficient experience exists from which to establish just how far a decline in bond prices would have to be pushed in order to achieve this objective. During 1969 and 1970 it seemed as if gilt-edge yields of nearly 10% proved to be the level at which buyers were tempted back into the market, but changes in expectations with regard to inflation and government policy could result in different levels of turning point. In addition, there is little evidence of the effect which such a dramatic rise in interest rates would have on the whole structure of the financial system.

While this argument over alternative methods of managing the national debt and the exercise of greater control over one further component of the money supply may appear inconclusive, there seems little doubt that the debate itself has already succeeded in bringing about a certain change of emphasis in monetary policy. All the evidence from the dramatic decline in bond prices in early 1969, followed by a strong recovery in the latter half of that year, and an equally dramatic collapse and recovery in the spring of 1970, points to a much reduced degree of intervention by the Bank of England in the market. As a result, there was a smaller impact on the money supply compared with what may have been expected from previous experience. It is certainly too early to gauge the longer-term repercussions of this apparent change in policy, but at this stage two tentative conclusions seem justified. Firstly, long-term rates of interest will prove more volatile in the future; secondly, the change in emphasis from a more to less 'orderly' market is liable to have the effect of keeping these same rates at a rather higher level than would otherwise be the case.

Even if this analysis proves correct, however, the recent change in policy still makes it virtually impossible to assess those short-term changes in the money supply resulting from transactions in government debt. Support for this conclusion is already available from policy decisions taken in 1969/70 (at a time when the government was committed to a fixed limit to D.C.E.). The size of the government's financial surplus, coupled with the duration and severity of the credit squeeze on the private sector, could be taken as reflecting not so much a conversion to the efficacy of control over the level of demand in the economy via D.C.E., but rather, and more simply, the need to provide the maximum amount of room for manoeuvre in the light of the uncertain outcome of operations in the gilt-edge market.

Fortunately for those engaged in forecasting, this conclusion is not quite so discouraging as might appear at first sight. Even if forecasts of the future *demand* for government debt are surrounded by such a high degree of uncertainty, both in the short and the long term, a more accurate assessment is possible of the factors affecting *supply*. Here all the evidence currently points to a much reduced borrowing requirement, at least through the first half of the 1970s. The crucial factor in this context will be the borrowing requirement of the public sector as a whole. This is determined by the likely capital spending programme of the public authorities on the one hand, and the volume of savings that can be generated through taxation and operating surpluses of the nationalized industries on the other – the latter being largely dependent upon the prices charged to the public.

There are currently two important reasons for suggesting that over the next few years at least the public sector will in fact not need to call upon external finance on anything like the same scale as in the past decade:

1) A number of public-sector bodies are unlikely to be faced with such large-scale investment programmes as they were in the 1960s. These include two whose capital requirements have traditionally been particularly large, notably the electricity industry (where the present existence of more than adequate capacity implies a more modest rate of expansion in the future) and housebuilding.

2) The recent change in the policies to be pursued by public corporations, which include a raising of target rates of return on capital employed, also carries the obligation to raise a greater proportion of their capital requirements through the price mechanism. The across-the-board price increases introduced since 1968 have already raised the cash flows of the nationalized industries by a substantial amount, thus ensuring that a greater proportion of their capital requirements will be met from the consumer. The 5% price rise limitation introduced in 1971 will temporarily interrupt this process.

For these reasons, there are good grounds for supposing that the public sector's overall borrowing requirement will not rise to any important extent from its current level. This in turn will give the authorities the power to exercise greater control over the national debt, which, other things being equal, must provide some impetus towards a decline in long-term interest rates. However, as we have seen, the rate and overall extent of any such decline will still remain closely linked to the wider objectives of monetary policy in its new guise.

BANK DEPOSITS

Having discussed the impact of the government's borrowing requirement on the monetary system and having outlined certain factors likely to influence its magnitude in the future, one can then integrate this public-sector component into the overall framework of the elements affecting the growth in the deposits of the banking system, as shown in Table 28.

It will be immediately apparent that in addition to lending to the public sector, the other major influence on the rate of growth of bank deposits is changes in the volume of advances made to the private sector under the old adage found in nearly all economic textbooks – 'each bank advance creates its own deposit'. In a free, uncomplicated system, changes in lending would be dependent upon the banks' liquidity requirements, together with their analysis of the risk factor in lending. The risk factor in making advances has to be balanced against the obvious incentive to employ as large a proportion as possible of bank funds in higher yielding assets. In practice, however, the situation is not as simple as this, since the ability of the banks to increase their total lending at will is limited by a number of constraints.

Table 28

Changes in Financial Assets/Liabilities of the Banking Sector

£ million

	Lending to public sector	Lending to private sector	Net liabilities to non-residents	Non-deposit liabilities	Net deposits of U.K. residents
1962	+115	+497	−132	−99	+381
1963	+73	+673	−67	−54	+625
1964	−381	+950	−107	−74	+388
1965	+429	+490	−43	−156	+720
1966	+220	+111	+264	−125	+470
1967	+571	+568	+79	−34	+1,184
1968	+73	+685	+242	−65	+935

In the first place, the banks' traditional policy has been to charge similar rates of interest (all directly linked to Bank Rate) to particular categories of borrowers. They have never, therefore, attempted to seek additional borrowers by a competitive lowering of rates, which in any event might not lead to any proportionate increase in the volume of borrowing from the banking system as a whole. As a result, the volume of lending extended by the banks still depends in large part on the strength of demand for funds from suitable borrowers.

In addition, new lending techniques which might have boosted the demand for funds have been few and far between in the post-war period; personal loan schemes are possibly the only important exception. This is in no way intended as a criticism, for one of the reasons why the banks have not taken a greater initiative is the fact that controls on the volume of bank lending have been an almost permanent feature of monetary policy throughout the post-war period. The official explanation for such a policy was touched upon earlier – namely that one of the problems facing the authorities in pursuing an effective monetary policy has lain in the growing difficulty of selling large quantities of public-sector debt at times when national economic policy has required the deflation of demand and a contraction in the rate of growth in the money supply.

When such a situation prevails, the banks' role of providing 'residual' finance for the public sector takes on added importance. By the same token, however, it also generates an additional volume of liquidity (through the take-up, directly or indirectly, of Treasury Bills) upon the base on which the banks expand their lending. At some points in the past the banks also had such large holdings of liquid assets that, even when conditions favoured large sales of bonds by the Bank of England, this could never be sufficient to put severe pressure on bank liquidity. It was exactly for this reason that Special Deposits were introduced. These deposits are placed with the Bank of England and excluded from the funds from which the bank liquidity ratios are calculated. The Special Deposits are thus effectively sterilized.

Despite official requests to limit the overall volume of lending, bank advances have nevertheless risen at a significantly faster rate than deposits over the past decade. This is shown in Chart 14. This also illustrates the extent of the resulting reduction in the banking system's liquidity ratio, coupled with the decline in the importance of the banks' holding of gilt-edged – the other principal illiquid asset held by the banks.

The trend over the 1960s has not been regular, however. Advances rose at an exceptionally rapid rate in the years up to 1965 when the advance/deposit ratio stood at 55%, 10 percentage points more than in 1960. The banks made large-scale sales of investments – almost for the first time since the war – to accommodate the increase in advances. Even so they found considerable difficulty in meeting their liquidity ratio requirement, notwithstanding the fact that the latter had been reduced from 30% to 28% during the intervening period.

Thereafter, mainly as a result of credit restrictions, a partial return to the previous pattern was achieved. Bank lending rose only slowly between 1965 and 1967, during which period a small increase in investment/deposit ratios was achieved. Liquidity ratios would also have shown an improvement but for the re-activation of Special Deposits which were progressively increased to account for 2% of total deposits. The situation changed

Chart 14

DISTRIBUTION OF DEPOSITS

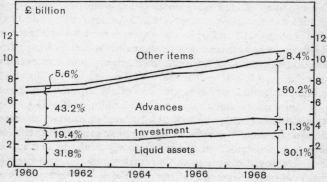

again in 1968 and 1969. In the former year, a large central government borrowing requirement was more than matched by sterling receipts from external transactions arising out of the balance of payments deficit (i.e. the take-up of debt by the overseas sector), while in the latter year the banks' liquidity came under even greater strain as a result of the turn-round in the central government's finances, and the emergence of a very large public-sector surplus. The effect of this surplus was not only to reduce sharply the volume of liquid assets available to the banks through the Treasury Bill issue, but also to produce a run-down of deposits as funds were drawn out of the private sector. It was for this reason that fears were expressed of a particularly acute credit squeeze in the first quarter of 1970, at the height of the tax-gathering season. That this did not occur (or at least not to the extent anticipated) was the result of an inflow of funds through the emergence of a balance of payments surplus, including a large inflow of capital from abroad. This illustration again emphasizes the importance of the external payments position on the internal money supply.

This brief résumé of developments within the banking system since 1960 provides the background from which some conclusions can be drawn for arriving at a forecast of the future level of bank lending and bank deposits. From the evidence, it would appear as a broad guideline that the banks have come to regard a ratio of advances to deposits of about 50% as an appropriate long-term policy. The ratio is inevitably bound to fluctuate in the short term with changes in the demand for credit, itself a function of the level of economic activity and the business cycle.

The 50% ratio is not as arbitrary as might appear at first sight. It is in the banks' obvious interests to employ as large a part of their funds as possible by way of advances, since these represent the asset on which the highest rates of return can be achieved. The constraint lies rather on the extent to which the proportion of funds employed elsewhere can be further reduced, and here, in sharp contrast to the general trend of the early 1960s, the scope is now strictly limited. Not only has the crucial liquidity ratio already fallen to a level which gives little room for further manoeuvre, but it is also clear that the redeployment of the banks' illiquid assets – as between investments on the one hand and advances on the other – cannot continue indefinitely and is most unlikely to be carried much further. The London Clearing Bank's investment/deposit ratio had already fallen to 10·3% by the end of 1969 – a figure which was close to the practical limit that can be applied over the foreseeable future.

With gilt-edged yields at high levels, not only is the rate of return on such investments close to that available on bank lending, but the reduction in the banking system's liquidity itself increases the relative attraction of holding funds in a form which is more quickly realizable than an advance. It must also be borne in mind that the banks' investments include some private-sector securities which are more in the nature of a fixed asset than a realizable gilt-edged stock.

For all these reasons, the inescapable conclusion seems to be that the rate of growth in bank advances from now on must come more into line with the underlying growth in bank deposits. The scope for increasing advances at the expense of liquidity, or for a further switch in the deployment of illiquid assets, will no longer be an important factor. It is in fact significant that this prospect already appears to be leading to some reconsideration of monetary policy as directly applied to the banks. In particular, the need to rely on restrictions on the overall level of bank lending is being questioned.[1] It is admitted by the authorities that such controls, when imposed over any length of time, tend to distort the structure and efficiency of the banking sector; it might also be added that they are hardly designed to improve the structure and efficiency of the whole of the national economy.

The most obvious alternative to the present system would be for the authorities to eliminate all direct controls and substitute an active and flexible policy in respect of liquidity ratios (possibly through more frequent changes in Special Deposits requirements), thereby regulating bank lending at one remove. There seems little doubt that such a change has begun to take place. This was hinted at in the 1970/71 Budget statement, but it is likely that a complete change will be introduced only gradually. Any such change must also automatically lead to a re-assessment of the structure of the banking system itself, including the extent and nature of the competition not only between the commercial banks and other financial institutions, but also between individual commercial banks. Competition cannot, however, be discussed simply in terms of lending outlets; it must also take into account the cost of borrowing, and this is discussed below in connection with forecasting short-term interest rates.

1. New regulations with regard to bank liquidity ratios have now, in fact, been brought into operation.

FORECASTING THE LONG-TERM RATE

From the whole of the preceding analysis, the main items from which forecasts of the long-term rate of interest can be compiled can be summarized as follows. On the supply side the factors which point to a slower rate of future growth in the money supply are essentially:

1) The transformation of the central government's finances from a position in which substantial borrowing requirements were necessary to one where borrowing will be on a relatively more modest scale.

2) A change in the emphasis in the management of the national debt, from one of the regular intervention in the market to one of less support for bond prices, even at the cost of more volatile movements and higher interest rates.

3) A slower rate of growth in bank lending as the latter becomes more of a function of the underlying growth in bank deposits, and less a function of a redeployment of assets.

It follows from this that given a consistent rate of growth in the national income at current prices (i.e. the demand for money), any reduction in the rate of growth of the supply of money must tend to move the general level of interest rates upwards. However, as previously noted, since 1965 rates have moved well out of line with the levels indicated as appropriate by changes in the velocity of circulation. The principal reasons were the expectation of devaluation from 1964 onwards, the anticipation of a rise in retail prices above the long-term trend, a general loss of confidence in government economic policy (as reflected, for example, in the exceptionally large borrowing requirements of 1967 and 1968), all coupled to the persistent weakness of sterling up until the first quarter of 1969.

The forecaster is left with one final problem – that of assessing for how long these special factors will continue to influence interest rates in the period ahead. But once a conclusion is reached on this point, forecasts based on established projections for the demand and supply of money and the velocity of circulation remain as valid as at any time in the past.

SHORT-TERM INTEREST RATES

While there is an obvious connection between long-term and short-term interest rates, in the sense that both tend to move in the same direction over varying periods of time, it is nevertheless not possible to make forecasts of short-term rates along the same lines. The problem of forecasting short-term rates must in fact be counted as an even more inexact 'science' than in the case of long-term rates, success being primarily dependent upon the correct 'reading' of monetary policy not only in the United Kingdom but also abroad, above all in the United States.

The importance of this international aspect is essentially a phenomenon of the 1960s, reflecting not only the influence of the United States on the world economy (and that of New York as the world's main financial centre) but also the result of the restoration of external convertibility to most European currencies in 1958. It is mainly through the international Eurodollar market (which arose out of this convertibility) that credit pressures in the U.S. are now transmitted to the rest of the world. This can be seen from the trend of U.S. and U.K. Treasury Bill rates, as well as the equivalent Eurodollar rate.[1]

The events of 1969, however, provided a warning that Eurodollar rates are not invariably a simple function of short-term rates in the United States. At certain points in time the pressure on the liquidity of the U.S. banking system becomes so acute that the cost at which it is in a position to obtain funds from alternative sources becomes of secondary importance. Two useful measures (excluding the obvious one of the amount of U.S.

1. It is argued, and with some justification, that Treasury Bill rates on both sides of the Atlantic are not always the best indicators of overall market pressures in so far as they are influenced by government financing and certain other special factors; but this is essentially a refinement and for most purposes they can be taken as adequate yardsticks.

bank borrowing in the Eurodollar market) of the extent to which the Federal Reserve is driving the American banking system into this kind of dilemma are the volume of Certificates of Deposits outstanding and changes in the banks' 'free' or net borrowed reserve position.

Nevertheless, in more normal circumstances it will be clear that Eurodollar rates tend to lie between those ruling on U.S. and U.K. Treasury Bills. One reason for this pattern stems from the fact that the flow of international funds is never solely determined by straight interest rate differentials, but also by the cost of 'insuring' or 'hedging' against exchange rate changes. The importance of this factor as a component of the true difference between short-term rates in the two main money markets can be seen in Table 29.

Table 29

Differential between U.S. and U.K. Rates

Quarterly averages (% p.a.)

		U.S. Treasury Bill rate	U.K. Treasury Bill rate	Straight differential	Forward discount on sterling	Covered differential
1968	i	4·97	7·27	+2·30	−4·21	−1·91
	ii	5·62	7·11	+1·49	−5·59	−4·10
	iii	5·27	6·77	+1·50	−2·15	−0·65
	iv	5·87	6·66	+0·79	−2·75	−1·96
1969	i	6·24	7·45	+1·21	−2·68	−1·47
	ii	6·17	7·90	+1·73	−4·95	−3·22
	iii	7·23	7·89	+0·66	−4·85	−4·19
	iv	7·73	7·80	+0·07	−0·69	−0·62

+ In favour of London.
− In favour of New York.

Notwithstanding the influence of international factors on a wide range of U.K. short-term interest rates, the crucial rate for most practising business economists is, of course, still Bank Rate. This is because changes in Bank Rate have usually served as an early-warning signal of imminent changes in economic policy – both on the monetary and fiscal side – and because of the traditional link between Bank Rate and commercial bank lending rates. The traditional importance of Bank Rate as a 'leading' indicator has, however, also been due to the fact that throughout most of the 1960s changes represented a response to the U.K.'s balance of payments position at a time when the latter was the main constraint on the economy.

There is little evidence to suggest that the authorities even considered Bank Rate (*vide* Radcliffe) as exercising any direct or immediate impact on the overall level of demand through an expansionary or restrictive effect on the demand for credit. Since the international money market has already reduced the relevance of Bank Rate as an influence on the 'competitive' position of short-term rates in London, it is inevitable that its relevance as an instrument of purely domestic policy should be called into question again.

Recent events in fact support the conclusion that the significance of Bank Rate within this latter context has already begun to weaken further. As far as the banking system is concerned it is more widely appreciated that keeping Bank Rate at a level out of line with those rates determined by 'free market' forces certainly does not assist, and can even obstruct, measures to control the volume of bank lending. Such a situation as ruled in 1969 – when the cost of bank credit was up to 2 percentage points cheaper than funds available from other sources – placed the banks in an almost impossible position in their attempt to bring their volume of advances down to within the official ceiling. It is significant that they took this opportunity to raise their prime lending rate to $1\frac{1}{2}\%$ over Bank Rate. Even more significantly, some other banks (admittedly accounting for only a small proportion of the total volume of U.K. credit) simultaneously adopted a base rate more closely related to costs incurred in obtaining deposits in arriving at the rates to be charged on loans.

Given that bank profits are likely to come under considerable pressure over the next few years, it is no doubt unrealistic to anticipate any reduction in the absolute difference between their borrowing and lending rates in the future. This does not rule out the probability of greater flexibility however. The inevitable outcome of any change in policy with regard to limits on the overall level of bank lending as a measure of monetary policy and the substitution of a policy regulating liquidity ratios will force the banks to adopt more flexible rates.

Such a move would almost certainly lead to more aggressive bidding for funds by the clearing banks. There has been a progressive decline of the banks' market share in total U.K. deposits during the 1960s, notwithstanding a dramatic increase in the proportion of their funds held directly in interest-bearing accounts at deposit rate or through their subsidiary companies operating in the 'open' market.

If this analysis is correct, it follows that those engaged in making forecasts of short-term interest rates are faced with the prospect of more volatile movements in the future, with such movements taking place over a much wider range of different sources and outlets for funds. Fortunately this does not necessarily imply that the already difficult problem of short-term interest rate projections will become even more intractable, for a more compact and less fragmented market will tend to reflect the free play of market forces.

CHAPTER 6

Forecasting Public Spending and the Budget

BY C. D. BARNARD
AND JAMES MORRELL

Since the beginning of the Second World War, the role of the state in the management of the economy has become of increasing importance. Before 1940 it is broadly true to say that the government saw its main functions as providing for defence and education, the maintenance of law and order, and similar regulatory functions accepted as the responsibility of the state. Each year the Budget provided for the revenue to meet the anticipated expenditure and in this respect was principally a fund-raising operation. The possibility of controlling the economy through changes in taxation and spending was understood by very few people and did not gain acceptance at the political level until late in the 1930s.

Since 1940, the government has exercised a far more important role in controlling the economy. Not only does it raise money in the Budget to pay for its expenditure on current and capital account, but it also has to consider the problem of managing demand in the economy so as to maintain full employment, and achieve an adequate balance of payments position. It also has the problem of managing monetary policy and the national debt. In other words, governments over the past thirty years have been compelled to use the Budget to control the economy, as well as to raise revenue.

During the 1960s the amount raised by the government through the Budget for current-account spending has increased significantly as a proportion of the country's Gross National Product, as is shown in Chart 15. This is a reflection of the increasing importance of government spending, not only in the social sense but also as an important factor in the balance between the total

Chart 15

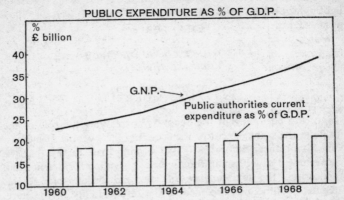

PUBLIC EXPENDITURE AS % OF G.D.P.

supply of goods and services likely to be available to the nation, and the total demand likely to be made on those supplies.

FORECASTING PUBLIC SPENDING

Expenditure for which the government itself is responsible falls into two broad categories – current and capital. Capital expenditure, such as housing grants to local authorities and the building of new hospitals and schools, is considered in Chapter 11. In this chapter, an analysis will be made of government expenditure on current account. In the national income accounts this item is listed as 'public authorities' current account expenditure'. Under this classification 'public authorities' include the central and all local governments, but the nationalized industries are excluded.

The three main components of spending are defence, National Health Service and education, and the manner in which these items have grown since 1960 is illustrated in Chart 16. The 'other' category shown in the chart comprises all the remaining items on which the government incurs expenditure of a non-capital nature. The chief items in this category are current spending on roads (such as repair, maintenance, drainage and lighting), police and prisons, fire services, sewage and refuse disposal, and the cost of collecting taxes.

Many of these items are paid for partly by the local authorities from rates, with the balance met by the central government. In 969, for example, 60% of this expenditure was made by the

Chart 16

BREAKDOWN OF PUBLIC SPENDING INTO MAIN CATEGORIES

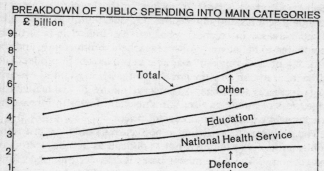

central government and 40% by local authorities, though much of the local authorities' expenditure was financed by the central government.

There are two important factors which help the forecaster in dealing with this section of the economy. Broadly speaking, both political parties agree that the government's expenditure on current services must be kept in line with the average annual increase in the country's economic growth. Thus, if in real terms the government anticipates an annual average increase in total national output of 3% during the next three or four years, it will plan to increase expenditure in real terms by about the same proportion. This helps to set the broad limits within which government spending is likely to develop in the medium term.

Annual increases may be significantly higher – or lower – than the increase in output, not only in real terms, but also in current prices. About 40% of public authorities' current expenditure is paid out in wages and salaries, and much of it, unlike manufacturing industry, is in categories where productivity gains are small. Thus an above-average rise in wages and salaries in the economy at large will tend to produce a faster rise in public spending than in the rest of the economy.

The best example of this is education, where the number of teachers required is broadly related to the number of persons attending schools and universities. In education, it is difficult to effect increases in teachers' productivity. Indeed it is virtually impossible to define and measure teachers' productivity, and the difficulty of achieving a measurable improvement in productivity is the main reason why the government is so reluctant to concede wage increases to teachers. The static nature of productivity in wide areas of public service is an important factor in forecasting government expenditure at current prices.

The problem of forecasting in both current and fixed prices for public authority spending is not as difficult as in other sectors of the economy. The government bases its slender published forecasts on future expenditure in fixed prices. The business forecaster has to anticipate what the relevant rates of inflation will be each year to translate the official forecasts into current prices. In the Budget accounts, of course, the figures for the year in question are always shown in current prices, so that some clue to official forecasts of price changes can be gleaned from a study of the Budget estimates and the official economic forecast.

The second factor which has made forecasting this sector less difficult was the decision of the government in April 1969 to publish its intentions for public expenditure for the next five years. The government proposed that 'there should be published towards the end of each calendar year a White Paper which will present to Parliament the results of the government's consideration of the prospect for public expenditure'. Although these forecasts are published in real terms, and therefore do not allow for the effects of inflation, the White Paper provides the forecaster with a firm base on which to make his own estimates.

In making these estimates, probably the most important factor is an assessment of which political party is likely to be in power in the years ahead. This is important, because it can affect both the pattern and the level of government expenditure considerably. By and large, it is true to say that Conservative governments aim to limit the amount of current spending as far as is practical, whereas Labour governments believe that spending on welfare items should increase as much as the country's economy will bear.

An example of this occurred after Labour was returned to power in 1964. In current prices, expenditure increased by 9% both in 1965 and 1966, and by 10% in 1967. In real terms, the highest increase was in 1967 when it rose by 5%, considerably more than the increase in national output, which in that year rose by 2%. Following the balance of payments crisis in 1967, however, the Labour government cut back significantly on its current spending, and in 1969 expenditure, in real terms, actually fell by 1%.

These figures suggest that it is not possible to establish any fundamental rules for forecasting in this sector whichever party is in power. Even fixed commitments, such as the need to provide more school places or hospital beds, are subject to retrenchment in difficult periods. As well as using the annual publication of government expenditure for five years ahead, it is necessary to adjust the forecast figures at frequent intervals to take into account prospective changes in the economic climate and the pronouncements of politicians.

CURRENT-ACCOUNT SPENDING

Considerable changes occur in the rate of growth of government expenditure from year to year. In any analysis, however, it is essential to break down total expenditure into its main components. Table 30 shows how the larger individual sectors of current spending developed during the 1960s. The main item is defence, which accounts for some 25% of total current expenditure.

Table 30

Public Spending by Main Categories

£ thousand million: share of total %

	Defence	%	National Health Service	%	Education	%	Other	%	Total
1960	1·58	37	0·75	18	0·66	16	1·26	30	4·25
1961	1·68	37	0·80	17	0·71	15	1·39	30	4·59
1962	1·80	37	0·82	17	0·80	16	1·43	29	4·92
1963	1·85	36	0·88	17	0·88	17	1·59	31	5·18
1964	1·93	35	0·95	17	0·94	17	1·70	31	5·51
1965	2·06	34	1·06	18	1·05	17	1·87	31	6·04
1966	2·15	33	1·16	18	1·18	18	2·09	32	6·57
1967	2·34	32	1·27	18	1·30	18	2·35	32	7·25
1968	2·37	31	1·37	18	1·42	18	2·54	33	7·70
1969	2·42	30	1·46	18	1·53	19	2·70	33	8·10

Defence

Defence provides a good example of the difference in approach of the two major political parties. After 1964, the Labour government aimed at slowing down the rate of increase in defence spending. Table 30 shows that between 1967 and 1969 spending on defence increased slowly. Allowing for price rises, there was a reduction in spending in real terms. The withdrawal of the armed forces from east of Suez contributed to the decline in defence spending, and the Labour government's plans were for a complete withdrawal in the early 1970s. The Conservative administration may well reverse this policy and enter a joint defence system with other Commonwealth countries. Clearly this will increase defence spending. Since it is not always possible to get reliable estimates of how much plans such as these are likely to cost, it is necessary to make an estimate, and include this in the forecast. It is essential in forecasting to try and anticipate political changes of this kind and to cost out the effects of the assumed changes.

Education

Spending on education has overtaken spending on the National Health Service since 1966. Education will undoubtedly be the fastest-growing major item in government expenditure in the 1970s. Not only will the raising of the school leaving age to sixteen in 1973 mean an additional number of children at school, but an increasing number of children will be passing through the schools during the 1970s. Education is such an important political issue that both parties are firmly committed to spending an increasing share of total government revenue on this item. Taking into account the two factors mentioned above, forecasting does not present too many problems. The biggest element of uncertainty is the rate of increase in the next few years in teachers' salaries – by far the most important single factor in educational cost. Forecasts, however, are made by relating growth in teachers' salaries to growth in earned incomes in the economy at large.

The Health Service

Forecasting expenditure on the National Health Service presents different problems, not so much on the total expenditure, which will probably rise in current prices by more than £100 million per annum, but on the net cost to the Exchequer. The public already pays a charge for dental treatment and for medical prescriptions. Prescription charges are more likely to rise under a Conservative government, and account must be taken of this in framing the forecast.

'Other' Spending

The 'other' items in Table 30 amount to about 35% of total current government expenditure and have been increasing on average during the past few years at a faster rate than the total. Expenditure on roads has been rising substantially and will continue to do so. Other large increases can be expected in spending on police and prisons, so that the total spending on the residual 'other' items will probably continue to increase at a faster than average rate during the next few years.

Having analysed the major categories of spending separately, in both current and constant prices, one can check the series against the figures at constant prices shown in the government's White Paper. It must not be assumed that a different figure from the government's estimates is necessarily wrong. If different assumptions from those of the government have been made, then obviously a different figure will result. What is essential is that the assumptions made are checked regularly, as conditions can change rapidly, and any change in either the record or the assumptions will need to be reflected in the forecast.

FORECASTING THE BUDGET

In 1969, public authorities' current expenditure accounted for just over 20% of the Gross Domestic Product. The Budget accounted for over 40% of the total. Chart 17 shows how this

Chart 17

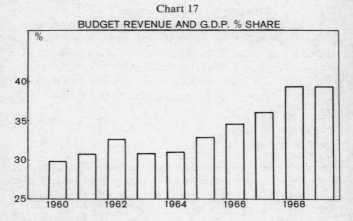

BUDGET REVENUE AND G.D.P. % SHARE

percentage increased during the 1960s. The increase was not planned as part of long-term policy, but was dictated by two main factors: firstly, the amount of money required by the government to pay for its spending programmes, on both current and capital account; and secondly the 'surplus' above this figure decided upon to enable the government to control the economy. These two factors are quite separate.

With the acceptance of the Budget as an instrument of economic management, government expenditure and taxation have risen steadily, and it has become increasingly clear that these two items have an important influence on the general level of output and distribution of resources. As a result, government forecasts made before the Budget now estimate the potential growth of resources and demand in the year ahead, including their effect on the balance of payments position. If these resources are expected to be in balance with the growth in demand at the existing level of taxation, then the Budget will probably be neutral. But if demand is expected to grow too slowly, then the government can take action through the Budget to stimulate the economy. If

Table 31

Consolidated Fund Summary

£ million

Current income		Current expenditure	
Taxation raised by:			
Inland Revenue	8,475	Civil Supply services	10,512
Customs and Excise	4,635	Defence	2,280
Motor vehicle duties	430	Supplementary provision	141
Selective Employment		Miscellaneous	593
Tax (gross)	2,042		
Miscellaneous	542		
	16,124		13,526
		Current surplus transferred to	
		National Loans Fund	2,598
			16,124

the growth in demand is expected to be excessive, then it may be necessary to apply restraint by means of tax increases.

Before examining the main factors in forecasting the Budget, it is helpful to see how the 1970 Budget was set out with regard to income and expenditure (Table 31).

On the income side the Inland Revenue collects income tax and surtax from private individuals, and corporation tax from companies. In addition, it is responsible for collection of capital gains tax and death duties. Customs and Excise is responsible for indirect taxes covering tobacco, purchase tax, oil, spirits, beer and wine. The other big item on the income side is Selective Employment Tax. This is shown gross, and where repayments are made these are shown on the expenditure side under the supply services heading.

The expenditure figures mainly consist of payments under Civil Supply services. This is made up of current expenditure on goods and services (discussed earlier in this chapter). Defence is shown separately. The Consolidated Fund is not the whole of the Budget, however, and National Insurance benefits and other current grants to the personal sector, subsidies (mainly on food) and interest on the national debt have also to be brought into the total.

It will be seen that the surplus on the Consolidated Fund account is transferred to the National Loans Fund. The government makes loans to nationalized industries and other public and private corporations from the Fund, thus supplementing other borrowing of the public authorities. What is left at the end of the financial year, after satisfying all capital as well as current transactions, is the net surplus or deficit on the government account. A surplus will be used to repay public debt or conversely the authorities will need to borrow. Thus if loans and payments from the National Loans Fund exceed the money transferred from the Consolidated Fund, then the government becomes a net borrower from the market, and increases the national debt.

Economic Management

Having briefly examined the government book-keeping system, we return to the two main factors which arise in forecasting the Budget. It has been noted that the government must first estimate its total expenditure for the forthcoming year. It then has to decide on the state of the economy. If the economy is strong and the balance of payments sound, it may consider that the amount raised in revenue need not necessarily equal its expenditure, and consequently budget for a deficit. The balance will then be made up by increasing the government debt, and borrowing in the market. On the other hand, if the economy is overheated, and the balance of payments weak, the government may wish to budget for an excess of revenue over expenditure, to give it tighter control over the economy. In the first instance the authorities will attempt to take less money off the general public via taxation than is being put back into the system via its own spending, thus increasing purchasing power and demand. In the second case the process is reversed and the general public's purchasing power curtailed. The implications of such developments on monetary policy and the money supply are discussed in Chapter 5.

The amount of surplus or deficit will be determined by considerations of economic management. Either way, the government does not necessarily have to raise all its revenue by taxation, though taxation revenue only is shown in the Consolidated Fund account. However, the most important factors in forecasting the shape of the Budget are the estimates of revenue and expenditure. Forecasting for large sectors of current expenditure has already been outlined above. To see the problem as a whole it is necessary to consider the National Insurance Fund and the capital transactions. Public authorities' capital expenditure is discussed separately in Chapters 10 and 11, but the receipts under capital account such as revenue from estate duties are discussed in the context of the Budget.

The National Insurance Fund

National Insurance contributions are paid by employers, employees and the self-employed. The contributions should properly be regarded as a form of taxation, for although National Insurance originated as a scheme to provide future welfare benefits, such as pensions, sickness benefits and unemployment relief, the scheme has seldom been viable in the sense that future pensions have been fully provided for from previous contributions and the interest earned on the fund.

Most countries now treat social security benefits and social security taxes as a set of current transactions and the idea of a 'funded' system has largely been abandoned. This is also true of the U.K. As a consequence National Insurance contributions have come to be regarded as a form of taxation, which can be varied as part of the system of economic management. The same is true of benefits and the timing of increases in benefits has been dictated less by the state of the revenue than by the social and economic background.

To understand the full budgetary implications, therefore, National Insurance contributions must be taken into account along with other 'transfer' payments (income transferred by the authorities from one section of the community to another). These are shown in the accounts as 'current grants to the personal sector' and include pensions, supplementary benefits, rate rebates, unemployment benefits, redundancy compensation and so on.

Public Sector by Economic Categories

In the annual 'Financial Statement and Budget Report' issued at the time of the Chancellor's Budget speech, all the public-sector transactions are brought together in a single table showing the analysis by economic category. The value of the presentation is that the public sector's activities can be viewed as a whole, with all the implications of tax changes as well as spending changes and economic influences reflected in the figures. Table 32 is taken from the report for 1970/71.

Current Receipts

Under 'current receipts' it will be seen that National Insurance contributions as well as local authority rate income is shown separately from the central government's income from taxation. In addition, the gross trading surpluses of the public bodies are shown, and these items represent the profit (or loss) of the nationalized industries and public corporations, and are struck before depreciation and tax. In other words these figures show the actual cash surplus of the public enterprises. Similarly, the rent item, representing the income on the public authorities' housing account, is shown before providing for depreciation. The interest item, which has grown rapidly in recent years, represents the income on the substantial loans made to outside bodies. However, when compared with the interest payments on the national debt shown on the spending side of the account, it can be seen that receipts of interest are heavily outweighed by payments.

Current Expenditure

The total of current spending as outlined earlier in the chapter is shown in the table under the two heads of central and local government. Subsidies are also divided in this way, although local authority subsidy payments are relatively small. Interest on the national debt is of huge proportions and has been forced up by the severe rise in interest rates. Interest rates have risen continuously from 1946 and rose particularly sharply between 1966 and 1969. It now appears that rates may have peaked and for this reason the national debt interest burden may not rise significantly in future. In forecasting this item, account is taken of prospective interest rates and the likelihood of the national debt increasing or decreasing. The chances are that in the 1970s the national debt will not grow significantly and debt interest may even decline to a small extent.

Current grants to the personal sector are also shown under central and local government headings. This large item of redistribution of income is largely comprised of pension payments.

Table 32

Public Sector Transactions by Economic Category

£ million

	1970–71 estimate *After Budget changes*
Current receipts	
Taxes on income	7,504
National Insurance contributions, etc.	2,700
Taxes on expenditure, central government	6,678
Local rates	1,854
Gross trading surplus[3] –	
Central government and local authorities	132
Public corporations	1,629
Rent[3]	1,141
Interest, dividends, etc.	312
TOTAL	21,950
Capital receipts	
Current surplus[3]	5,293
Taxes on capital	854
Capital transfers	22
Loan repayments from overseas governments	26
Receipts from certain pension 'funds' (net)	52
Adjustment for accruals of –	
Taxes on expenditure	−40
Subsidies	—
Import deposits	−417
Miscellaneous capital transactions (net)[5]	−206
Borrowing requirement (net balance)[6] –	
Central government[7]	−611
Local authorities[8]	295
Public corporations[9]	55
Net borrowing by Northern Ireland central government	17
Total	−244
TOTAL	5,340

1. Differences from the figures given in Table 8 of the Financial Statement and Budget Report 1969–70 (H.C. 211–15 April 1969) reflect changes of classification.
2. Includes selective employment tax.
3. Before allowing for depreciation and stock appreciation.
4. Includes British Broadcasting Corporation, Independent Television Authority and Covent Garden Market Authority.

	1970–71 estimate After Budget changes
Current expenditure	
Current expenditure on goods and services–	
Central government	5,377
Local authorities	3,750
Subsidies–	
Central government	831
Local authorities	95
Debt interest	2,045
Current grants to personal sector–	
Central government	4,211
Local authorities	168
Current grants abroad	180
Total current expenditure	16,657
Current surplus[3]	5,293
TOTAL	21,950
Capital expenditure	
Gross domestic fixed capital formation–	
Central government	610
Local authorities	1,790
Nationalized industries, etc.[4]	1,567
Other public corporations	149
Increase in value of stocks–	
Central government	58
Nationalized industries	−29
Capital grants to private sector	841
Net lending to private sector	170
Loans to overseas governments	96
Drawings from United Kingdom subscriptions to international lending bodies	17
Other net lending and investment abroad	25
Cash expenditure on company securities (net)	46
TOTAL	5,340

5. Includes re-financeable export credits and unidentified items.
6. Defined as in 'Financial Statistics'.
7. Includes borrowing of £215 million in 1969–70 and £8 million in 1970–71 to finance redemption of nationalized industries' stock.
8. Borrowing other than from central government and public corporations.
9. Includes redemption of stock.

It will, therefore, continue to grow as pension levels are raised and as the number of pensioners grows. Current grants paid abroad include British aid to other countries.

The Surplus

When total current spending is subtracted from total current receipts a large surplus figure is thrown up. In the 1970/71 estimate this was put in excess of £5,300 million – a huge figure representing the community's savings through the public bodies, i.e. the central government, the local authorities, the nationalized industries and other public corporations. This residue, or savings, is available to finance capital spending, and in the table the item is transferred down to the 'capital receipts' part of the account.

Capital Receipts

The savings on current account represents virtually the total net receipts on capital account. Taxes on capital are treated as capital receipts and these include death duties, gains tax and stamp duties. Import deposits are shown in this instance as a large capital outgoing, since it was envisaged that the deposits would be progressively repaid during the fiscal year. The borrowing requirement (net balance) is shown separately for the three main public-sector divisions, and in the residual item representing the difference between total capital receipts and total capital expenditure.

Capital Expenditure

The capital spending of the central government, local authorities and nationalized industries is shown for investment in building work, plant and machinery, as well as for changes in inventories and stocks. These items are forecast separately and are discussed in later chapters. Capital grants to the private sector (which are to be largely discontinued) have reached substantial proportions and these are principally investment grants to industry. The capital expenditure account also includes a certain amount of lending both at home and abroad.

The Borrowing Requirement

For 1970/71 the estimates showed a surplus of capital receipts over capital spending of £244 million (given in the table under capital receipts but shown as a minus). How this figure was made up is shown in Table 33. In other words if all the funds were put

Table 33
Borrowing Requirements
£ million

Central government	−611 (i.e. a surplus)
Local authorities	+295 (deficit)
Public corporations	+55 (deficit)
Northern Ireland government	+17 (deficit)
TOTAL	−244 (surplus)

into a single account the central government's revenue surplus would be enough to meet all the capital account deficits of the other three bodies, the net result being that public authorities as a whole would not be borrowing from the general public but would effectively be paying off part of the accumulated borrowing which makes up the national debt.

This section of the estimates is of great importance in that it largely determines monetary policy and exercises a preponderant influence on the money supply. Its relevance is discussed in Chapter 5. In attempting to predict the Budget, therefore, an overall view of the public-sector accounts is required. Only in this way is it possible to take into consideration the main influences on economic policy and management and to reach conclusions on the final shape of the public account. The size of the public sector's overall surplus or deficit (borrowing requirement) is a key factor and the various strands of forecasts of the Budget must be made consistent with the overall assumption of the size of the net borrowing requirement.

The Supply Services

The detail for the Budget accounts is as follows. The bulk of the expenditure from the Consolidated Fund is on Supply Services. Not only is expenditure on goods and services for civil and defence purposes met out of this, but also grants by the government in support of the National Insurance Funds, local authority services (education, local health and welfare services etc.), the National Health Service, agricultural subsidies and most of the overseas aid programme. Since estimates of Supply expenditure have to be submitted to Parliament early in the calendar year, the forecaster's job in this respect is relatively straightforward. In addition, it may, and probably will, happen that additional or supplementary estimates have to be put to Parliament by government departments later during the year, where the original estimates are too low.

Other items on the expenditure side consist of service on the national debt and grants to Northern Ireland. The servicing of the national debt does not cover the total cost relating to payment of interest on outstanding government debt. It covers the balance necessary after allowing for the payment of interest on loans from the government, and the profits of the Issue Department of the Bank of England.

The payment to Northern Ireland is similar to grants to local authorities in England, Wales and Scotland. It is quite a significant sum – in the 1970/71 Budget it amounted to £272 million – but is not subject to large fluctuations.

Consolidated Fund Income

Having determined the anticipated level of expenditure, the income side of the account is difficult to forecast. Since the bulk of revenue has to be raised through taxes, the forecast requires political as well as economic judgement.

Taxation is divided broadly into two groups – direct and indirect. 'Direct' implies a tax on incomes; 'indirect' a tax on consumption. In the national accounts the only items shown separately from these two main groups are motor vehicle duties and Selective Employment Tax. All sources, however, have to be considered in determining any possible change in taxation, and it is as well to keep in mind that the authorities are always interested in the possibility of a new type of tax which will either help raise more revenue more effectively or reduce highly unpopular and less efficient taxes. Unless political parties are prepared to discuss in public the possible introduction of new taxes – and there are increasing signs that this is the case – forecasting in this field is bound to be hazardous.

On the other hand, taxes may be abolished. Selective Employment Tax and purchase tax are to be abolished and replaced by Value Added Tax. Other possibilities are the abolition of stamp duties and the reform of capital gains tax.

Tax Changes

The main problem in forecasting the Budget is to determine what changes are likely to occur in direct and indirect taxation. The main items of direct taxation are income tax, surtax, corporation tax, capital gains tax and death duties. Chart 18 shows that direct

Chart 18

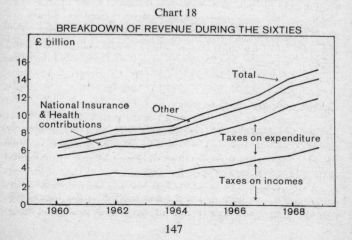

BREAKDOWN OF REVENUE DURING THE SIXTIES

147

taxation is the largest single item in the revenue accounts. Consequently, changes in taxes on income tend to have the largest impact on the economy through the immediate effects on the total amount of disposable income in the hands of the public.

Both parties are now committed, where and when possible, to reducing the total level of direct taxation, and this is of value in constructing long-term forecasts. In forecasting any possible short-term Budget changes, however, the forecaster must first determine whether the economy in the year ahead is likely to require stimulating or dampening down. If it requires stimulating then a reduction in direct taxation is not necessarily the Chancellor's most likely choice. Higher pensions, for example, will stimulate spending or cuts in indirect taxation will result in a selective impetus to spending. Cuts in direct taxation will have a more general effect. Both parties may tend to favour a reduction in income tax, since this will benefit the largest number of persons, and have the greatest appeal to the electorate.

Inland Revenue Items

The income tax system is particularly complex and may well be simplified in the next few years. It is difficult for the forecaster to anticipate the exact timing and pattern of changes. Much depends on the load of work facing the Inland Revenue department. The transfer of accounts to computers should enable the Inland Revenue to simplify the system, though it will certainly take some years to produce worthwhile results. In the meantime the forecaster must assess in which areas of the income tax structure changes are most likely to occur.

It is important for the forecaster to gauge these items as accurately as possible. If there is likely to be a change in revenue from income tax, the economy may be affected in different ways. There is, for example, more likely to be an increase in personal savings if the higher tax rates are reduced, rather than if the personal allowance is increased. This is because the increase in personal allowance gives all tax payers a marginal increase in disposable income. A large part of this is likely to be spent.

Although surtax is treated separately from income tax, it is really only an extension of income tax. It is possible that this tax will be integrated into income tax with a graduated increase for higher incomes.

There remains the problem, both in income tax and surtax, of the differentiation between earned and unearned income. Broadly speaking, whenever changes are expected in income tax, these have more usually occurred in regard to earned income. Changes in taxation on unearned income have been fewer, except where connected with adjustments for age relief. But the total yields from earned and unearned income can be estimated separately and any likely adjustments calculated.

Corporation tax is also administered by the Inland Revenue. Introduced in 1966, this tax was intended to differentiate company taxation from personal taxation.

The third main tax which Inland Revenue collects is death duties. The yield tends to fluctuate with the level of the stock market, since the value of estates at the time of death reflects to some extent the level of security prices. Capital gains tax is also collected by Inland Revenue.

Customs and Excise

Inland Revenue collects approximately 50% of all tax revenue, whilst Customs and Excise accounts for 25% of the total. Both parties are agreed that indirect taxes should account for an increasing share of total taxation, and the forecaster has the problem not only of assessing the chances of changes in present taxes, but of estimating where and when new indirect taxes are likely to be applied.

At present there are four main heads of Customs and Excise taxation. These are purchase tax, oil duties, taxes on alcoholic drink and taxes on tobacco. The tobacco tax, which now yields over £1,000 million, presents little difficulty to the forecaster. Demand for tobacco products is not markedly sensitive to price changes, provided these are roughly in line with the general level of price changes. Since many smokers are addicted, spending on tobacco remains at a fairly constant proportion of consumers' spending, and this facilitates a tolerably close forecast of receipts from tobacco tax.

Duties on oil have been increased heavily during the past few years and this trend is likely to continue. Most of the tax yield is derived from petrol duties, and yet petrol in the U.K. is still as cheap as in any country in the Common Market. In France and Italy petrol prices are considerably higher. The future movement of this tax is, therefore, likely to be upwards especially in view of two important factors. First, oil supplies have to be imported and are, therefore, a considerable item in the import bill. With the balance of payments of major concern to the U.K. authorities a limitation of import growth through increasing the tax on petrol has obvious attractions. The main disadvantage of this approach is that the price of oil and petrol has a direct bearing on the costs of production and thus on export prices and the cost of living. Secondly, the vehicle population will continue to increase. This will inevitably lead to further problems of road congestion, so that the government may be encouraged to increase petrol tax in an effort to discourage both congestion and pollution. The revenue from oil duties is, therefore, likely to continue to increase strongly. In 1970, the yield topped £1,300 million, and this could well rise to exceed £2,000 million before the end of the decade.

The fourth largest group of taxes collected by Customs and Excise is the duty on spirits, beer and wine. The yield on these items is of the same order as that from tobacco. The tax on spirits, however, cannot be increased without regard to yield, as the higher the price the greater the effect on consumption. On the other hand, duties on wines have been increased significantly during the past few years and sales by volume have continued to increase. This is a reflection of changing living standards. The movement in taxation in this field in the future is still likely to be upwards, though probably not to the same extent as taxes on petrol and oils.

S.E.T. and Import Deposits

There is one final problem in forecasting government receipts and expenditure under the Budget. During the Labour government of 1966/70 certain items were introduced which presented a problem in book-keeping. These were Selective Employment Tax and Import Deposits. In both of these cases money was refunded after a period of time. The policy aim was to withdraw an additional sum of money from the economy in an effort to intensify the credit squeeze. Import Deposits were planned as a temporary measure to check imports and ease the payments problem and were abolished from December 1970.

In the accounts for S.E.T. the total sum collected was shown under government receipts. Refunds were then charged to expenditure under Supply Services. In the case of Import Deposits, however, the figure was shown under the taxation heading, and where repayment exceeded payment the figure was shown as a negative item. As a result, the estimate for revenue under Customs and Excise for the year 1970/71 is shown in Table 31 as £4,635 million, although total gross receipts for Customs and Excise was expected to yield £4,952 million. This net receipts figure allowed for £425 million in repayments under Import Deposits.

The Intensity and Importance of Budget Forecasting

It is probably true to say that more work is done on forecasting for the Budget than any other item in the national economy. From Christmas onwards a variety of articles appear to enlighten the taxpayer and the Chancellor as to what changes are desirable. It is not too difficult to forecast by how much the Chancellor will increase or reduce total taxation, since the state of the economy gives a fairly clear indication as to how much scope he has for manoeuvre. The difficult problem lies in pinpointing which taxes are likely to be changed. In forecasting the Budget, it is worth the effort of examining every single item on taxation to consider whether or not a change is practical. The

Chancellor has a wide variety of items from which to choose. It must not be forgotten that in the months leading up to the Budget the Chancellor will receive deputations and recommendations from a considerable number of lobbies, each of which will, no doubt, present a convincing argument as to why their particular field requires assistance. Taxation, although primarily a revenue raiser, can and does produce anomalies in the economic system which may require amending. It must be kept in view that the administrative requirements, both in terms of parliamentary draftsmanship and Inland Revenue time, of a major change in the tax system are so severe that no more than one substantial change a year can be accommodated.

Forecasting government current account expenditure is the problem mainly of forecasting three major items. Forecasting the Budget is far more involved. It keeps many people at the Treasury and Revenue Departments occupied for a large part of the year. The external forecaster will find the subject requires close study, for the assumptions made as to prospective changes in economic policy and management will be critical to the forecasts, both of the economy as a whole, and of the individual business sectors.

CHAPTER 7

Forecasting Costs and Prices

BY JAMES MORRELL
AND T. LAUGHARNE

Many firms assume that inflation of costs will be offset by inflation of their own selling prices. While this may be true over the
long run and for the economy at large, it is certainly not the case
in the short run, nor is it true for the individual firm.

The great majority of firms display a cyclical tendency, and
generally costs rise faster than prices at one stage of the business
cycle and vice versa. A sound forecast of the cycle, therefore, will
be of great assistance to the firm, not only in providing warnings
about the timing and magnitude of cost increases, but also of the
desirability and optimum timing of selling price increases. Moreover, one firm's prices are another firm's costs: therefore a set of
forecasts of cost changes for the economy at large will automatically throw up the means of forecasting price changes for
the economy. Given this type of analysis the individual firm can
then relate its own historical cost experience to the history of
costs and prices in the economy and from this evidence construct
meaningful forecasts of its own cost movements. The analysis
then becomes a major factor in determining the firm's pricing
policy.

Far too little effort has been made in British business in the past
to master this problem of cost and price analysis and to apply the
lessons in such a way as to optimize profits over the course of the
business cycle. Straight-line assumptions for future cost and price
movements are of little value in any cyclical situation, for the
firm runs the risk of a serious 'undershoot' of its cash flow and
profit projection when margins are being squeezed in the 'down'
phase of the cycle. This chapter is concerned with an analysis
of cost developments, their causes and magnitudes, and the
mechanism of passing cost changes on into price changes. By

analysing the post-war history of costs and prices for the U.K. economy it is possible to develop a forecasting system both for the economy and the firm.

THE COMPOSITION OF COSTS

There are three main categories of costs. These are

a) labour costs, including wages and salaries, taxes relating to employment such as National Insurance contributions and Selective Employment Tax, pension provisions and 'fringe' benefits;

b) materials, including basic and raw materials, semi-processed materials bought in, and fuel and power – whether in the form of electricity, gas, oil or coal;

c) service costs, such as rent, rates, postage, telephone, advertising.

One thing stands out from this broad analysis of costs, namely that labour costs are preponderant. Apart from direct labour costs, purchases of materials and services from other firms also incorporate labour costs. One unit is in effect buying labour from another, so that in the economy at large labour accounts for nearly 80% of all costs of production. This is in sharp contrast to the individual firm, where direct labour costs will seldom account for more than half of total costs.

In the national income accounts, income from employment accounts for nearly 70% of total domestic incomes. This share has tended to increase in recent years at the expense of profits, so that labour incomes have a dominant influence within the economy both as a share of costs and as a share of incomes. In the cost structure, however, prime costs can be broken down between home labour and imports and, for the purpose of forecasting, estimates of future movements in home labour costs per unit of output and import prices will largely explain all cost movements.

Thus the starting point of the forecast is employment incomes.

However, this comprises items other than wages and salaries, and employers' contributions to pension funds, National Insurance contributions, Selective Employment Tax and Regional Employment Premiums have to be taken into account. If the total

Table 34

Labour Costs per Unit: Total Economy 1969

£ million

Wages and salaries	24,326
Employers' contributions	2,431
Forces' pay	543
Total income from employment	27,300
Adjustment for S.E.T. and R.E.P.	494
TOTAL LABOUR COSTS	27,794

of these items is divided by an index of Gross Domestic Product measured by volume of output, then labour costs per unit of output in the whole economy can be derived (Table 34). This data, divided by G.D.P., is plotted in Chart 19 from 1950 onwards.

Chart 19

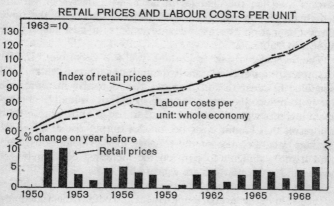

RETAIL PRICES AND LABOUR COSTS PER UNIT

In Table 35 the unit labour cost index numbers are set out together with import prices, which constitute around 20 to 25% of prime costs. Given, therefore, forecasts of labour costs, G.D.P. in volume terms and import prices, a forecast of total costs in the economy can be constructed.

Table 35

Costs and Prices in the Total Economy
(1963 = 100)

	Labour costs per unit	Import prices	Total costs	All prices
1964	102·6	103·2	102·7	102·7
1965	107·4	104·6	106·8	106·8
1966	114·7	106·0	112·9	110·5
1967	117·3	106·8	115·1	114·6
1968	122·1	119·1	121·5	117·8
1969	129·2	122·1	127·7	122·0

The relationship between costs and prices for the period 1964–9 for the economy as a whole can also be seen in the table. After a short parallel movement, costs have tended to outstrip prices, thus squeezing profits. This movement is not typical, however, and in the twenty-year period from 1950 to 1970 prices have always matched the changes in costs, with delays of varying length depending upon the special circumstances of the time. Over this period the average movements in cost factors are shown in Table 36.

The averages mask important cyclical variations. If, for example, the authorities need to dampen down home demand and spending in order to curb imports, the repressive measures are likely to reduce the rate of growth in output. Initially, employment incomes will probably continue to rise at a strong rate, with the result that labour costs per unit of output rise at an above average rate. Because of the tougher market conditions firms find it more difficult to pass on the increased costs in higher prices and profit margins are squeezed.

The second round effect of the restrictive government policies is then seen in the level of employment and employment incomes.

Table 36

Costs and Prices 1950–70

Average annual rate of increase

	%	*Average weight*
Total labour bill	7·1	
Divided by: Change in output	2·7	
Equals: Unit labour costs	4·3	77%
Import prices	2·2	23%
Total unit costs	3·8	100%
Change in prices	3·7	

Wages rise less rapidly and a more normal rise in costs ensues. Finally, as the economy is re-expanded output rises at an above average rate while the labour bill increases more modestly, so that unit labour costs then rise at a below-average rate. This cyclical pattern is of the greatest importance to the individual business.

THE IMPACT OF TAXATION

The major means of correcting imbalance in the economy will be changes in taxation, thus inducing the cyclical movement discussed above. In fact the tax changes themselves may well produce important cost changes. Notably, increases in National Insurance contributions and the dramatic introduction and increase in Selective Employment Tax have produced a marked effect on business costs. This can be seen in Table 37.

In other respects tax changes have a more immediate bearing on prices. Thus an increase in duty on beer, wines, spirits, tobacco, or petrol and oil will show up immediately in retail prices. The same will be true of changes in purchase tax, so that tax changes will produce direct changes in costs and prices as well as indirect changes in prices after a time lag. This is illustrated in Table 38, setting out the tax changes contained in the Budget of March 1968 and the ultimate effect of the measures.

157

Table 37

Employers' National Insurance Contributions and Selective
Employment Tax

Weekly amounts per adult male employee

	s.	d.	
June 1963	9	8	
March 1965	12	11	
December 1965	13	4	
September 1966	38	4	S.E.T. introduced @ 25s.
February 1967	38	9	
October 1967	41	0	
May 1968	41	6	
September 1968	54	0	S.E.T. raised to 37s. 6d.
July 1969	54	6	S.E.T. raised to 48s. 0d.
November 1969	65	11	
July 1970	66	11	

TIME-LAGS

In constructing price forecasts, therefore, it is necessary to calculate three sets of influences:

a) tax changes (i) on costs, (ii) directly on prices
b) changes in wages and salaries
c) changes in material costs

The time-lags will vary but by and large follow an obvious pattern. When allowance is made for the movement of raw materials through to final consumption it will be seen that the materials and goods are held in stock first by the importer, then by the manufacturer, then by the wholesaler, and finally by the retailer.

This stock pipeline has a life of about ten months taking the average for the whole economy, but in addition there will be time-lags in adjusting selling prices in response to cost changes. Many

Table 38

Impact on the Retail Price Index – Tax and Price Effects:
the March 1968 Budget

Purchase tax increases:
Clothing, furniture and household utensils	from 10% to 12%
Confectionery, ice cream and soft drinks	from 16% to 20%
Cars and most other durables	from 27% to 33%
Jewellery and furs	from 27% to 50%
Tape recorders	to 33%
Pre-recorded tapes	to 50%

Effect on prices	about $+\frac{1}{2}$%

Customs and Excise duties:
Spirits	up 2s. 6d. a bottle
Heavy wines	up 1s. 0d. a bottle
Light wines	up 6d. a bottle
Tobacco	up 2d. for 20

Effect on prices	about $+\frac{1}{4}$%

S.E.T.
Selective Employment Tax	up 50%

Effect on prices	about $+\frac{1}{4}$% – after a time-lag

Motoring Taxes
Car licence	from £17 10s to £25
Petrol tax	up 4d. a gallon

Effect on prices	about $+\frac{1}{2}$%

TOTAL EFFECT OF ABOVE	about $+1$% on retail prices within a year $+1\frac{1}{2}$% in two years

producers have to plan changes in selling prices with considerable care. Administrative problems tend to make price changes infrequent in that a time interval of perhaps a year is allowed between successive price increases. All in all, therefore, there may be time-lags of up to two years between a change in costs and the final absorption of the cost movement in final selling prices for the economy at large. The lags for labour costs and import prices are shown in Table 39. In addition, a column may be added

Table 39

The Build-up of Retail Price Adjustments to Changes in Costs

Time-lags for cumulative cost effects to work through to retail prices

	Cumulative effect by quarters	Labour costs	Import prices: basic materials	Import prices: manufacturers' goods
		%	%	%
Year 1	1st	0	0	0
	2nd	46	0	51
	3rd	74	52	75
	4th	86	76	87
Year 2	5th	91	88	92
	6th	93	94	97
	7th	94	96	98
	8th	96	98	99

for specifix tax changes and the three influences built into the forecast of price changes. From this it will be apparent that a correct analysis of cost changes will provide a nearly automatic forecast of price changes for up to two years ahead.

MANUFACTURING COSTS

The method for forecasting manufacturing industry's costs will be the same as that outlined above for the whole economy. Given a forecast of labour costs in the economy, a similar forecast for manufacturing can be derived by ratioing out growth in the past and applying the ratio forward with adjustments for either expected factors, or changing trends. For example, the ratio of annual growth rates for wages and salaries over the ten years 1958 to 1968 for manufacturing compared with the total economy was 1·08. That is, if wages and salaries are forecast to grow by 7·3% per annum in the total economy, then on the basis of past relationships wages and salaries in manufacturing industry would grow by 7·9%. Of course, as there are structural shifts in the economy (e.g. size of labour force) this kind of ratio needs to be adjusted. In the period up to 1975 it is expected that wage and salary movements in manufacturing will mirror more closely those in the total economy.

Other adjustments also need to be made such as assumptions about policy on Social Security Tax and Regional Employment Premiums. In any forecast it would be wise to allow for the phasing out of R.E.P.s by 1974 and to allow for increases in National Insurance and Social Security Taxes.

The record of labour costs in manufacturing from 1964 to 1969 is shown in Table 40. Dividing these past figures by figures

Table 40

Labour Costs in Manufacturing

Years	Wages and salaries	Employers' contributions	S.E.T. and R.E.P.	Total	
	£m.	£m.	£m.	£m.	% change
1964	6,346	447	–	6,793	+9·3
1965	6,922	519	–	7,441	+9·5
1966	7,348	581	+104	8,033	+8·0
1967	7,450	626	−252	7,824	−2·6
1968	8,013	697	−174	8,536	+9·1
1969*	8,614	743	−142	9,215	+8·0

* 1969 part-estimated

for manufacturing output gives labour costs per unit for manufacturing industry (see Table 41), and the same procedure with forecast data also produces a forecast of labour costs per unit.

The next step is to produce a forecast of material costs, taking

161

Table 41

Labour Costs per Unit of Output – in Manufacturing and
the Total Economy

Years	Labour costs in manufacturing		Labour costs in total economy	
	1963 = 100	*% change*	*1963 = 100*	*% change*
1964	100·6	+0·6	102·5	+2·5
1965	106·5	+5·9	107·2	+4·6
1966	113·2	+6·3	114·6	+6·9
1967	110·3	−2·6	117·2	+2·3
1968	113·3	+2·7	121·9	+4·0
1969	118·2	+4·3	128·7	+5·6

as a guide the Board of Trade's series, Price Index Numbers of
Basic Materials and Fuels Purchased by Manufacturing Industry.
Chart 20 shows the Board of Trade series together with the import unit value index. The two series show a close similarity. This
is because import prices feature as the predominant factor in
determining basic materials prices. The series is also affected by
movements in labour costs per unit of output in home industry
supplying the manufacturing trades. Therefore, to produce a

Chart 20

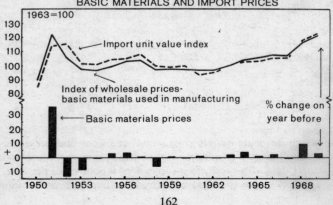

BASIC MATERIALS AND IMPORT PRICES

forecast of basic material and fuel price trends a forecast is required not only of import prices but also for labour costs. In some years more weight has to be given to one rather than the other, but on average the appropriate weighting is about two-thirds import price changes and one-third labour costs. This relationship is illustrated in Table 42.

Table 42

Basic Materials and Fuels – Wholesale Price Index

Years	Labour costs per unit in manufacturing		Import prices		Basic materials and fuel prices	
	1963 = 100	% change	1963 = 100	% change	1963 = 100	% change
1964	100·6	+0·6	103·9	+3·9	104·1	+4·1
1965	106·5	+5·9	103·9	nil	105·4	+1·2
1966	113·2	+6·3	105·8	+1·8	108·0	+2·5
1967	110·3	−2·6	105·8	nil	107·5	−0·5
1968	113·3	+2·7	117·5	+11·1	117·3	+9·1
1969	118·2	+4·3	122·3	+4·1	121·3	+3·4

Having produced a forecast of both labour costs per unit in manufacturing and basic materials and fuels prices, the two series can be linked together to give an estimate of the total cost change for manufacturing industry. In fact for U.K. manufacturing industry as a whole, costs comprise almost exactly 50% labour cost and 50% material and fuel cost. Thus a simple average of the forecasts for labour and materials will produce a forecast for total prime costs.

DETERMINATION OF PRICES

The forecast can now be moved from cost to price changes. A great deal has been published on price forecasting and it can be accepted that useful results can be obtained from regression analysis using data on labour costs adjusted for productivity trends, a measure of materials prices and a measure for the

163

pressure of demand. In Chart 21 a measure of the demand for labour is shown as a guide to the overall pressure of demand in the economy. Although this approach is a crude approximation of demand it will be seen that there is some correspondence between changing pressures in the labour market and changes in labour costs. However, the question of how prices are determined must first be examined before discussing method.

Chart 21

COSTS, PRICES AND PRESSURE OF DEMAND

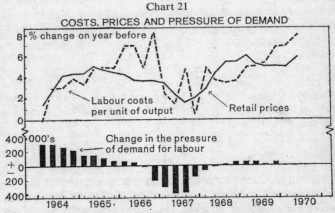

In times of full employment and full capacity working it is argued that excess demand leads to a rising price level. Demand for goods bids up prices. Firms try to meet the higher demand by increasing production and in order to do so raise the prices they are willing to pay for materials and labour. In this way wages, and after a time other money incomes, rise. This stimulates excess demand. In a modern economy there are leaks in the process, particularly as imports are usually available to supplement home demand. But, nevertheless, excess demand still generates a rising price level.

This argument attributes price inflation to demand/pull, and attempts have been made to test the theory. As we have seen, a relationship is assumed between variations in price and variations in the level of demand, usually measured by unemployment. In some work figures for unemployment are coupled with unfilled vacancies and the result termed an index for excess demand for labour. It has been shown that until 1969 a high proportion of the variation in money wages was associated with variations in the level of unemployment or excess demand for labour. This seems powerful evidence in support of a demand/pull theory of inflation, yet it is by no means a completely satisfactory explanation. This matter is discussed more fully in Chapter 8.

Another explanation of rising prices is propounded by the cost/push theory. It is argued that the price of goods and labour can rise independently of the level of demand and so lead to an increase in the price level. This line of approach is often pivoted on the cost of living: an increase in prices stimulates compensatory wage increases, which in turn lead to higher prices. Thus a wage/price spiral ensues. However, as a 1% increase in wages leads to a less than 1% increase in prices the spiral is a diminishing one, unless there are further shocks to restimulate it.

An acceptable view of the inflationary process must combine demand/pull and cost/push influences. But apart from this there is a good deal of debate over the role of the money supply – is it a determining factor or not in the general level of prices? It can be argued that the avoidance of excess monetary demand will lead to price stability. But it could also be argued that if the money supply is stabilized in the long run, the more efficient use of money will cause the velocity of circulation to rise and inflation will continue. It is undeniable, however, that conditions of excess money supply lead to an easy climate for passing on price increases, and on the other hand a tight money supply inhibits this. As the money supply in a modern economy operating at full employment is nowadays usually controlled by the monetary authorities, the degree of control they exercise must be watched and allowed for when forecasting costs and prices. A reasonable assumption for the U.K. in future years would seem to be that the authorities will allow a 6% per annum increase in money supply.

It is apparent, therefore, that the authorities are able to regulate conditions in such a way as to affect demand, costs, the availability of money and – indirectly – prices. In some cases the government may directly influence prices both through tax changes and by control of public-sector pricing policy. Beyond this, however, the government's influence will be felt through the regulation of the economic climate. 'Too much money chasing too few goods' is still a sound and simple explanation of one form of inflation. By the same token, if the authorities create a shortage of funds, competition will intensify and traders will be able to charge only such prices as the market will bear.

To summarize the arguments, although the pressures working for cost and price changes can be estimated, and whereas it will be true in the long run that businesses will recover cost increases through higher prices, the process is by no means automatic. Where an industry has surplus capacity, competition will be fierce and some firms will be unable to raise prices freely. In addition, at each phase of the business cycle, the ability to change prices will vary. Therefore, in this form of forecasting, once the general long-run trends have been established, the greatest attention has to be paid to the detailed analysis of the timing of the business cycle.

MANUFACTURING PRICES

To return to the estimation of manufacturing costs, given the forecast of labour and material costs, it is then possible to translate the overall cost forecast to price forecasts, making due allowance for the government policy measures and cyclical factors referred to above. Two sets of price forecasts are required. Firstly, a large part of manufacturing production will be sold at home. Secondly, manufactured goods are exported and prices of manufactured exports will depend upon conditions in overseas markets.

The first step must be the construction of the forecast for home prices, and this can be done in such a way as to produce a forecast of the wholesale price index for home sales. The record of both home and export prices from 1964 to 1969 is shown in

Table 43. The series are also illustrated in Chart 22, covering the period from 1950 to 1970.

Table 43

Home and Export Price Indices

Years	Wholesale home prices		Export prices	
	1963 = 100	% change	1963 = 100	% change
1964	102·9	+2·9	101·9	+1·9
1965	106·8	+3·8	104·8	+2·8
1966	109·6	+2·6	108·7	+3·7
1967	110·9	+1·2	109·6	+0·8
1968	115·3	+4·0	118·3	+7·9
1969	119·8	+3·9	122·1	+3·2

Export prices obviously move in the same direction as home prices, but generally move up less rapidly. An exception was the period following the 1967 devaluation. Short-term expectations for overseas markets are fairly well documented and a fuller discussion of this problem is contained in Chapter 4. The O.E.C.D. *Economic Outlook* contains excellent summaries of

Chart 22

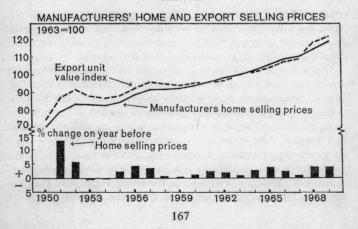

MANUFACTURERS' HOME AND EXPORT SELLING PRICES

short-term prospects for leading industrial economies which form Britain's major export markets.

Taking the analysis as a whole the forecaster can then produce a schedule of estimates, covering some years ahead, showing data for costs, home selling prices, export selling prices, profit margins and changes in profits (as discussed in Chapter 9). This will, of course, show any cyclical pattern expected to occur. Such a schedule gives the businessman an invaluable guide to both cost trends and pricing policy. The years in which it should be possible to move up prices will be identified as well as years when this is likely to be more difficult. Similarly, years which might be suitable to push up export prices, and years in which it might be prudent to exercise restraint, will be more easily identified.

CONSUMER PRICES

For many purposes it is necessary to take the forecast of manufacturing prices further and to construct estimates of consumers' and retail prices. Many manufacturing firms are concerned not only with ex-factory or wholesale prices, but also with distributors' margins, possible purchase tax changes and the resultant effect on the consumer market, and finally the retail price paid by the consumer. Wage negotiations, too, may in some cases be dependent upon changes in the index of retail prices, and it is certain that the price level, or cost of living, is of great importance in determining wages and salaries.

The index of retail prices is designed to measure changes in prices, between a base year and other periods of a 'basket of goods' representing most household purchases (there is now available a separate old age pensioners' index). The index is based on data collected in the annual family expenditure survey and monthly data collected by the appropriate Ministry – currently the Department of Employment and Productivity.

Yet the index is not wholly representative of the total range of consumers' spending. It leaves out, for example, prices of durable goods such as new cars, installation of central heating, and miscellaneous items such as garden plants, air tickets and so on. All these items are included in the consumers' spending implicit price deflator, usually called the consumer price index. This index is current-weighted and much wider in scope than the retail price index, and should, for these reasons, be preferred to the retail price index as a general measure of price change. However, in practice the two indices move in a similar way and since 1958 have moved together very closely. This is illustrated in Table 44, showing movements in the respective indices since 1950.

Table 44

Indices of Retail and Consumer Prices

(1963 = 100)

Year	Retail prices		Consumer prices	
	Index	*% change*	*Index*	*% change*
1950	61·1		64·9	
1951	66·6	9·0	71·0	9·4
1952	72·8	9·3	75·2	5·9
1953	75·0	3·0	76·7	2·0
1954	76·4	1·9	78·2	1·9
1955	79·8	4·5	81·0	3·6
1956	83·8	5·0	84·7	4·6
1957	86·9	3·7	87·5	3·3
1958	98·5	3·0	89·9	2·7
1959	90·0	0·6	90·8	1·0
1960	90·9	1·0	91·8	1·1
1961	94·1	3·5	94·5	2·9
1962	98·0	4·3	98·2	3·9
1963	100·0	1·9	100·0	1·8
1964	103·3	3·3	103·2	3·2
1965	108·2	4·7	108·0	4·7
1966	112·5	4·0	112·0	3·7
1967	115·3	2·5	114·9	2·6
1968	120·7	4·7	120·1	4·5
1969	127·3	5·5	126·4	5·2
1970*	135·0	6·0	133·5	5·6

* Estimated

The wholesale price index for manufactured goods sold is closely linked with the retail price index in a large proportion of retail sales consisting of manufactured products. Even agricultural output is indirectly included, as so much foodstuff is sent for further processing by manufacturing industry.

The main weights of the retail price index are shown in Table 45, with the changes in weighting between 1963 and 1970. The extent to which the importance of food in the index has declined will be noted.

Table 45

General Index of Retail Prices: Weights

Item	Weight in 1963	Weight in 1970
	%	%
All food	31·9	25·5
(of which seasonal foods)	(6·3)	(4·7)
Alcoholic drink	6·3	6·6
Tobacco	7·7	6·4
Housing	10·4	11·9
Fuel and light	6·3	6·1
Durable household goods	6·4	6·0
Clothing and footwear	9·8	8·6
Transport and vehicles	9·3	12·6
Miscellaneous goods	6·3	6·5
Services	5·6	5·5
Meals bought out	–	4·3
	100·0	100·0

Differences in movements between the retail and wholesale price index reflect changes in distributors' margins. For example, when resale price maintenance ended, margins were affected. More importantly, purchase tax is levied on the wholesale price and thus appears in the retail price, but not in the wholesale price index. The two series for recent years are shown in Table 46. Over the period 1963 to 1969 retail prices rose by 4·1% per annum on average, compared with only 3·1% per annum for wholesale prices.

As might be expected, there has been a good deal of similarity in the movement of the wholesale and retail price indices, but to forecast the retail price index adequately a different approach is required from relying solely on a forecast for wholesale prices. The most satisfactory method is to disaggregate the series into

Table 46

Wholesale and Retail Prices Compared

(1963 = 100)

Year	Wholesale home selling prices		Retail prices	
	Index	% increase	Index	% increase
1963	100·0	–	100·0	–
1964	103·3	3·3	102·9	2·9
1965	108·2	4·7	106·8	3·8
1966	112·5	4·0	109·6	2·6
1967	115·3	2·5	110·9	1·2
1968	120·7	4·7	115·3	4·0
1969	127·3	5·5	119·8	3·9

broad groupings, forecast each group's price trends separately and then to weight the groups together into the overall index. This forecast can then be cross-checked with the previously determined wholesale price index and tested for consistency.

The retail price index can usefully be broken down into four main sections. Food, which can be further subdivided into seasonal foods and non-seasonal foods, can be forecast on a trend basis, with some reference to weather and harvest prospects when determining the current year's forecast. Allowance also has to be made for factors such as changed systems of agricultural price support. Minor changes are currently being effected, but larger changes will obviously accompany Britain's entry into the E.E.C.

The weight of food items in the all-items index is currently 25·5%; the changes since 1963 are shown in Table 47. Over the eight years 1962 to 1970, food prices rose by an annual average of

3·8% compared with 3·9% for both all other items and for the total index.

Table 47

Index of Retail Prices (a)

(*16 January 1962 = 100*)

Year*	All items		All food items		All items except food	
1963	102·7	+2·7	103·8	+3·8	102·2	+2·2
1964	104·7	+1·9	105·4	+1·5	104·3	+2·1
1965	109·5	+4·6	110·3	+4·6	109·2	+4·7
1966	114·3	+4·4	113·0	+2·4	114·8	+5·1
1967	118·5	+3·7	117·6	+4·1	119·0	+3·7
1968	121·6	+2·6	121·1	+3·0	121·9	+2·4
1969	129·1	+6·2	126·1	+4·1	130·2	+6·8
1970	135·5	+5·0	134·7	+6·8	135·8	+4·3

* Figures for January each year

The three other main items to be forecast are shown in Table 48. Alcoholic drink and tobacco both suffer from large tax imposts. The other heading covers the other items and is referred to here as the 'residual retail price index' (R.R.P.I.). In general the trends in the drink and tobacco prices are fairly stable apart from changes in excise duties.

In 1970 the weights for drink and tobacco in the total index were 6·6% and 6·4%, and for the R.R.P.I. 61·5%. Thus the residual items account for almost two-thirds of items in the retail price index, and cover spending on housing, fuel and light, durable goods, clothing and footwear, transport and other goods and services. Over the eight years shown, prices rose on average by 3·9% per annum for R.R.P.I., compared with 4·6% and 4·0% for drink and tobacco and 3·9% for the total index.

The R.R.P.I. can be forecast by relating past price changes to movements in labour costs adjusted for productivity trends, and by movements in import prices by major classes. On the basis of relationship in the period 1963 to 1969, the full response to an increase in labour costs per unit, or import prices, involved on average a lag of about two years, although, as was shown in Table 39, in some cases about half the final effect is through into prices within six months. There is a good deal of recent evidence to suggest these lags are contracting, particularly with regard to wage costs. Employers are now much more alert for the need to move prices quickly in response to cost increases in order to protect profits.

Table 48

Index of Retail Prices (b)

(*16 January 1962 = 100*)

Years*	Alcoholic drink		Tobacco		Residual items (R.R.P.I.)	
1963	100·9	+0·9	100·0	–	102·7	+2·7
1964	103·2	+2·3	100·0	–	105·1	+2·3
1965	110·9	+7·5	109·5	+9·5	109·0	+3·7
1966	119·0	+7·3	120·8	+10·3	113·7	+4·3
1967	125·4	+5·4	120·7	−0·1	118·2	+4·0
1968	125·0	−0·3	120·8	+0·1	122·2	+3·4
1969	134·7	+7·8	135·1	+11·8	129·4	+5·9
1970	143·0	+6·2	135·8	+0·5	135·4	+4·6

* Figures for January each year

The four main components of the retail price index can then be amalgamated into a single forecast, and cross-checked for consistency with the previously determined wholesale price index. A separate forecast for consumer prices can now be prepared using the forecast of retail prices as a base. Table 44 listed past data for retail and consumer prices, and a marked similarity is evident. Retail prices can give a good guide to consumer prices provided adjustments are made to allow for abnormal years of durable goods sales. Prices of these items usually rise less rapidly than retail prices, so that in a year when there is a sharp cyclical upswing in sales of cars and appliances, the consumer price index will rise less than the retail price index.

So far forecasts for consumer prices and export prices have

been derived. In order to get a price forecast for the economy as a whole (the G.D.P. deflator), forecasts for government spending prices and investment goods are required. Public authorities spending is closely, though not solely, determined by employment and wage and salary trends, and the price deflator for this sector can be related to labour cost movements. Similarly investment prices can be related to wholesale prices.

BUSINESS FORECASTING

The significance of the cost and price forecasts for the whole economy can be assessed by the individual firm only from an analysis of the relative price movements of the items with which it is mainly concerned. Whether these are labour or material costs, or wholesale, export or retail prices, the experience of the individual firm or industry can be compared with the national averages for those items. Bearing in mind that major trends or relationships change only gradually, a past relationship is a valuable tool for forecasting purposes.

For example, in the case of labour costs, where because of local circumstances firms in a district have been obliged to grant wage increases well in excess of the national average, it is as well to assume that this relationship will hold in the future planning period. The forecast of national wage movements can, therefore, be modified for the district and firms concerned.

The same will apply to selling prices. Where prices have risen less than the national average in the past it is probable that special factors, such as strong competition or a rapidly expanding market or new technology, have influenced prices. Since these factors will probably continue to operate in the near future, a similar market performance is likely.

The importance of this kind of analysis to both marketing and buying is obvious, but without an underlying set of forecasts for costs and prices for the economy at large, it will not be possible to develop confident forecasts for the individual firm. The same will be true for purposes of planning. A business plan must be couched in realistic prices current in the years under review, for cash flows and profits are current price-valued amounts. A consistent set of price forecasts is, therefore, a necessity in many aspects of modern business.

CHAPTER 8

Forecasting Incomes and Spending

BY R. J. HALL

Consumer spending accounts for over half of Britain's imports and, directly or indirectly, 55% of Britain's total output of goods and services. Industry's dependence on consumption goes further, since decisions on both public and private capital spending rest heavily on forecasts of consumer demand for goods and services.

From this chain of dependence a strong case can be made for governments to concentrate on manipulating consumer spending when seeking to regulate the overall growth of the economy. Changes in hire-purchase controls, for example, either increasing minimum deposit requirements or reducing the maximum repayment period, have an almost immediate effect on durable goods – the most dynamic sector of consumer spending. This is soon followed by a reaction on other forms of consumer spending, capital spending and business confidence generally. Hire-purchase controls have proved to be rather a blunderbuss weapon but none can deny their sharp impact.

Changes in spending work their way through the economy by producing changes in income. An extra £1 a week spent by 1,000 consumers at a supermarket leads to increased overtime and commission earnings for the manager and staff, to increased demands on suppliers in order to replenish stock levels (or even increase them in anticipation of further increased spending) and a whole sequence of increases in incomes and output.

Changes in spending can and do arise from changes in the proportion of income that is spent and also from changes in hire purchase and bank debt. But, except in the very short term, the principal engine of changes in consumer spending must be changes in personal incomes.

INCOMES

Of total personal incomes, before tax, 70% is from employment, 8% from self-employment, 12% rent, interest and dividends, and 10% pensions, benefits and grants from central and local government. Some of this is income in kind, some 'imputed' income such as rent on owner-occupied houses, and some (e.g. dividends received by pension funds) is not cash immediately at the disposal of the consumer. It also includes employers' National Insurance contributions, which only as an accounting nicety can be counted as part of personal incomes. Thus, while consumer spending is the dominant component of total spending, employment incomes are the prime base of consumer spending.

Table 49

Income from Employment

£ million

	1958	1968	Increase
Wages and salaries	12,135	22,450	+85%
Forces' pay	395	542	+37%
Employers' contributions:			
National Insurance, etc.	398	1,102	+177%
Other	542	1,173	+116%
TOTAL	13,470	25,267	+88%

There are simple arithmetic relationships between output, output-per-man-hour (loosely termed 'productivity'), income-per-man-hour, total employment (measured in man-hours) and total wages and salaries. For example in 1966 output rose by 1·9% and 'productivity' by 3·1%. Thus total man-hours worked fell by

$$\left(\frac{1\cdot019}{1\cdot031} - 1\right) \times 100\% = 1\cdot2\%$$

Income-per-man-hour rose by 8·4%, and so total wages and salaries rose by

$$1\cdot084 \times 0\cdot988 \times 100\% = 7\cdot1\%$$

The causal relationships, however, are not so simple. Given the rate of output growth, the higher the productivity the lower employment becomes. But employment changes cannot be large in any normal circumstances. In peace-time conditions overtime working can be increased only within a fairly low upper limit. In some industries rather larger changes can be made in the opposite direction, by short-time working, for a limited period. More permanent reductions in average hours worked cannot diverge far from the rate at which workers' preference for increased leisure increases.

EMPLOYMENT AND PRODUCTIVITY

Turning to the numbers employed, governments almost everywhere are committed to maintain full employment. Although the level of unemployment that is deemed 'politically acceptable', i.e. consistent with a full-employment policy, can, and does, vary from time to time and place to place, unemployment will not be allowed to rise far before the instinct of self-preservation compels a democratically elected government to stimulate output growth and hence reduce unemployment by increasing demand for labour.

The supply of labour is also inelastic, that is to say, a change in the number of workers required by employers does not induce a proportionately large change in the number of workers seeking employment. This is particularly marked in Britain, with a slow natural increase in population and strict immigration control. Occasionally wholly abnormal circumstances can lead to a sharp reduction in the labour force by emigration, as, for example, from Ireland during the nineteenth-century potato famine and from East to West Germany in the 1950s.

The possibility cannot be ruled out that international financial co-operation may one day fail to avert a really damaging slump in world trade. Barring this, it must be concluded that large changes in employment are well nigh impossible. The largest change in Britain in recent years was a fall of $2\frac{1}{2}\%$ in 1967 follow-

178

ing the introduction of Selective Employment Tax and during a tough credit squeeze.

While total employment is notably inflexible, such changes as do occur are generally in the same direction as changes in the rate of growth of output. Flexibility is further increased by the observed link between output and 'productivity'. The word is put in quotes because, as we have seen, what is measured is output-per-man-hour. Changes in this may arise from changes in the effective effort or skill of the labour force, as a result of a productivity deal or a longer-term improvement in the quality and education of the labour force. They may also arise from improvements in the quality of management and organization, and from improvements in the quality and quantity of capital equipment.

The true productivity of a firm, industry or whole economy is the relationship between its output and input of all resources – including not only quantity and quality of labour, management and capital, but also social and institutional factors not at all readily measurable. If such a relationship can be envisaged, the rate of change in the productivity of any one resource (or 'factor') is the percentage by which output would be increased if the input of the resource in question were increased by 1% and the input of all other resources were held constant. Clearly, quite apart from the unreliable nature of the economic data, the intangibility of the social and institutional factors make the calculation of academic rather than practical interest.

EMPLOYMENT AND PRODUCTIVITY IN THE SHORT TERM

As well as the long-term causes discussed above, productivity can also change as a result of an important short-term variation in the degree of capacity utilization. When there is an up-swing in activity, i.e. an increase in the rate of growth of output after a period of decline, it is normal to expect some increase in output to come without any increase in man-hours employed. This is because plant and labour are being used more intensively. Beyond

this stage, a further output increase is likely by increasing overtime working, and up to a point this may also show up as an
improvement in the rate of productivity growth. If output still
continues to grow, however, more plant will be required and more
labour to man it, and the rate of productivity growth will tend to
fall back.

When the output cycle enters its downward phase, the process
is reversed. First average hours worked are reduced, immediately cutting the growth of productivity unless overtime working
has been excessive. Then numbers employed are reduced, by
checking recruitment and laying-off men.

The productivity cycle can be seen from Chart 23, covering the

Chart 23
PRODUCTIVITY AND INCOMES

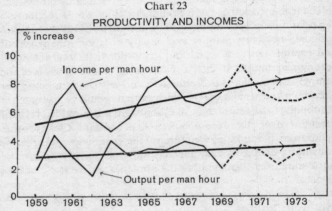

1959–64 period. Output growth picked up during 1959, leading
to a relatively large increase in average hours worked. Output
accelerated in 1960 but hours worked did not, and a very large
productivity gain was achieved. The economy then became overheated and the brakes were applied in 1961. Output growth
slackened and average hours were cut, but at first numbers
employed increased further. There was therefore a sharp fall in
productivity growth. Output slackened further in 1962, when
unemployment mounted, short-time working increased and

productivity dipped further. Then, after an appalling winter, output growth was stimulated during 1963. The year's output increase was achieved with hardly any extra labour and productivity accelerated. Output grew even more in 1964, at the cost of substantial increases in capital equipment, and employment – in terms of both numbers and average hours – and productivity growth eased back once again.

Subsequently the cyclical pattern was broken. Substantial reductions in normal hours were negotiated in 1965 and this appeared to result in a genuine productivity gain. Then in July 1966 a most severe deflationary policy was introduced. Up till then, progressive tightening of the screws on the economy in October 1964, April and June 1965 and April 1966 had not created more unemployment. Perhaps employers suspected the Labour government would reverse policies if unemployment started to rise and those who had let labour go would then find themselves short. If so, the July 1966 measures produced a change of mind. Selective Employment Tax began to change employment policies. In addition increased redundancy payments affected the readiness of employers to lay off workers and – probably more important – the ability of the unemployed to endure longer periods of unemployment in order to find the right job rather than take the first opportunity open must have resulted in more people staying unemployed.

A combination of these factors led to a decline in total employment during 1966 and 1967 of a magnitude unprecedented since the war. Output growth was reduced in 1967 but did not cease. So, while on the past cyclical experience the forecaster would have expected a decline in productivity growth, the combination of institutional and politico-psychological factors led to a greater increase than in any year of the decade except 1960 and 1963.

The cyclical pattern seemed to re-emerge in 1969 with a downturn in both output and productivity growth. Cautioned by previous experience, the forecaster must therefore assess the likelihood of further distortions and consider whether any longer-term factors will change.

LONG-TERM TRENDS IN EMPLOYMENT AND PRODUCTIVITY

The potential supply of labour changed during the 1960s. In the earlier part of the decade, both net immigration and the U.K.-born population of working age increased. Neither rose in the second half of the period. Without immigration controls, immigration would have risen faster in the late sixties but most probably not as fast as in previous years, when the pressure of demand for labour was much higher.

At the same time, although the natural domestic supply of labour virtually stopped growing, demand for labour fell. The total of those actually employed plus those registered as unemployed dropped below the potential working population as calculated from the age distribution and past 'activity' proportions in each age group. The gap was made up by young people staying extra years at school, by earlier retirement and by slower growth in employment of married women. If the demand for labour had been higher, the supply was there to meet it. If the supply had been a little higher, it is unlikely that unemployment would have been higher, or that the government would have been obliged to stimulate demand. Only if supply had been much greater would the situation have been significantly different.

The natural supply of labour will not change until 1973, when the school-leaving age is raised. After this once-for-all drop, a slow increase will ensue. There seems no possibility that immigration will be liberalized unless and until the U.K. joins the European Economic Community. From the evidence of the 1960s and earlier, it appears that the supply of labour will not, however, be a limiting factor on economic growth for some years, except in the highly unlikely event of output growth being stimulated far beyond any previous heights. It also appears that unemployment will not be so high as to embarrass the government – taking the period as a whole. Such is the potential reserve of labour that raising the minimum school-leaving age may not cause any general shortage even in the actual year of transition.

Another longer-term factor is the trend in average hours worked, compounded from hours per week and days worked per year. Hours per week actually worked (not normal hours, i.e. hours worked at basic rates) tended to fall during the 1960s for the first time since the end of the war. It may be assumed that weekly hours will continue to fall and that annual holidays will be further increased. Thus average hours worked will decline in the first half of the 1970s by about 0·2% a year on average. Precisely when the negotiated 'normal' week will be shortened cannot be predicted far in advance. But it is certain that some further reduction will take place before 1980.

Chart 23 shows a straight line through the productivity cycles to indicate the trend in productivity growth. Refined economic calculations and crude comparisons between similar stages in successive cycles indicate that the growth of productivity has tended to accelerate slowly. There was a spurt, taking 1965 to 1968 above the trend, which was associated with the drastic labour shake-out discussed above. It may be assumed that in the first half of the 1970s the rate of acceleration will fall back, leading to a trend rate of productivity growth of $3\frac{1}{2}$ to $3\frac{3}{4}\%$ per annum by 1975.

The chart shows the actual figures barely up to trend during this period. It is quite possible that were output allowed to increase faster, say by $3\frac{3}{4}\%$ rather than $3\frac{1}{4}\%$ a year, the actual productivity performance would be better. That is to say, the faster growth would not be wholly met by extra employment. However, given balance of payments and debt repayment constraints on output, the available reserve of manpower (and woman power) and no fundamental institutional changes, there seems little reason to forecast any major divergence from the productivity trend illustrated.

Yet there is one minor favourable factor to take into account. The fact that a smaller number of new entrants to the labour force will require training in future years compared with the past will probably increase the productivity of the labour force as a whole by a little. Apart from this no fundamental effects on output and productivity growth are in view.

The actual path around the trend illustrated in Chart 23 suggests a check to output growth in 1972 following overheating in 1971. Productivity growth is shown to fall in 1972 to be followed by a pick-up in output and productivity in 1973 and 1974. The eventual out-turn may be differently timed or have a quite different shape, but the point of making a year-by-year forecast is not to pretend that changes can be precisely pin-pointed, but to ensure that medium-term forecasts are consistent with a plausible time path. As short-term movements occur they can be checked against the longer-term forecasts and the forecasts revised.

Productivity trends over the really long term – ten, twenty, thirty years – are much harder to predict. So many institutional factors may change that for most purposes the best that can be done is to postulate a range on either side of a projection of the current trend.

WAGES AND SALARIES

Chart 23 shows income as well as output per man-hour. For past years income per man-hour is simply total wages and salaries divided by man-hours worked. In 1966 for example, wages and salaries grew by 7·1% and hours worked fell by 1·4%. Thus income per man-hour rose by

$$\left(\frac{1\cdot071}{0\cdot986} - 1\right) \times 100\% = 8\cdot6\%$$

There is no very obvious trend, but it is quite clear that income per man-hour has accelerated appreciably more than productivity. It also has a marked cyclical pattern with peak rates of growth in 1961, 1966 and 1970.

In the first period shown there appears to be a connection between the productivity cycle and the income per man-hour cycle. The 1960 peak in productivity was followed by an income peak in 1961 and the productivity low in 1962 was followed by an income low in 1963. This seems logical; workers receiving the benefit of increased productivity in higher wages a year later. There is, however, no correspondence between the series from 1964 to 1969. In the forecast period changes in the two series are shown to be in the same direction, but without a time-lag and without any very close fit. Productivity must have some bearing on incomes, at least in the long run, even though there are other factors affecting the short run.

In forecasting labour incomes it is necessary first of all to examine what relationship incomes have to basic wage rates. The Department of Employment and Productivity compiles and publishes an index of basic hourly wage rates for all workers in all industries. In general the rates included are nationally negotiated minimum rates of pay. Obviously actual average hourly income is raised above the minimum by agreements at plant level, bonuses and pay at overtime rates. What is not so obvious is why actual income should *grow*, as it has by over 1% a year more than basic rates.

Furthermore the gap has widened, as is shown in Table 50.

Table 50

Wage Drift

% p.a. increase

	Hourly wage rate	Income per man-hour
1959–64	5·0	6·2
1964–9	5·8	7·5

Part of the explanation is faster reduction in normal hours than in actual hours, i.e. increased time worked at overtime rates. But another part is to be found in the operation of incomes policy. In 1965 wages rates rose by 6·3% and income per man-hour by 7·5% – a fairly normal gap of 1·2%. Wages accelerated in the first half of 1966; then in July came the wage freeze. The wage rate index did not change during the second half of 1966 and rose only slowly in the next six months of severe restraint. But actual income received did not freeze so hard, and thawed rather more quickly. Thus for 1967 as a whole while the wage rate index increased by 4·0% and incomes per man-hour rose by 6·9% – a wide gap of 2·9%. After another wage spurt during 1968 further attempts were made to restrain income growth and in 1969 wage rate growth was held to 5·4%. Again the gap widened and income per man-hour increased by 7·2%.

WAGE RATES

It may be assumed that during the 1970s wages are not restrained by such blanket direct government action as in the past. Underlying the forecast shown in Chart 24 is an assumption that incomes will grow by about 1·2% a year faster, on average, than wage rates. But what determines the growth of wage rates?

Chart 24
EMPLOYMENT AND INCOMES

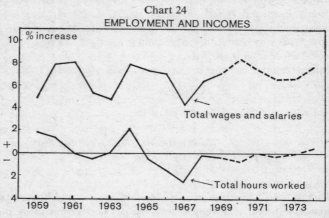

There are two divergent schools of thought. One argues that the price determinant of wage rate settlements is the balance of supply and demand in the labour market. As the supply of labour, in the short run at least, is relatively static and inelastic, this concentrates attention on changes in the demand for labour. This can best be measured by changes in unemployment and unfilled vacancies. Statistical relationships have been calculated covering long periods between the rate of growth of wage rates, the unemployment percentage and the rate of change in unemployment, and discussed in an important article by Professor A. W.

186

Phillips.[1] The theory developed from such observations led to the following policy arguments: Inflationary wage increases can be avoided if total demand and output is managed in such a way as to hold unemployment at 2–2½% and to increase output at the underlying rate of growth of productive capacity of the economy as a whole. The weakness of such a theory is that it depends to a large extent upon the definition used as to the real level of un-employment and also upon measurement of changes in pro-ductive capacity. The latter is incapable of precise measurement in the British economy.

Alternatively more weight can be attached to institutional factors, in chief the bargaining power of trade unions. Certainly the experience of 1969 and 1970 appears to support this school. Unemployment remained at its highest level since the war and yet wages rose faster than ever before. At the same time, in the U.S.A. wages rose very rapidly despite a severe monetary squeeze which brought about a sharp rise in unemployment. Wage 'explosions' also rocked France, Italy, Germany and Japan as well as the smaller industrial economies. This line of thought leads to advocacy of incomes policies, i.e. either legislative or exhortatory intervention in the bargaining process. The awkward truth, however, is that the British wage explosion followed a switch to greater reliance on incomes policy.

Returning to Professor Phillips' article, it seems to have been forgotten that he noted his relationship did not hold in periods of exceptionally rapid increases in import prices. In these periods the effect of the rising cost of living on trades unions' determina-tion to seek wage increases, and employers' readiness to grant

1. Such relationships are known as 'Phillips' Curves' after Professor A. W. Phillips, who in an article (*Economica*, November 1958) demon-strated that, if allowance is made for time-lags to reflect the increasing institutionalizing and hence protracted nature of wage negotiations, the basic relationship had not changed in almost 100 years. He concluded that at the time of writing a condition for price stability (allowing for produc-tivity growth) was a 2% unemployment rate. Additional studies since that date have led to varying conclusions. See "The Change in the Relationship between Unemployment and Earnings Increases: A Review of Some Possible Explanations", *N.I.E.S.R. Review*, November 1970.

them, appeared to be greater than the effect of employers' competitive bidding for labour. This seems to fit 1969 and 1970, when the wage explosion followed the rapid rise in import prices in 1968 – consequent upon the 1967 devaluation.

Furthermore, emphasis on incomes policy had drawn more attention to comparative rates of wages and wage increases. If anything, this has stimulated the pressures for wage increases. Moreover, there is a marked trend towards more sophisticated bargaining by the unions in response to pressures by members and a greater degree of knowledge about labour factors up and down the country. More emphasis on the actual purchasing power of money wages led to dissatisfaction over growth in the standard of living in the years immediately following devaluation and determination to redress this by seeking much larger pay increases than hitherto.

Assuming no further devaluation and a faster rate of output growth in the first half of the 1970s, the 1968–70 period may prove to have been a once for all adjustment period. The next adjustment period to be prepared for is on U.K. entry into the E.E.C. Should this occur the two important factors will be changes in the cost of living resulting from changes in taxation and agricultural systems and greater awareness of comparative wage levels on the Continent.

The conclusion is that in estimating future labour incomes the forecaster should start from a basic relationship between wage rates and the demand for labour, building into this relationship a trend to reflect the increasing sophistication of the negotiators and the growing importance of bargains covering a much longer term than merely one year or eighteen months. A relationship appropriate to the first half of the 1970s is:

$$W = 3\tfrac{1}{2} + \frac{6}{u_{t-1}} + \frac{t}{10}$$

where $W = \%$ increase in hourly wage rates on corresponding quarter of previous year

$u_{t-1} = \%$ unemployed in previous quarter

$t =$ time in quarters from first quarter 1969

This equation implies an inverse relationship between unemployment and wage rates, and also a trend adding 0·4% to the average wage settlement, cumulatively year by year. On this basic relationship the forecaster must superimpose special factors peculiar to the period for which he is forecasting. The conclusion is that, unless unemployment is at a particularly high level, inflationary wage increases will be the order of the day.

SELF-EMPLOYMENT

The growth of incomes from self-employment fluctuates considerably in the course of the business cycle. Professional people, sole traders and partnerships are not so able as employees to push up the selling price of their services. Their incomes, however, do benefit more directly and fully from an improvement in business. An example of this is the earnings of stockbroker partnerships. On an upturn in stock exchange turnover, stockbrokers' commission rises much more than costs, a large part of which (e.g. office overheads, research department costs) are inflexible, at least in the short term. The converse occurs in a bear market when the volume of trading falls.

Farmers account for rather less than a quarter of income from self-employment. These fluctuate but without any direct connection with the general business cycle. The weather, and hence quality and quantity of the harvest, and the generosity (or otherwise) of the government's price review are the all-important factors.

There is a long-term decline in the number of small trading businesses; the family grocer is submerged by the supermarket; the one-man shop is swallowed by a multiple chain. This is reflected in slower growth of income from self-employment compared with income from employment.

RENT, DIVIDENDS, INTEREST

Of rent, dividend and net interest receipts by persons, a growing proportion (currently over a quarter) is accounted for by receipts for life assurance and pension funds. The remainder, some 9% of total personal income, comprises miscellaneous small items. The largest single item is the imputed rent of owner-occupied dwellings. As this is also an expenditure item in the official statistics, it presents no problems for the forecaster.

The other items are dividends from private shareholdings, rent (largely from houses) and receipts of interest from National Savings, other government securities, building societies and finance houses, etc., less payments of interest to building societies etc.

Table 51

Income from Self-Employment and Property

£ million

	1958	1968	*Increase*
Self-employment	1,786	2,840	+59%
Rent from owner-occupied dwellings	364	933	+156%
Rent, interest, dividends, receipts of pension funds	343	1,154	+236%
Other rent, dividends, net interest, etc.	1,154	2,212	+92%
TOTAL	3,647	7,139	+95%

No detailed breakdown of these items is published but it seems clear that interest is the largest component of the last item in the table, with dividends second and rent a poor third. It is forecast, therefore, on the basis of predictions of personal savings, company profits and the level of interest rates.

PUBLIC GRANTS

One of the fastest-growing sectors of income is that from National Insurance benefits and grants from public authorities. The rapid growth is due to the increasing number of old-age pensioners and improvements in the scale of social security and supplementary benefits. It is also swollen by increased numbers of grants for university students and others in further education. The only cyclical element in payment of grants is unemployment benefit, the total of which is obviously high in years such as 1963, when unemployment was high. But even since the introduction of earnings related benefit this is not a large item in the total.

The two problems in forecasting pensions and grants are the long-term rate of increase and the timing of increases in the scale. It is certain that the retired population will increase and highly probable that the real value of pensions and other social security benefits will continue to increase slowly through the 1970s. Within this period it is likely that pension contributions will be stepped up so that in the longer term the real value of pensions will grow faster. Increases in scale tend to occur every other year with variation to take account of electoral considerations.

Table 52

National Insurance Benefits and Other Public Grants

£ million

	1958	1968	Increase
Pensions	715	1,675	+134%
Unemployment benefit and redundancy pay	54	195	+261%
Other social security	258	674	+161%
Supplementary benefit	121	421	+248%
Education	90	358	+298%
Family Allowances	129	270	+109%
Other	40	94	+135%
TOTAL	1,407	3,687	+162%

NATIONAL INSURANCE

Turning now to deductions from personal incomes, the first is National Insurance and health contributions. These have been increased in step with social security benefits. It is probable that during the 1970s a new system of finance for the health and social security schemes will be developed. If a social security tax, as was foreshadowed for 1972, is introduced, this will simplify forecasting – given percentages of wages and salaries would be taken for the employers' contribution and deducted for the employees. If a larger part of health or other services are to be financed directly by users, instead of from contributions by all, this would show up in the national incomes accounts as a reduction in contributions and an increase in consumers' spending.

TAX

Income tax is, of course, the most important deduction from income. The figures in Table 53 for disposable income show how taxes have tended to take an increasing share of incomes, particularly in the years of the last Labour government. The standard rate of income tax was increased in 1965, but there are three more important reasons for the increase in the total tax bill.

First, as national productivity rises so incomes rise. With a progressive tax system this means more people move into the tax-paying classes and more rise into the higher tax brackets.

Second, inflation has the same effect. In fact, inflation has tended to rise faster than productivity. This can be offset, and from time to time has been partially offset, by raising the level of personal tax allowances, and so excluding those on low incomes from tax-paying altogether. It can also be done by raising the level of income at which tax rates increase, for example, as the lower limit for paying surtax was raised in 1962. However, these adjustments have usually been only partial and have lagged behind inflation of incomes.

Third, in the second half of the 1960s, there were fewer new entrants – school leavers and immigrants – into the labour force, fewer part-time workers and slower growth in the numbers of married women at work. Thus there were fewer low incomes and the tax slice of total incomes rose.

For these reasons, income tax receipts have a natural buoyancy. In contrast, indirect taxes rise as fast as spending in the case of purchase tax and less rapidly in the case of specific duties on beer, tobacco, petrol, etc. unless the rates of tax are raised. Income tax has become increasingly unpopular and the forecaster may take it as certain that during the 1970s there will be switches away from direct[1] to indirect taxation. This does not mean that the share of total incomes taken by income tax will fall, still less that the income tax total will fall, but that it will not accelerate as it did in the second half of the sixties.

Such switches may well increase savings by a little and so fractionally reduce spending. More significantly it will alter the pattern of spending, the change depending on the shape of the indirect tax mix.

DISPOSABLE INCOME

The final, relatively small, deduction from incomes is payment abroad of taxes and transfers. Personal disposable income, as the residual is called, grew steadily at an average rate of $6\frac{1}{4}\%$ a year during the 1960s, with some tendency to accelerate as inflation accelerated after devaluation in 1967.

CREDIT

Disposable income is supplemented by credit to form total spending power. The most significant sources of consumer credit are hire purchase and bank lending. Both were severely restricted for much of the 1950s and 1960s. Far and away the peak year was

1. Surtax is only a minor item in the direct tax bill.

1959, when credit added some 2% to spending power. Given un-trammelled development – which seems unlikely – no doubt credit would grow towards the U.S. level, where it frequently adds 2% to consumer spending power in a year.

Table 53

Disposable Income

| | £ million | | | % change | |
	1959	1964	1969	1959–64	1964–9
Total income	19,630	27,671	38,489	+41	+39
Less:					
National Insurance	897	1,444	2,249	+61	+56
Taxes on income	1,776	2,801	5,173	+58	+85
Transfers and taxes paid abroad	11	42	109		
Disposable income	16,946	23,384	30,958	+38	+32

The significance of credit, however, is in its variation from year to year. Even in the U.S.A., where less resort has been made to credit controls as an instrument for fine tuning of the economy, year-to-year variations in credit have had widespread reper-cussions through the economy. In the U.K. spectacular results have been achieved. Changes in hire-purchase controls, backed up by comparable directives to the banks about personal loans, have a short sharp effect on consumer spending. Furthermore they have a quite disproportionate effect on sales of durable goods. This can be criticized on the grounds of equity. It can also be criticized as a damaging attack on industries with above average productivity and export potential.

It may well be that in future more attention will be paid to longer-term consequences of credit controls and that less-frequent interventions will be made. If this is so, growth will be steadier and forecasting credit changes a relatively small component of the overall forecast.

SAVINGS

Of total spending power 7 or 8% is not spent but saved. It may seem reasonable to expect that as time goes on and people become richer on average, the proportion of income pre-empted by necessities will fall and that which is saved will rise. At first sight the historical statistics bear this out. Savings, measured as the difference between spending power and actual spending, is shown by the official statistics to have increased its share of spending power persistently throughout the post-war period.

This increase in the 'savings ratio' was more apparent than real for two reasons. First, at the end of the war the liquidity of the personal sector was abnormally high; cash had been accumulated which could not be spent because of rationing and controls. During the ensuing decade, as rationing and controls were lifted and as this surplus cash was used up, the savings ratio rose. It was not so much that a rising proportion of income was being saved but that savings from the past were being run down – a process that could not continue indefinitely.

Second, the subsequent rise in the savings ratio is a statistical illusion. Reference has been made in Chapter 3 to the problem of revisions to the official data. In the case of personal incomes and spending, the former are more often than not revised upwards, but are sometimes revised downwards, while spending is always revised upwards. There is a simple reason for this. New goods and services are constantly coming on to the market and new outlets are being opened. It takes time for the official statisticians to catch up with them. When they do, upward revisions must be made to the back statistics of total spending. When allowance is made for this, the apparent growth of the savings ratio from the mid-1950s to the mid-1960s disappears.

Taking this into account, the theory on which forecasts of savings are made is that higher income brings a greater sense of security and hopes of still higher income to come. This, together with ever-widening consumer choice, leads to a greater willingness to go into debt, rather than save, so as to enjoy the fruits of future income now. During the 1970s the U.K. economy will move closer in pattern to that of the U.S.A., where incomes are higher, consumer debt very much higher, and the savings ratio the same.

SAVINGS OUTLETS

A fairly stable long-term trend in the savings ratio, however, does not preclude significant cyclical variations. In examining these it is helpful to look at the uses to which savings are put. Savings can be classified as either 'planned' or 'unplanned'. Planned savings include acquisition of paper assets such as stocks and shares, National Savings and building society deposits, repayment of mortgages, cash outlays for house purchase, and contractual savings such as life assurance and pension contributions. Unplanned savings may include changes in bank deposits and cash stowed away under the mattress.

Contractual savings are rising rapidly and comparatively steadily. As incomes rise and more employees are included in pension schemes, rapid growth seems certain to continue, whether or not the state system is substantially widened and deepened. Saving for house purchase is also on a steeply rising trend as prices rise and better quality housing is demanded. By contrast, acquisition of paper assets is marked more by sharp cyclical fluctuations than long-term growth.

A critical determinant of these fluctuations is the state of the stock market. A stock market boom diverts some funds from other forms of savings (e.g. building societies and idle current-account balances), but it may also attract new savings and increase the savings ratio. In parallel with this increase in planned savings, a short-term increase in unplanned savings is to be expected. A stock-market boom usually occurs during an upswing in economic activity. At such times productivity rises sharply and wages run ahead of prices. Wage earners take time to adjust spending to higher spending power and so the savings ratio rises. The process goes into reverse in the downswing. The stock-market turns down, investors may take profits (partly to finance spending at a time of tight credit and to pay tax bills) and wage earners save less as income growth falls below the boosted rate of spending growth. Many odd quirks in the savings ratio occur from time to time, but in general it is safe to assume that around a stable trend there will be upward fluctuations in boom years and downward ones in depressed years.

CONSUMER SPENDING

In this chapter attention has been concentrated on forecasting incomes. This is the most difficult area. The deductions from incomes to arrive at disposable income are easier to forecast. For the longer term, given the comparative insignificance of credit changes and a stable savings ratio, total spending must grow at a very similar rate to that of disposable income.

When adjusted for price changes, consumer spending is a most important component of total output on which, in turn, the forecast of incomes rests. This re-cycling of flows of income and spending through the system is outlined in Chapter 2. For the purpose of this chapter it is sufficient to note that for the long term the spending forecast follows simply from the incomes forecast.

SHORT-TERM FORECASTS OF SPENDING

In the shorter term the problem is more complex. Spending cannot be forecast simply as a residual. The reason for this is that, while it is fairly easy to forecast the *direction* of changes in the savings ratio and consumer credit, the magnitude of these changes cannot be predicted with assurance in isolation. A direct forecast of consumer spending has to be matched with the savings forecast. More often than not revisions will then have to be made to both forecasts.

A further complication is that, as explained above, the official data for the recent past cannot be trusted. Chapter 3 shows how the figures of consumer spending may be revised to form a basis for forecasting. Given this basis, what indicators may be used for a direct forecast of spending?

The broadest indicator is the monthly index of retail sales, published by the Board of Trade some five or six weeks after the end of the month. This index is based on a sample of all shops, including gas and electricity showrooms and mail-order houses. It does not cover car sales. Altogether about half of consumer spending is accounted for by retail sales. As an indicator of total spending, however, the index has three drawbacks. First, it tends to grow only three-quarters as fast as consumer spending in total. Second, by excluding cars, half of the most dynamic sector of spending – durable goods – is excluded. Third, the seasonal pattern is different. It is easy to allow for the first; the second and third can be met by drawing on other indicators.

DURABLES

Chart 25 shows the dynamic course of spending on durables. Peaks and troughs generally coincide with those in total spending, but are much more marked. Spending on durables, whether a first purchase or a replacement, can always be postponed if expectations about future income deteriorate and brought forward if expectations rise. And so greater than average fluctuations are natural. But the situation has been aggravated by use of changes in hire-purchase controls and purchase tax rates in short-term management of the economy.

Lifting of restrictions on hire purchase provoked a durables boom in 1959 which was transformed into a slump in 1961 after re-imposition of controls and increased purchase tax. Purchase tax on cars was cut twice in 1962, and 1963 saw another boom. In 1965 and 1966 hire-purchase controls were tightened and spending on durables fell. In 1967 controls were relaxed, only to be tightened again after devaluation. Early in 1968 the Chancellor promised higher taxation in April – a signal for a gigantic 'beat-the-Budget' boom, to be followed by a mid-year slump. Tighter hire-purchase controls, a more severe squeeze on the supply of credit and still higher purchase tax produced a deep slump in 1969.

If durable goods continue to bear a disproportionate share of the burden of changes in management of the economy, excessive fluctuations will remain. If not, the changes will be less dramatic

Chart 25

CONSUMER SPENDING

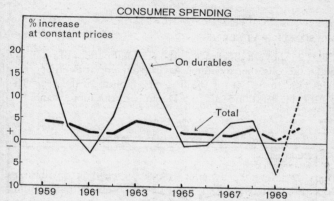

and it is probable that fluctuations in total spending will also be reduced. Durable goods will in either case still account for most of the fluctuations in consumers' spending.

Sales of domestic appliances and furniture are indicated by the durable goods shops sector of the retail sales index. Monthly statistics of new registrations of cars are published by the Ministry of Transport about three weeks after the end of the month. Further monthly information in the motor market is provided by the Board of Trade statistics on the turnover of motor traders and by Hire Purchase Information statistics on hire purchase deals, both of which show separately new and used vehicles. These statistics reveal whether sales of durable goods are growing faster or slower than the long-term trend.

As well as long-term models, there are short-term econometric models of varying sophistication and complexity which purport to measure the effects of income, changes in income and changes in hire-purchase terms and purchase tax from which scientifically based forecasts may be derived. Forecasting durables, however, remains very much an art. While formal models are useful and techniques are improving all the time, someone with a good nose for current trends and likely changes in government policy may still produce the best forecast.

SEASONAL PATTERNS

Chart 26 shows a difference in the seasonal pattern of retail sales and total consumer spending. Apart from a poor February, retail sales tend to be flat for the first nine months of the year. Then a steep acceleration leads to a December peak more than a third

Chart 26

THE SEASONAL PATTERN

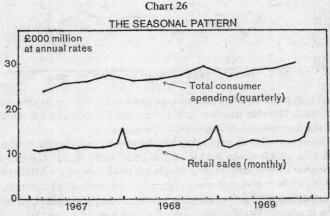

above the year's average. Total spending registers some growth in the middle of the year and a less pronounced Christmas peak than retail sales.

This difference arises partly from car demand, which is usually at its highest in the second quarter and lowest in the fourth, and partly from services, some of which (e.g. holidays and travel) are more in demand in the summer. Published monthly statistics for services include the turnover of the catering trades, including public houses and the motor trades' sales other than of vehicles, i.e. petrol, servicing and repair work, etc. Changes in demand for services are fairly predictable, but the weather has an important bearing, for example, on electricity supply and public house trade. An unusually fine May will see record beer sales and little use of electric fires. From time to time other variations may occur. In the early months of 1970, wages rose sharply but retail sales were flat. Instead, the first sign of a rising tide of spending was found in the turnover of public houses.

From these various strands a direct forecast of consumer spending can be built up to be matched with the short-term income and savings forecasts. Finally, forecasts at constant prices are derived using the price forecasts described in Chapter 7.

SPENDING IN THE LONGER TERM

Turning to the longer term, the forecast of consumer spending is derived from the incomes, saving and credit forecast. With the addition of a forecast of prices, a summary such as Table 54 can

Table 54

Consumer Spending

% per annum growth

	Previous 10 years	Previous 5 years	Next 5 years
In current prices	6·1	6·2	7·5
Average price level	3·4	4·1	3·9
Revalued at constant prices	2·6	2·0	3·5

be made. Five-year and ten-year periods are chosen, since the average length of the post-war U.K. business cycle has been nearly five years. Aggregate forecasts are of interest but limited value to the industrial business. The giant company, or one with a diverse range of consumer products, will find it valuable to measure its own progress over the past five and ten years against that of consumer spending in total, and to relate its forecast to the aggregate forecast. Most businesses, however, will gain maximum benefit from disaggregated forecasts of spending.

CATEGORIES OF SPENDING

Forecasts of an individual category of spending can be made by simple (or complex) projection of past trends or by relating it to one aggregate variable such as total industrial production. But it is safer to construct forecasts for each category that are consistent with the aggregate forecast. There are several stages in this process. Whether all are necessary will depend on the degree of detail required, the accuracy required (or possible), and the special factors relevant to the individual categories of interest to the business.

First, total spending is divided into about ten major categories, such as food, clothing, fuel. For each, growth over the past five and ten years is calculated and related to the aggregate growth. Taking clothing for example, a picture such as Table 55 emerges.

Table 55

Spending on Clothing and Footwear

	Past 10 years		*Past 5 years*	
	% p.a. growth	ratio to total spending	% p.a. growth	ratio to total spending
In current prices	4·4	72%	3·8	61%
Prices	2·1	62%	2·3	56%
At constant prices	2·3	88%	1·5	75%

Thus we see that over the past five years spending on clothing at constant prices grew 75% as fast as total consumer spending while clothing prices grew only 56% as fast as average prices.

202

On the basis of these past relationships and making a few broad assumptions, such as one that clothing prices will increase relatively faster in the future because wages in the clothing industry will grow at an above-average rate, a first forecast of spending on clothing is made (Table 56).

Table 56

Clothing and Footwear over the Next Five Years

	Ratio to total spending	% p.a. growth
In current prices	67%	5·0
Prices	70%	2·7
At constant prices	63%	2·2

The other nine categories of spending are treated in the same way. Small adjustments will then have to be made to ensure that the parts add up to the whole before proceeding to the second stage of disaggregation. In the above example, clothing and footwear may be subdivided into footwear, men's and boys' wear, and women's, girls' and infants' wear. The approach is similar to the first-stage analysis, but more detailed information can be incorporated. Allowance can be made for eccentricities in the cycle of clothing sales, liberalization of low-priced imports, peculiar fashion trends, etc. More or less sophisticated statistical and econometric methods may be used at this stage if the data and the methods can be shown to be suitable. The result may, however, cast doubts on the Stage 1 disaggregation and necessitate revised forecasts for the major categories.

Subsequent stages lead to forecasts of particular commodities or services rather than categories; for example, within the forecast of footwear a forecast of fashion boots may be required. Specialized knowledge of the market and of fashion trends is then called for, but the most reliable forecasts will be related to the trend of spending on footwear, on clothing generally and to consumers' spending in total.

A general guiding principle with which to close this chapter on incomes and spending is that in the long term the British scene seems certain to move closer to that of the U.S.A. This implies above average growth in services, leisure goods and durables and below average growth in food as a whole and basic necessities. Those goods and services which today are the preserve of the rich will tomorrow be mass-produced for the average customer.

CHAPTER 9

Forecasting Profits

BY SANDRA MASON

WHY MAKE PROFIT FORECASTS?

Profits are a key indicator of business performance. Most companies make some attempt to forecast future profits and these will reflect the impact of pricing decisions, cost increases or reductions and will show both the company's financing needs and its overall viability.

For an individual company, profit forecasts are an automatic derivative from sales and cost predictions. Once adequate forecasts have been made of the company's total sales revenue and total costs, the profit forecast can be derived as a residual:

$$\text{profit} = \text{total revenue} - \text{total cost}$$

The profit figure thus derived has to be adjusted for such items as depreciation, financing charges and taxation; but the most important element in the resulting net profit figure, the gross trading profit, has already been obtained.

Why then is it important to look at profit forecasts for industry as a whole, as well as at future trends in sales and costs? One reason is that consideration of general trends in profits can provide the business executive with a useful check on the sales and cost forecasts he has derived for his own business. A comparison of the general trends in profits with the forecasts for his own business will show the extent to which he is assuming, explicitly or implicitly, that there are special factors of various kinds working either for or against him. These factors may relate to particular price and cost trends or to projected changes in market shares. The manager may be completely justified in assuming the existence of such special factors, but the availability of a bench-mark, such as a general profit forecast, can help him to consider the matter more objectively.

The other main reason why the manager should use forecasts of the general trend of profits in the economy, and in individual sectors and industries, is that knowledge of these trends will help him forecast other variables of considerable importance to him. Profits are highly responsive to the cyclical movements in the economy. They play an important part in the dynamics of the economic system, and an understanding of the likely trends in profits is a key element in any realistic economic forecasting system.

The importance of profits in the general economic system derives from a number of particular influences which are also of interest to the firm. The profit trend has a significant influence on the general business climate. This is in part psychological in character but is naturally related to the effect of profit changes on the liquidity of companies. This in turn has a considerable effect on both stocking and investing decisions by industry. The close relation between corporate cash flow and private-sector capital investment was illustrated in Chart 2 (p. 25). Where a company's business is to any degree affected by decisions by other companies, profit forecasts can obviously help to make sales predictions more accurate.

The usefulness of profit forecasts in sales predictions is reinforced if the general forecasts can be supplemented by those for particular sectors or industries. The greater degree of detail enables the firm to examine more closely the expected position of both its customers and competitors. It can then assess their likely behaviour in response to the expected conditions, and the consequent effect on itself.

An additional area where profit forecasts are indispensable is in relation to the stock-market. The changes in profits earned are closely related to movements in equity prices (see Chart 27). This relationship has an important role in any overall forecast for the economy and financial flows. It is also of particular significance for a quoted company concerned about the level of its share price and for any company planning to raise money on the stock exchange in some form or other. Any manager aiming to plan ahead his company's financial needs will have to make allowance for the likely level of stock-markets and their influence on the possibility of raising further outside capital. This type of forecast is notoriously difficult to make and general profits forecasts can be a considerable help to this end.

Chart 27

PROFITS AND THE EQUITY MARKET

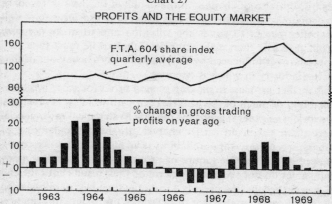

THE NATURE OF PROFITS AND SOME GENERAL FORECASTING PROBLEMS

It is as well to realize at the outset that accurate profit forecasts are not easy to obtain. This results from the very nature of profits, particularly their extreme cyclicality and the fact that they are by definition the residual difference between two much larger items, total revenue and total costs. Even small errors in the forecasts of revenue and costs become magnified into substantial errors in the forecast of residual profits. This difficulty arises in other types of forecast – the best-known example being that of the trade balance – and there is no easy way round it.

The extreme cyclicality of profits derives from the lags in the economic process, particularly in the adjustment of production and employment to demand, and in price changes to those in costs. If all adjustments in the system took place instantaneously there would not be an extreme profit cycle; hence accurate profit forecasting is vitally dependent on success in forecasting the size of the time-lags in the adjustment process. This in turn depends on a good understanding not only of past experience in this regard, but also of changes in the habits of business in response to economic conditions. For this reason the executive may well be better placed to assess the situation and to make accurate profit forecasts than many outsiders, though he must take care not to be over-influenced by his own company's behaviour or that of the industry in which it operates.

A further problem in making general profit forecasts is the unreliability of much of the historic data with which it is necessary to work. The general problems relating to statistical raw material were discussed in an earlier chapter. In the particular case of profits, some degree of unreliability is an almost inevitable consequence of the volatile nature of profits and the fact that many companies do not accurately determine their results until the end of specific accounting periods. Given the time-lags in publication of these figures, any system of collecting up-to-date information on profits, as soon as they are earned, is likely to be subject to considerable inaccuracy. The size of this problem, as indicated by subsequent revisions to the published figures for U.K. gross trading profits, is shown in Table 57. It is clear from this that preliminary figures have tended to overestimate the final result and any forecaster must make allowances for the likely direction of revisions when using the preliminary data.

FORECASTING TRADING PROFITS

The first and most important stage in making overall profit forecasts is to obtain the forecast of what are called 'gross trading profits', that is profits on U.K. trading alone excluding any other forms of income arising either in the U.K. or from trading abroad, and before allowing for depreciation, interest, taxation and any other additions or deductions. Once the figure for gross trading profit is available, supplementary forecasts can be made of the other items normally entering into the profit and loss

Table 57

Revisions to Gross Trading Profits

Quarterly figures £m		First published figures	Latest published figures	Difference*
1965	i	1,133	1,170	+37
	ii	1,150	1,234	+84
	iii	1,087	1,148	+61
	iv	1,196	1,226	+30
1966	i	1,124	1,134	+10
	ii	1,230	1,179	−51
	iii	1,071	1,094	+23
	iv	1,097	1,048	−49
1967	i	1,137	1,116	−21
	ii	1,242	1,228	−14
	iii	1,172	1,053	−119
	iv	1,291	1,263	−28
1968	i	1,325	1,242	−83
	ii	1,387	1,325	−62
	iii	1,259	1,159	−100
	iv	1,322	1,339	+17
1969	i	1,232	1,184	−48
	ii	1,348	1,351	+3
	iii	1,197	1,161	−36
	iv	1,361	1,361	nil

* Latest − first

account in order to derive net profits or cash flow or whatever precise formulation of profits is required. The method by which this transition from the gross to the net profit position is carried out is often called the 'cascade' system and the problems involved are considered in some detail below. For the moment, however, consideration will be confined to the forecasting of gross trading profits.

The question of forecasting trading profits can, in practice, be approached in three main ways. The first of these considers profits as a form of income and derives the profit forecast as a residual from forecasts of other items in the incomes table covering the whole economy. This is known in the national income accounts as the factor incomes table. The second approach looks at the profit forecast as the residual item from forecasts of the value of output and total costs in the corporate sector, these forecasts being derived from those for the economy as a whole. The third method derives a forecast of profit margins per unit of output from forecasts of unit costs and prices and then relates this forecast to that of total output in volume terms to obtain a figure for total profits.

Each of these approaches will be examined in turn. They have in common the fact that they are all concerned with money rather than volume flows; they differ principally in the information they use and the nature of the simplifying assumptions made with regard to the relationship involved in the economic system. The use of more sophisticated techniques is considered briefly later in the chapter.

THE FACTOR INCOMES TABLE

Total national product can be looked at not only as the sum of the net output of all sectors of the economy or of the total of all expenditure on that output, but also as the total of all the factor incomes derived as a result of the production of the output. The main types of factor income normally identified in this total and their relative sizes in recent years in the U.K. are shown in Table 58. It is evident from this table that the categories identified correspond quite closely to those normal in company accounting. The only item not included in the factor incomes table which would be deducted from sales revenue in a company's trading account is the cost of raw materials. Its absence is explained by the fact that in the national income accounts total product or factor incomes is defined as the value added in production, not the gross sales, thus avoiding the duplication that would result if total sales figures for all companies or sectors were to be aggregated. For simplicity, the total of factor incomes has been shown before allowing for stock appreciation and ignoring the residual error in the national income accounts; the question of stock appreciation is discussed below, that of the residual error was considered in a previous chapter.

Table 58

Factor Incomes Table

£ thousand million

	1964	1965	1966	1967	1968
Total domestic income*	29·37	31·52	33·02	34·44	37·05
less income from employment	19·70	21·26	22·74	23·62	25·27
less income from self-employment	2·34	2·53	2·67	2·77	2·84
less rent	1·70	1·87	2·02	2·18	2·36
equals total profits	5·62	5·87	5·60	5·87	6·58
divided into					
gross trading surplus of public corporations and enterprises	1·02	1·09	1·14	1·23	1·46
gross trading profits of companies	4·60	4·78	4·46	4·64	5·12

* before allowing for depreciation or stock appreciation

The form in which Table 58 is laid out indicates the way in which the forecast of profits by this method is derived. The figure for incomes from employment is a normal ingredient of most economic forecasts, since it is required for the forecast of consumers' spending. Deduction of this from the value of the total Gross Domestic Product gives the total of profits plus rent and income from self-employment. This total must then be allocated between rent and self-employment income on the one hand and

211

profits on the other. Finally, the total of profits must be divided between public-sector and private-sector enterprises.

The question of allocation can be approached from a number of ways, and unless strict, formalized relationships are used, it is very much a matter of individual study and interpretation. However, a useful system which can be applied in many other areas of forecasting is to look first at the longer-term growth rates for the various items and project these, allowing for any likely changes in relationships, to some terminal year. In doing this it is most important to ensure either that the years used for growth rate calculations are at similar stages of the economic cycle, or that some previous smoothing of cyclical movement has been carried out. Having made the projections to the final year of the forecast period, explicit allowance can be made for cyclical movements in the intervening years. This will be done on the basis of the expectations for the economy as a whole, and the normal cyclical developments in the individual types of factor income.

At every stage in this process it is vitally important to consider whether there are any particular factors likely to alter the historical pattern of relationships. The forecaster should take into account other relationships or items of information likely to be helpful with regard to the forecast of individual items. An example of this is the government's policy in relation to the profits and deficits of the nationalized industries and changes that have taken place in individual industries as a result. As another example rent and self-employment incomes also enter into the forecast for consumer spending and the figures used should be consistent in the two cases.

THE COMPANY SECTOR FORECAST

Corporate profits can also be estimated by subtracting incomes from employment in the corporate sector (i.e. the total wages and salaries bill plus other labour costs such as National Insurance and S.E.T.) from the value of the output of the corporate sector. In using this method there is no need to make separate forecasts of the other elements in the factor incomes table. But it is necessary to examine the relationship of corporate sector output and labour costs to those in the economy as a whole. Generally speaking, the corporate sector has in the past been much more volatile than other sectors; this is particularly so in the case of output, and is illustrated in Chart 28 with respect to gross product as well as employment incomes.

Chart 28

CORPORATE GROWTH IN THE ECONOMY

In trying to forecast the cyclical movement it will again be necessary to project the overall growth rate for a period and then to superimpose on this the likely cyclical movements. Possible shifts in the relative importance of different sectors of the economy should be considered, such as whether public-sector output is likely to be restrained in favour of the private sector, or whether wages in the public sector are likely to be held down by comparison with the private sector. The relative movements in prices in the public and private sectors must be considered.

UNIT COSTS, PRICES AND OUTPUT

The third approach to profit forecasting has the advantage that it does not depend directly, like the previous two, on an examination and informed projection of historic trends and relationships. Even so it has its own drawbacks; primarily, that it is crucially affected by the accuracy of the cost and price forecasts used, and highly dependent upon the efficiency with which the analyst recognizes the shifting relationships between unit costs and prices.

By this method the profit forecasts are obtained by applying the forecasts of unit costs and prices to weights reflecting the relative importance of the main items in the corporate trading account. The weights required can be obtained from the census of production data and although the census does not cover the whole of the corporate sector, only a minor adjustment is necessary to allow for this. Price changes are normally related to weights for total output, not value added as in the first approach. Cost forecasts and weights must therefore make explicit allowances for costs of raw materials, as well as labour. The price data used must be for wholesale not retail prices, but excluding the effects of changes in indirect taxes.

Table 59 shows, in simplified form and on historic data, how the calculations are carried out. The derived weighted index for unit costs is subtracted from that for unit prices to give an indicator of unit profit margins. This is then combined with the change in volume of output to give the movement for total profits. In this last step there may again be problems of coverage. Ideally the coverage of the volume figures should be identical with that of the cost and price data, but this can be difficult to achieve in practice. However, though coverage problems can be a source of inaccuracy in forecasts made using this approach, it is clear from the example shown that the general picture given is a reasonably accurate one.

THE COMPROMISE FORECAST

Each of these three approaches to forecasting trading profits suffers from some disadvantages. These arise from difficulties in obtaining data (particularly the necessary supplementary forecasts) and in establishing the precise nature of the simplified

Table 59
Use of Cost and Price Data to Estimate Profits

	Price changes %	Price index 1963 = 100	Cost changes %	Cost index 1963 = 100	Profit per unit index 1963 = 100	% change in profit per unit	Volume of output % change	Estimated total profits % change	Actual gross trading profit % change
1964	+2·5	102·5	+2·7	82·1	20·4	+2	+5	+7	+12
1965	+3·4	106·0	+4·0	85·4	20·6	+1	+3	+4	+4
1966	+2·6	108·8	+5·8	90·4	18·4	−11	+2	−9	−7
1967	+1·4	110·2	+2·2	92·3	17·9	−3	+2	−1	+5
1968	+5·1	116·0	+5·2	97·1	18·9	+6	+4	+10	+9
1969	+3·6	120·1	+5·1	102·1	18·0	−5	+2	−3	nil

relationships to be used for forecasting purposes. In practice, therefore, it is often desirable to make use of all three approaches simultaneously. They are thus used as a check on one another and a compromise forecast can be derived.

This compromise method has certain additional advantages where the trading profit forecast forms part of a wider forecasting system. Comparison of the three forecasts provides a check not only on the method of forecasting employed, but also on the consistency of the information fed in in each case. Hence the forecasts indicate the degree of consistency in the forecasting framework as a whole, particularly as between the forecasts of total output and incomes on the one hand and those of unit costs and prices on the other.

MORE SOPHISTICATED TECHNIQUES

The three approaches to trading profit forecasts have been outlined in terms of simple arithmetical relationships such as the ratios and disparities between growth rates. Obviously, however, profit forecasting can be and has been approached in a more sophisticated manner, making use, for example, of econometric techniques to establish useful predictive relationships.

Theoretically any of the three methods discussed can be used as the basis for this type of forecasting system. The econometric models which incorporate a profits relationship (of which there are relatively few) most commonly use some modification of the second or third approaches. Profits are related to total output and employment incomes, or to unit costs, prices and output. In addition some indicator of the cyclical phase of the economy, such as unemployment or capacity working, may be included in the equation. By using this kind of approach the profit forecasts can be derived almost directly from information already available in the forecasting system. Some additional relationships must be specified, notably that between aspects of the corporate sector and the whole economy, but particularly with the third approach there is little additional data to be collected.

The advantages of the more sophisticated techniques in profit forecasting are, as with other types of forecasting, the ability to examine relationships in greater detail, the greater degree of objectivity once the forecasting system is set up, and, given the necessary computing equipment, greater ease in making the forecast in practice. However, the quality of the resulting forecasts remains critically dependent on the exact form of relationships specified and the reliability of the data used.

FROM TRADING PROFITS TO CASH FLOW: THE 'CASCADE' SYSTEM

Once trading profits have been forecast, various other definitions of profits can be derived by a process of addition and subtraction known as the cascade system. This is not the only way to derive net profits and cash flow from trading profits. A simplified system could be adopted using a form of direct relationship between the items involved – similar, for example, to that used to derive forecasts for the company sector from those for the economy as a whole. But the relationship between net profits and trading profits can be seriously upset by changes in business practices or legislation relating to depreciation or taxation, and there are no checks available on such forecasts as there are with those of trading profits. Hence it is usually desirable to make a full forecast of the main items involved in the corporate profit and loss account via the cascade system.

Table 60 shows the various items involved in the cascade system and gives some recent figures for the U.K. At some stages in the process of addition and subtraction, additional independent forecasts are required. At others it is only necessary to make an assumption as to the relationship between one item and a previous one, for example the level of the tax charge. The nature of the items involved and problems in forecasting the different items are discussed below for each stage in the process.

217

Table 60

Companies' Appropriation Account

£ million

	1964	1965	1966	1967	1968
Gross trading profits*	4,601	4,778	4,455	4,637	5,117
+ Rent and non-trading income	1,053	1,222	1,343	1,461	1,676
+ Income from abroad	1,296	1,452	1,417	1,450	1,766
= Total income	6,950	7,452	7,215	7,548	8,559
− Depreciation†	993	1,087	1,189	1,210	1,300
− Interest‡	756	908	1,088	1,224	1,478
= Pre-tax profits	5,201	5,457	4,938	5,114	5,781
− U.K. tax payments	703	656	694	1,027	1,068
− Overseas tax payments	512	552	555	563	726
− Additions to tax reserves	304	22	481	269	517
= Net profit	3,682	4,227	3,208	3,255	3,470
− Dividend	1,520	1,735	1,687	1,576	1,630
= Retained profit	2,162	2,492	1,521	1,679	1,840
+ Investment grants	–	–	–	199	410
+ Depreciation	993	1,087	1,189	1,210	1,300
+ Additions to tax reserves	304	22	481	269	517
− Profits due abroad (net of U.K. tax)	227	247	210	222	319
= U.K. cash flow	3,232	3,354	2,981	3,135	3,748

* Including stock appreciation (see text)
† Capital consumption figures (see text)
‡ Including preference dividends

STOCK APPRECIATION

In calculating the profits of a company, changes in the value of stocks can have a significant effect. The same is also true in relation to the total profits for the corporate sector. When there are violent changes in the level of raw material prices (for instance at a time of currency devaluation) this can have a marked effect on the trends in profits. This factor must, therefore, be taken into account in general profit forecasts.

Although the figures quoted earlier for total national product were assumed to include stock appreciation, this was primarily for simplicity of exposition. Normally the figures for Gross Domestic Product, either historic or forecast, are given after deducting the stock appreciation element, since this does not correspond to any physical output in the economy. Thus an amount representing the past or future appreciation must be added in to the profit forecast if the estimates are to correspond to actual company experience. This can be done either by adjusting the G.D.P. figures before making any calculations, or by direct addition to the profit forecast of that proportion of stock appreciation normally attributable to the corporate sector.

Historic data for stock appreciation are available in the national income accounts. In making forecasts, expected price changes for raw materials and semi-finished goods need to be related to the total level of stocks held by the corporate sector; historic details of the latter are also in the National Income Blue Book, but attention should be paid to changes not only in expected stock levels but also in valuation practices.

OTHER INCOME

Other income of companies comprises two items, income from abroad and rent. As was shown in Table 60 these are of approximately equal size and together they form an appreciable proportion of total income. They are thus important elements in the overall profit forecast.

'Income from abroad' assumes particular importance at times of currency revaluation. After the 1967 devaluation of the pound U.K. company income from abroad rose sharply. This item does not relate to exports but consists of profits earned by British companies or their overseas subsidiaries on operations overseas.

It is important to remember that the income in question is not necessarily remitted to the U.K. It belongs, however, to British companies. The historic data in the Blue Book is based on balance of payments figures and is shown net of depreciation. 'Income from abroad' in total is normally rather more stable than home trading profits, reflecting the wide geographical spread of Britain's overseas interests. There is, however, a cyclical movement related to some extent to conditions in the U.S.A. This is hardly surprising in view of the great significance of the U.S. economy in relation to the trade of other countries.

Forecasts of this item have to be made with an eye to general world economic conditions, with a particular emphasis on countries such as the U.S.A., Canada, Australia and South Africa – all countries where Britain has large interests. Account must also be taken of changes in currency levels and in currency regulations which might over a period alter the pattern of overseas investment. Forecasts should also be reconciled with those for the balance of payments.

The income shown as rent is earned very largely by companies in the financial sector. It is defined as the interest and property earnings on loans made by companies to other sectors. The bulk of the large loans made by companies to one another is self-cancelling. Fluctuations in rent are related to the size and cost of loans made to the personal and public sector by banks and other financial institutions. Forecasts need to allow for such things as the likely trend in interest rates and developments in monetary policy generally.

DEPRECIATION AND INTEREST

In making the transition from total income to pretax profits it is necessary to deduct both depreciation and interest charges. Depreciation presents the more difficult problem, since estimates have to be made for the past levels as well as forecasts for the future. The national income accounts give no precise figures for past depreciation charges by companies. An estimate is shown of capital consumption and this differs in concept and practical definition from depreciation as normally calculated by companies. It provides a first approximation which can be adequate for some purposes; but it appears to underestimate the actual figure of depreciation, since the tax charge shown by relating income net of capital consumption to corporate tax payments and additions to reserves is lower than would be expected. The Blue Book also shows the figures for depreciation allowances against tax for the company sector, but here again the figures will not correspond to actual depreciation provisions.

To obtain estimates of depreciation consistent with the other Blue Book figures for companies, an indirect approach deriving depreciation as a residual is necessary. The method is to estimate the level of the tax charge and use this to derive a figure for pretax profit consistent with the size of the tax accruals given. Depreciation is then the difference between this pre-tax profit figure and total income after deducting the interest paid. The estimated figures can be checked by companies with published data on depreciation for quoted companies, such as that collected by the Board of Trade, though allowance must be made for the fact that the latter data covers both a different group of companies and a different time period from the Blue Book figures.

The factors influencing the choice of which type of depreciation estimates to use are discussed further in relation to taxation and cash flow. In forecasting future depreciation, account needs to be taken of both the age structure of the capital stock, which is closely related to the levels of investment in recent years, and any changes expected in the practices relating to the charging of depreciation.

Interest charges are much simpler to handle. Adequate historic figures exist, though it is important to realize that the national income figures do not include interest payments from one company to another, such as those by industrial companies on bank loans. Equally they do include payments on loans by other sectors to various financial institutions, notably interest paid on bank and building society deposits. The forecasts will be influenced by the level of interest rates and general monetary conditions as well as changes in company borrowing habits. After the introduction of corporation tax, for example, companies increased their borrowings substantially.

TAXATION

In considering taxation, it is necessary first to make the distinction between tax accruals and tax payments. The distinction is necessary because of the U.K. practice of assessing companies to taxation somewhat in arrears. As a result, tax payments can be delayed for several years behind the year to which they actually refer. Since it is normal for companies to make provision in any year for tax likely to be payable in due course on the profits earned in that year, two sets of data are available for taxation in any year – the payments actually made in the year and the accruals or liability for that year. The latter are shown in the Blue Book as the sum of the payments for the year and additions to reserves for future payments.

Problems in forecasting tax are closely related to those already mentioned in connection with depreciation. If the historic figures for taxation are related to pre-tax profits derived by deducting capital consumption as depreciation, the resulting tax charge will be significantly different from the rates actually in practice. To forecast from this starting point would require a clear understanding of the reasons for this difference, something which is in practice difficult to obtain. Hence it is probably best to opt for one of two alternative approaches.

The first is to make use of the capital consumption figures that are published as a best estimate of depreciation and then calculate the corresponding historic tax charge for the year in question using estimated tax rates applied to the derived pre-tax profits. The second is to use the available figures for tax accruals and to calculate from this the historic depreciation charge.

In both cases, estimates must be made of the rate of tax charged on profits in any given year. For past years, these estimates will be based on knowledge of the rates in force and of the workings of the corporate tax system; as mentioned in connection with depreciation, the figures can be checked against other published data for quoted companies. For the future, views on likely changes in fiscal policy for reasons of economic management have to be combined with consideration of possible wider changes in the overall tax structure for political reasons.

The choice between which of the two approaches to forecasting tax accruals should be used depends largely on the use to which the forecast is to be put. If the purpose is to obtain an indicator of earnings trends to relate to the general economic picture or to stock-market trends, then the first method is very adequate and has the advantage of requiring less work, since the figures used, other than the tax rate estimate, are already published. But, if the aim is to obtain an estimate of company liquidity that will tie up immediately with published data, then the second approach must be used.

This will be the case if the ultimate aim of the forecast is to show cash flow. Here, historic material is available but, if the forecast is to tie up with this data, tax and depreciation must be based on the published figures. It is important to remember also that, in this type of forecast, what is required is future tax payments not accruals. These lag one or two years behind the accruals and the forecast figures must be adjusted accordingly.

DIVIDENDS, INVESTMENT GRANTS AND CASH FLOW

Published dividend payments in the Blue Book on both preference and ordinary shares relate to payments actually made during the year. They are thus the correct figure to use in relation to cash flow forecasts but need to be adjusted for accruals to dividend reserves if they are to be related to the figure of earnings for a particular year. In making forecasts, it is probably best to approach the question by looking first at expected dividend declarations or accruals and then adjust these to a cash flow basis if required. The forecasts will obviously be strongly influenced by the general trend shown by the forecast of net profits as well as by projected company liquidity positions and official policy with regard to companies' dividend pay out.

As can be seen from Table 60, investment grants represented quite a significant proportion of net profits and even more so of cash flow. Although companies' practice as regards the treatment of these grants varies considerably, and not all of them include the grants in earnings, they are sufficiently important to be taken into account in some degree in making year-by-year profit estimates. The replacement of grants by substantial first-year investment allowances against tax complicates the analysis and the forecast figures must obviously be related to the expected level of investment in the period considered.

The significant ingredients making up the cash flow forecast have now been considered. Owing to the self-cancelling of depreciation in the calculation, there is no serious problem with regard to the historic figures, though, as has been mentioned, tax payments must be used, and not accruals. The forecast figures will follow automatically from forecasts of the items already discussed. The only additional figure that may be required is the proportion of profits remitted or retained abroad. This will be necessary if a U.K. cash flow figure is required which may be the case either for consideration of internal liquidity or to relate to U.K. capital formation. Historic figures for this item are available; forecasts will depend on the size of profits earned overseas, attitudes to remittances and retentions especially on the part of the government, and these should be consistent with any forecast made for investment income flows in the balance of payments.

ALTERNATIVE COVERAGE OF FORECASTS

So far the discussion of profit forecasting has been related solely to forecasts covering the whole of the corporate sector and for the periods in which these profits are actually earned. For certain purposes it is desirable to obtain forecasts with a somewhat different coverage. This may be either for a particular group of industries or a special sub-group such as quoted companies only. It may also be desirable to look at profits from the point of view of the trends apparent as they are reported as well as when they are earned in real time.

Forecasts for real-time trading profits of a particular group of industries could in theory be derived by exactly the same methods as those used for forecasts of total corporate profits. But no factor incomes data are available for sub-groups of industry and corporate accounts are given only for the financial group and for industrial and commercial companies as a whole. This means that in practice if a manager wants to forecast profits for particular customer or competitive industries he must rely on the third approach discussed, using unit costs, prices and volume of output. His only alternative is to obtain forecasts of total revenue and costs from some other source and derive profits as the residual.

The process of translating forecasts of trading profits for a particular group of industries into real-time net profit or cash flow is also hampered by lack of data. The only historical information that gives an industrial breakdown of profit and loss accounts is that for quoted companies by reporting periods. For certain purposes this may be the type of data wanted. But the data has somehow to be linked with that for trading profits for all companies and real-time earning periods.

This linkage cannot be made directly, as no information is available on the real-time trading profits earned by quoted companies only. It can, however, be made indirectly, using information on the normal lags between earned and reported profits. It is known, for example, that reported profits summarized by the Board of Trade tend to lag some fifteen months behind profits currently being earned. This information can be used to adjust historic trading profits to approximate reporting periods. The relationship between quoted companies and all companies in a particular industrial group or in all industries can also be examined. The resulting relationship, together with the lag adjustment, enables forecasts to be derived on whatever basis wanted – for quoted companies or total industry group, real-time earned figures or on a reported basis. Once the necessary relationship or lags are established the forecasting approach will be some modification of the cascade system.

The Board of Trade data for quoted companies covers companies with assets of £0·5 million or more and of income of £50,000 or more in manufacturing, distribution, construction, transport and certain other service industries. Alternative coverage of quoted companies is available from other compilations, for example by the *Financial Times* and the *Economist*. This data can be used in place of that collated by the Board of Trade as a basis for forecasting. The system of forecasting is similar to that outlined, given the necessary information on coverage and lags between earned and reported profits. Providing adequate allowance is made for differences in coverage and lags, these alternative sets of data can be used as a check on the relationships between quoted and all companies derived from the Board of Trade figures.

FORECASTING PROFITS IN PRACTICE

To summarize, general profit forecasts can be of considerable value to the manager and it is well worth his while spending some time on them. His forecasts will inevitably be subject to some inaccuracy, but this can be minimized if he pays close attention to the following points, each of which is a big element in successful profit forecasting in practice.

a) The need for a clear understanding of the nature of the historic data available on profits and other variables of importance; of the definition of individual items and the limitations of the figures as a whole

b) The choice of a forecasting method that both reflects the nature of the data available and makes best use of knowledge of historic relationships

c) The carrying-out of a continual examination of the relationships involved in this forecasting method in the context of current developments, and the ability to modify these relationships quickly as and when necessary.

In addition the quality of the forecasts and to some extent the choice of the forecasting method will depend on the nature of the supplementary forecast data available from other sources.

The methods of profit forecasting outlined in this chapter have been developed to fulfil these requirements. The general approach is a highly flexible one which can be used both by the firm with limited resources available and the one with a fully fledged econometric forecasting system. It is also capable of elaboration as more detailed historic data becomes available and greater knowledge is obtained about the relationships involved.

Table 61 summarizes the data required if the system described is to be operated in full. The sources of historic data are easily available from official statistics.

Table 61

Data Required for Profit Forecasts

*Examples of where else used
in forecasting system*

I Forecast of gross trading profits	
a) *via factor incomes table*	
Total factor incomes	Total output
	Total expenditure
Incomes from employment	Consumers' expenditure
Rent and self-employment incomes	Consumers' expenditure
Gross trading surplus of public corporations and enterprises	Public sector accounts
b) *via company sector forecast*	
Total factor incomes or domestic product	see above
Incomes from employment	
c) *via unit costs and prices and output*	
Unit prices	Real incomes and expenditure and output
Unit costs	Unit prices
Volume of output	Total output, value and volume, unemployment and capacity working
II Forecast of net profits and cash flow	
a) Stock appreciation	Factor incomes table
b) Income from abroad	Balance of payments
c) Rent	Factor incomes table
d) Depreciation	Capital stock and investment
e) Interest	Consumers' expenditure
	Public sector accounts
f) Taxation and investment and grants	Public sector accounts
g) Dividends	Consumers' expenditure

CHAPTER 10

Forecasting Investment by the Public Corporations and Manufacturing Industry

BY B. ASHER
AND JAMES MORRELL

Since all investment requires planning, and the majority of investment spending is undertaken by a few large state and private undertakings, it would seem a relatively easy part of business forecasting to determine the level of capital spending in these industries. The reality is some distance from the logic: investment by manufacturing industry and the public corporations is surprisingly volatile in movement and varies considerably from the declared intent or planned commitment to investment.

The tendency over the last twenty years has been for the investment of both manufacturing industry and the public corporation to increase in importance in the U.K. economy. The share of national resources absorbed by these two sectors of industry has risen from 5·4% in 1950 to an estimated 8·1% in 1970. The upward trend has been anything but smooth; there have been severe recessions in manufacturing industry investment in 1958, 1962 and 1967, and sharp fluctuations in the rate of increase of public corporation investment with a decline in 1969 and 1970. The nub of forecasting is, of course, predicting correctly the turning points and extent of change in these cycles. The problem is to identify key leads and indicators and to ensure that their message is unvarying and clearly understood.

It is often suggested that much of the uncertainty regarding the future could be eliminated by making available better, more detailed and more frequently published statistical series. Improved orders figures and greater compatibility between existing statistical series would ease the forecaster's task, as would less secrecy on the part of the government. But those who put their faith in the weight of numbers to predict the future would be well advised to ponder on investment in this sector of the economy, particularly by public corporations. It is not the lack of statistical indicators or known plans that presents the main problem, but the reliance which can be placed on each of them in the light of the influence of short-term factors.

The public corporations, for example, are not free to invest in new plant and equipment just as they wish. Their plans are checked in two ways. Firstly, the Treasury sets objective rates of return to be earned on new investment projects, which certainly act as a filter to nationalized industries' investment plans. Secondly, and more importantly for the purpose of forecasting, the Treasury takes a view on the share of national resources that can be made available for public-sector investment, including nationalized industries. The first step in forecasting public corporation investment, therefore, is to determine the Treasury view of the overall level of public investment and how far this view will prevail against pressure from spending departments and industries.

PUBLIC-SECTOR INVESTMENT: POLITICAL FACTORS

Forecasting nationalized industry, central government and local authority spending must inevitably differ a good deal in predictive technique from methods used to forecast other forms of investment of other sectors of the economy. No purely statistical or econometric methodology can be adopted for forecasting this form of investment. A more political view is necessary. The amount of investment undertaken by government is not only the result of economic pressures, like the shortage of capacity or the profitability of capital expenditure, it reflects also the social and political priorities of the government and country. However carefully public investment plans are prepared to ensure the most productive use of resources, political factors must influence the decisions and, therefore, the level and rate of change in state investment. Looking back, political factors have caused even swifter changes in the individual capital spending programmes than in the overall level, and now make forecasting extremely hazardous, and certainly non-quantitative.

Most nationalized industry investment is undertaken according to long-term (five–ten year) plans. The scale of investment demands that this must be so. If, for example, the electrical power requirements of 1980 are to be met, power stations must be planned now, orders placed in the mid-1970s, or certainly not less than two or three years ahead of their required opening date. The same considerations apply for railway modernization, steel mills, natural-gas pipelines and most forms of state investment. The plans are not only published individually, but are aggregated by the government, and in the period 1961–4 and again since 1969 have been published in the form of a White Paper on Public Investment.

However, vulnerability to short-term changes in fiscal policy complicates the use of official forecasts of public and nationalized-industry capital spending. When changes in economic performance of the country, particularly in the balance of payments, have required some restraint on spending inside the U.K., governments have applied the brakes sharply in this area. The skill in forecasting then becomes a question of estimating how much the government will cut back its own spending programme relative to spending in the private sector, knowing which programmes are more vulnerable to political pressure than others, or which are more likely to be given strategic priority in the upturn.

THE NATURE OF PUBLIC CORPORATION INVESTMENT

A full description of the public corporations and their investment problems is beyond the scope of a single chapter. The list of public enterprises would stretch from the electricity authorities, which invest £600 million a year, to certain harbour boards, the B.B.C. and (until denationalized) the pubs of Carlisle. We are concerned here with those corporations who are the main

spenders, and account for the greater proportion of total investment. These are the power industries (electricity, gas and coal),
the railways, air corporations, the steel industry and the Post
Office. Investment by these bodies accounts for over 95% of all
the funds available to public corporations.

In the national income accounts investment spending is listed
as gross fixed capital formation. All replacements and additions
to buildings, plant, machinery and vehicles are included in these
figures. Sales and purchases of land are excluded, since they do
not require a fresh call on the nation's resources; so too are
maintenance costs associated with public housing and buildings.

The published quarterly statistics for public-sector investment
vary slightly from the remainder of U.K. fixed investment statistics, in that they include not only work completed, but certain
payments for work in progress. Given the large scale of many
public-sector investment programmes, progress payments, before
and during a planned programme, can be quite large and may
distort the quarterly movements in the statistical series.

THE POST-WAR EXPERIENCE

It is a feature of nearly all the public services that they are heavy
capital spenders. A unit of output from these industries generally
requires a very large capital input. If it was freely able to invest,
the amount of the economy's resources absorbed by the public
sector would be very substantial. The government tries to limit
the level to a fairly steady share of the nation's resources. Over
the last decade, however, public investment rose from just over a
third to nearly half of the capital expenditure in the U.K., and
much of this rise was associated with public corporation investment.

In a way the 1960s proved the golden decade of the public
utility. The investment undertaken in these areas was intended to
make up for years of neglect and inadequate investment in the
1940s and 1950s, as well as to keep pace with the very sharp rise
in standards required on public services, and to match increasing

demand. The increase in demand was so rapid during this period that it was necessary from time to time to put a stop to programmes and to seek new ways of limiting the amount of national resources flowing into the public sector.

The periods and the types of experimentation in investment management and control did not change significantly between the Labour and Conservative governments. It was the Conservative governments which shifted the nationalized industries from a break-even to a target return on assets basis of operation. The Labour government extended these criteria during the 1960s and in the last two years of their administration increased quite sharply the rate of return required by nationalized industries on their investment. Notwithstanding the attempts to reduce nationalized industry investment, it continued to grow as a share of national product and also as a share of total investment in the economy. This is illustrated in Table 62. These figures include the steel industry from the third quarter of 1967.

Table 62

Public-Sector Investment Share of
the National Product

	1958	1964	1970
Public-sector investment as a % of:			
Total U.K. investment	44	43	53
National output	7	9	11

Over the twelve years to 1970, a period comprising six years of Conservative and six years of Labour government, there were three major balance of payments crises and one major nationalization (that of the steel industry). Even so, public investment grew in volume terms at 7% a year during both six-year periods. In fact the individual annual increases in state investment showed sharp fluctuations. During this period national output grew by about 3% a year, with a slightly lower rate in the second half of the twelve-year period. Total investment expanded by 5% a year, with an appreciably slower rate in the second half of the period 1964–70.

The peak years 1961, 1964 and 1967 were years of strain on U.K. resources, when the demand for imports was high and balance of payments problems loomed. The trough years occurred when governments tried to relieve pressure on domestic resources and in particular to cut back public-sector spending, notably in 1962, 1968 and 1969. The pattern of investment year by year is almost the economic history of the 1960s in itself (see Chart 29).

Chart 29

INFLUENCE OF ECONOMIC POLICY

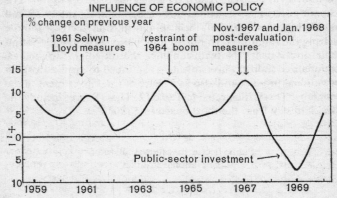

This does certainly not give an impression of uninterrupted expansion of public-sector investment, as has been suggested by nationalized industry and departmental programmes or White Papers. It shows much more clearly the impact of short-term economic policy changes on the level of investment.

Against this background of recurring balance of payments crises, it is difficult to assess the importance for public investment of having a particular party in office. Comparing the years 1959 to 1964 and 1965 to 1969 would not be entirely valid, for in 1965 the Labour government had inherited the previous administration's programmes. On the other hand 1968–9 were years of unusually severe restraint in government spending because of yet another balance of payments crisis. In all probability the Labour government did not have the opportunity in the 1960s to authorize public investment expansion at the rate it would have wished. The more pronounced tendency of Labour towards increasing public investment was not translated into an expanding public corporation programme while the Party was in office.

On the other hand, investment by the public authorities during the first half of the 1960s absorbed an increasing share of national resources. In successive years there proved to be a wave of investment from different industries and services. First, the power industries, then rail, finally gas and then the Post Office built up very large programmes. The constant momentum of increase tended to suggest that the rise in the public sector's share of national investment would be continuous. However, at the beginning of 1967 the largest single publicly owned capital spender, the electricity industry, began to cut back its investment spending heavily, as the prospect of over-capacity loomed ahead. With demand increasing at barely one-third the forecast rate, the industry estimated that a margin of spare capacity of 30% would arise by 1970 if the plant expansion plans made in the mid-1960s were carried through. There were also reductions in rail, coal and gas investment. These, however, moved more predictably since their programmes had previously risen to meet specific replacement needs and, in the case of gas, a major new discovery.

LESSONS OF THE PAST

Looking to this pattern of increase the problem for the forecaster is to determine whether it was possible to predict the downturn in electricity investment. Most forecasters in the early 1960s were forecasting that an ever-increasing share of national investment resources would be absorbed by electric power requirements. Secondly, was it possible to forecast the duration and intensity of the investment downturn?

Electricity demand in the U.K. is linked to both total output growth and the relative price of electricity. The electricity investment programme was revised in the early 1960s to meet the demands of an economy growing at an assessed rate of 3·8% a year. This would have approximated with a growth in electricity demand of 7–8% a year compared with the 5% increase of the 1950s. In fact the economy's growth rate from 1963 turned out to be under 3% a year and capacity was therefore prepared for a non-existent demand. After 1965 demand for electricity slipped back to under 5% a year.

A depressing influence on demand in this period was the very substantial price increases made to finance the heavy investment programme. Not unnaturally, consumers switched to alternative fuels. The failure of the economy to grow at the predicted rate and the sharp decline in growth of electricity in 1965 should have provided the basis for reassessing the investment forecast. At its lowest point the level of investment in electric power generation was down 40% from its 1966 peak and was such a sharp reversal that after it occurred the forecaster continually predicted another turning point to an upward trend. It will be obvious, however, that a better analysis of consumption demand and price elasticity would have warned the forecaster against over-optimistic assumptions.

The decline in electricity investment in 1967 was accompanied by the slackening in investment by other public corporations. By comparison these reductions were small beer and all fairly predictable. The static railway and coal revenues, and the completion of re-equipment programmes, required a lower rate of investment by these industries. The completion of the sea-gas grid and the associated works connected with the North Sea gas also resulted in reduced gas investment. Since 1967 the only increasing programmes have been for telecommunications and steel.

THE INDICATORS

The illustrations referred to above are concerned with the qualitative and random factors indicating change in public-sector investment. Equally the statistical series which correlate or provide a lead indicator for public-sector investment must also be examined. One should not, however, over-estimate the importance of the quantitative factors. Relationships are not stable; nor is it merely a question of detecting the government's undisclosed plans, for even governments may not be fully aware of the consequence of policy changes on public investment. To rely on government assessments, were they fully available, would be no formula for accurate forecasting, and to pay attention only to statistical indicators or government plans would still leave the problem of identifying major shifts in public spending.

As an example one can draw on the fastest-growing major public-sector programme in the last ten years, namely the Post Office telecommunications investment. This rose from 5% to 12% of total state investment between 1964 and 1970, and grew at an average rate of 17% a year. Any forecast of this programme at the beginning of the 1960s, and the priority accorded to it, would have been wrong, unless it had taken into account the important political sensitivity to Post Office telephone failings, namely, waiting lists and defective calling rates.

So far as the make-up of public investment is concerned, around half the total (excluding housing) is building work. A construction index indicator is published ahead of official investment figures by the Ministry of Technology. This serves as a useful indicator of the direction of public-sector investment. But the best short-term indicator is the statistical series of net new orders for construction by the public authorities. Since public-sector investment involves a high proportion of building activity, the level of orders is usually a sensitive indicator of the turning points and rate of change in public-sector investment as a whole. The net new order series can, however, occasionally prove unreliable, particularly prior to an official 'squeeze'. Orders will be placed which will ultimately have to be delayed or slowed. It is then that a clear view of the political factors and a knowledge of the demands on national resources (derived from the complete model of the economy) becomes invaluable.

A second indicator of some assistance, particularly in the first quarter of the year, is weather conditions. In the early months of 1970 a long wet spring suggested an abnormally low level of investment which in fact turned out to be true. Such an indicator is, of course, only a guide to the recent past and its use is limited to providing the most accurate base from which to forecast the future. More precise short-term leading indicators of public investment are provided by the industries that serve and sell to the public authorities, and both the order and delivery figures of the supplying industries will help to confirm the estimate of recent public-authority investment spending.

THE SUPPLY OF FUNDS

The availability of funds is also a major determinant of public-sector investment. A discussion of public-sector expenditure and financing can be found in the chapters on monetary policy and the Budget. The margin between the cash flow of the public sector and its investment programme, indicating its borrowing requirements, is a key factor in the Treasury's assessment of public investment programmes. It must be considered, therefore, as a major factor in forecasting. The borrowing requirement to finance public-sector programmes considerably complicates official debt management and monetary policy.

As is shown in Table 63 the tremendous increases in public-sector investment in 1964, and again in 1967, gave rise in those and the subsequent years to a very large increase in public

Table 63

Borrowing and Investment

£ million

	Annual change in public corporation investment	Official borrowing requirement
1964	+163	+165
1965	+106	+191
1966	+152	+237
1967	+214	+854
1968	−27	−494
1969	−145	−1,786

borrowing. Equally, in 1969 the sharp downturn in investment was one of the factors that contributed to the large net repayment of debt by the public sector to the rest of the economy. Although the financing of public-sector investment cannot provide a precise forecast of public capital spending, it is a very positive limiting factor and as such is an indicator meriting careful examination. The Treasury will probably limit the borrowing requirement during much of the 1970s and this will help provide a useful guide to the trend of the total level of public corporation investment.

LONG-TERM INDICATORS

The long-term indicators of public corporation investment are the well-documented plans of capital expenditure that each of the nationalized industries and relevant government departments maintain, and periodically revise. Over certain periods of the 1960s these programmes were integrated into a national plan by the National Economic Development Office. This process facilitated an examination of the demands public investment would make on national resources. In addition to the individual plans the government now issues annually a paper on public expenditure which predicts the level of public spending, on both capital and current account, for two financial years ahead with a trend estimate for a further three years.[1]

These programmes are based on certain assumptions about economic growth, the demand for public services and the ability of the industries and government departments to use the capital efficiently. Changes in each one of these factors can, and do, cause adjustments to the programmes either adversely or beneficially. For example, the failure of the British economy to expand at 3·8% between 1964 and 1967 was the single most important reason for the eventual cutback in public-corporation investment in 1968–9. Once started, the programmes were allowed to continue at the projected level, even though growth in the economy

1. *Public Expenditure 1969/70 to 1974/75;* Cmd 4578, H.M.S.O., January 1971.

was not occurring at the forecast rate; but by 1968 the whole level of the programmes was being sharply curtailed.

Equally, the investment programmes were restrained by raising the target rates of return on assets to be achieved by the industries. The successive increases in target during the 1960s led to sharper increases in the selling prices of nationalized industry and services. This had a great deal to do with the decline in the rate of demand and therefore affected future investment requirements. The consumer was, in effect, being compelled to finance future investment through the price mechanism.

The divergence from the plan was drastic in a number of cases and this is illustrated in Chart 30. The air corporations achieved

Chart 30

PUBLISHED PLANS AND ACTUAL INVESTMENT

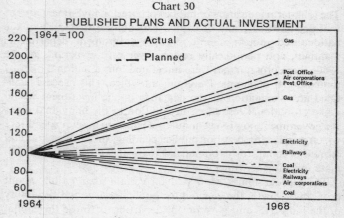

more than double the planned level of investment, but coal and railways undershot. It is clear, therefore, that the published programmes, whilst substantially realistic, must be carefully treated and evaluated for the impact of general economic and political factors. These programmes provide the clearest quantitative guides available of future levels of public investment. However, it must be recognized that different governments have different priorities, not only as regards the overall level of public investment, but also as regards the type of investment to be undertaken.

240

Judged by the figures, the Conservative governments of the 1950s gave much greater priority to nationalized industry investment and to electricity and transport in particular. Only in the last years of Conservative administration, from 1962 to 1964, was there an acceleration of the Post Office programme which, together with gas, formed the crest of public corporation investment in the Labour party's first few years in office.

FUTURE PUBLIC INVESTMENT

There seems little prospect of the total level of public-sector spending (excluding housing) rising faster than 4% a year in constant prices over the first half of the 1970s. The slow rise cannot be taken as a certain feature, however. Investment in public corporations is as popular as an anti-recession weapon as its curtailment is in times of restraint. The pattern of squeezes and relaxations by the government over the last decade suggests that cut-backs last five to six quarters, i.e. eighteen months (see Chart 31). Therefore, when circumstances permit and political pressures

Chart 31

THE DURATION OF SQUEEZES

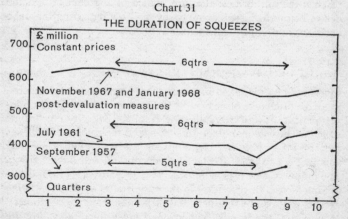

build up to increase demand, an expansion in public investment takes place. In this concertina of increase and squeeze public-corporation investment shares the general fate of all public-sector capital spending. This would suggest that public investment will rise in the early 1970s and any reductions the authorities may make in this period are likely to come from public investment in the central and local government areas. It will be apparent that forecasting public-corporation investment requires a fair 'nose' for politics. Whereas the corporation will plan the details of its programmes in much the same way as a private company, the private company will respond in its overall investment outlays to direct economic pressures rather than political pressures. In this sense the techniques for forecasting private investment are quite different.

Public investment is largely an independent variable in the economic system. Political and administrative decisions determine the trend of public investment, and it is only the realities of the economic situation which eventually cause a trimming of further increases in the total. To forecast these kinds of changes the analyst needs to understand the timing of reactions between a change in the economy at large, the evidence of this change as it reaches the authorities, the importance of the change and the delays before Ministers come to grips with a new situation, take decisions and implement them.

MANUFACTURING INVESTMENT

Investment by manufacturing industry, however, is very much a function of change elsewhere in the economy. In some areas investment decisions are made as a result of capacity constraints which encourage manufacturers to extend their plants. Decisions may be taken because the return on assets is high. They may equally depend upon the fact that corporate cash flow is rising. The inflow of new orders influencing expectations is also a determining factor. If, therefore, in the early stages of the forecasting cycle it is apparent that personal disposable income, consumers' expenditure, the level of exports and government spending are rising at a sufficient rate, then manufacturing investment will also tend to rise after a time-lag. This in turn will generate even faster growth of economic activity and so further accelerate the investment cycle.

This, however, is an over-simplified account of the economic process and in the U.K. economic environment there are a number of complicating factors. The government is interested in the level of investment because it determines the capacity of the country in future years and also the competitive efficiency of the British economy in relation to other major trading nations. Fiscal policy is shaped, therefore, to encourage investment. For example, industry is encouraged by a generous system of investment allowances, by a partial subsidy on wages and earnings in development areas, by loans from government agencies for investment purposes, by the building of factories which are loaned to and equipped by the manufacturer. Changes in these generous terms offered to industry clearly influence manufacturers' decisions when and where to invest, and must be taken into account in forecasting the level of industrial investment.

In the 1960s industrial investment in the U.K. accounted for a low proportion of national product compared with other countries. It also grew at a much slower rate than in major competitor economies. One reason for this has been the recurring balance of payments problem, which determined the rather long periods of stagnation and much shorter bursts of expansion in the U.K. economy. This sort of business cycle does not foster high investment. The recovery from the trough of the business cycle as the balance of payments improved was usually through a relaxation of credit restraints. Only in the later stages of the upturn did investment begin to rise under the pressures of high-capacity utilization. By this time in the cycle, the balance of payments was deteriorating once again, leading up to a further restriction of internal demand.

In this climate manufacturing industry has been continually forced to modify its plans. The stagnant economy discouraged it from promoting ambitious projects. Nevertheless, the scale of investment and the time required to complete major projects requires many industries to disregard a current critical situation in orders or profits, and to continue investing to ensure competitiveness and prepare capacity to meet future growth in demand. This was particularly noticeable in the plastics, chemical and oil-refining industries, where major manufacturers ignored the current economic situation in Britain in undertaking extensions to their capacity.

This contra-cyclical planning, only open to the largest firms, must be taken into account when considering the future level of investment in the U.K. The industries that have acted in this way are responsible for about half of U.K. manufacturing industry investment, and the individual large firms, straddling many industries as well as frontiers, are responsible for about 60% of all investment in the U.K. Clearly the actions of these large manufacturers dominating a few major investing industries can influence the trend whatever the general economic environment.

LEADING INDICATORS FOR MANUFACTURING INVESTMENT

Because the level of industrial investment is dependent upon the rate of economic change, there is no shortage of indicators to chart the short-term movements in industrial investment. The significant indicators are corporate profits, dividends, investment intentions as determined by periodic surveys, capacity shortages and the provision of industrial development certificates. Each of these indicators provides a fairly reasonable guide to industrial investment as a whole for about four quarters ahead. The method of correlating these with industrial investment varies, but in general a relationship is apparent from visual inspection of the figures, as can be seen from Chart 2 (p. 25), showing the close parallel in movement between profits and investment with a lead time of a year.

The amount of investment businesses are able to undertake depends largely on the amount of cash available to them. This is principally determined by gross trading profits. Profits will be supplemented by investment grants and subsidies. Payments of interest, taxation and dividends will reduce the cash flow available to the firm and the net flow of funds will exercise the greatest single influence on investment decisions.

Through the 1960s gross trading profits earned in the U.K. provided a reasonable advance guide to the level of investment in plant and machinery for about a year ahead. Because building work tends to be undertaken on much longer time horizons, the short-term cash flow of a company is not so relevant and certainly not as good an indicator. There are, of course, difficulties in using corporate cash flow for a forecast of this sort. Changes in corporate taxation or the investment allowance system can provide complications, but most of the changes are foreseeable from a proper evaluation of fiscal policy, and can, therefore, be written into the forecast.

It may be argued that since companies are able to raise funds via new issues on the capital market, they are, to this extent, isolated from the profits and investment cycle. However, examination of the pattern of investment financing shows this to be fallacious. Only a small part is financed by new issues. Up to 1969, the company sector succeeded in financing all its investment from retained cash flow. Moreover, if a company's profits have sagged it will be less well placed to make a new issue, and therefore the contra-cycle possibilities of new issue financing are strictly limited.

DIVIDENDS

Dividend declarations also give some clue to the subsequent climate for business investment spending. When they declare dividends after the end of a financial year, companies are already some months into a new operating year. The directors thus have some kind of indication of the current year's profits. They are unlikely to declare a dividend so high that they will be unable to equal it again in the current year. Dividend declarations, therefore, are not only a firm indication of last year's profits, but a very up-to-date pulse reading of the current and proximate profit situation. An index of dividend declarations can thus be used to improve the forecast of investment by companies in plant and machinery – again for about four quarters ahead. This particular indicator has been subject to distortions because of dividend limitations. Corporate dividends of necessity had to be held down, and so no longer provided a sensitive indicator of investment intentions. With the ending of dividend restraint in 1969, dividends rose at an unnatural rate, reflecting a catching-up process, and this too invalidated the use of declarations as a forecasting indicator. However, in normal circumstances the dividend index is a useful short-term forecasting tool.

By the same token, equity prices have some value as an indicator. Share price movements mirror dividend changes, and the state of business confidence reflected in the level of the stock market will re-inforce short-term investment spending forecasts.

INTENTIONS SURVEYS

Capital spending intentions surveys are conducted three times a year by the authorities. Comprehensive surveys are made of industry's capital spending intentions by the Department of Trade and Industry (previously Ministry of Technology and the Board of Trade). The surveys are undertaken in June, October and January, for the present twelve months and the coming year. These survey intentions are expressed in percentage terms and are published about two months after collection. They are revised with each inquiry.

This exercise has a reasonable accuracy, but is at its worst in charting the turning points in the investment cycle. In a sense this is a severe disadvantage, because within tolerable limits it is always possible to make an estimate of the upward movement in industrial investment. What is really required is the turning points of the cycle. This is particularly important to heavy-equipment manufacturers.

The failure to forecast turning points in the investment cycle stems from the nature of the questionnaire. Asking for absolute numbers in respect of investment spending, the questionnaire is probably completed by company accounts departments, using the firm's current budget. A change in the company's circumstances leads to a board-room decision to hold up, or accelerate, investment projects, but the budget, and therefore Ministry return, remains the same.

For this reason the independent C.B.I. industrial trends inquiry is a much better indicator. The inquiry is not a quantitative forecast, but it is comprehensive in that it asks manufacturers about their confidence of the future level of business, their view on cost and prices and order intake and their feeling about capacity utilization, as well as asking for their capital spending intentions on plant and machinery and building. If a manufacturer is generally pessimistic he is unlikely to be so inconsistent as to offer an optimistic answer on investment. The C.B.I. inquiry is a more reliable indicator of the turning points in the investment cycle, but not necessarily such a reliable indicator of the actual percentage movement of industrial investment through time. The Ministry surveys and the C.B.I.'s industrial trends inquiry combined provide a useful guide to industrial investment for about four quarters ahead, with this proviso: few people have any ability to forecast, and when questioned about the future most answers reflect the state of things at the present. The more pessimistic 'intentions' surveys have to be interpreted in this light. Similarly, the more optimistic surveys have to be pared down.

The C.B.I. and other surveys of capacity utilization provide another check to industrial investment, for the degree of capacity utilization is a reasonable guide to manufacturers' views on the need to increase their through-put by further investment.

The granting of industrial development certificates also provides a reasonably accurate guide to building work for industrial purposes. Industrial development certificates must be obtained by all firms wishing to extend or build new plants, and these figures are published quarterly by the Ministry of Works. In recent years changes in the law on use of land and betterment levy tended to accelerate the application for development certificates without actually leading to a real increase in investment. When these changes occur, it is difficult to quantify the impact on the investment prospects, so that on these occasions the published figures on industrial developments certificates are a less reliable guide. Nevertheless, if no major changes are expected in the rules of the game, the series will, once again, become a good guide to the building part of industrial investment.

LONGER-TERM FORECASTS

For the longer term the forecasting model for the whole economy and the movements in total output provide the best guide to the future level of industrial investment. Industrial investment relative to U.K. domestic product has been rising very slowly, reaching about 4·6% of G.D.P. in 1969, compared with 4·5% in 1960. The growth in the economy, therefore, is a key to the future level of industrial investment and, as was outlined in previous chapters, growth in the economy is determined by labour productivity and employment. Both of these are assessed at an early stage in the forecasting cycle, and in so far as they are influenced by investment can be adjusted in further reiterative processes of the forecasting model.

The growth in the economy is also subject to government planning and this provides further clues to the pattern and shape of future industrial investment. Industries, too, sometimes publish their investment plans. The oil-refining and motor-car industries are examples in that they issue future productive capacity figures from time to time.

Equally important in looking at investment over a period of years is to compare investment levels relative to the changes in total economic output over previous business cycles. There have been three major business cycles in the U.K. since the Korean war. One in the late 1950s, one in the early 1960s and one in the late 1960s. These cycles have been between four and five years in duration and rather shallow from the peak to the trough. The 1961/6 business cycle (measuring from top to top) was very much complicated by the adverse climatic conditions of the first quarter of 1963, which tended to make the trough much deeper than it would otherwise have been. Equally, it made the recovery through 1963/4 much more rapid than in the previous investment cycle.

However, it is unlikely that one business cycle closely resembles another, either in time or shape. Following devaluation in 1967 the investment business cycle was very much complicated by the tight credit squeeze, particularly in 1969 and 1970, and by the narrowing of profit margins. Also the unexpected wage movement in the latter part of 1969 and in 1970 exacerbated the pressure on profit margins. Whereas on previous cyclical expectations 1970 should have been a good year for corporate profits brought about by high-capacity utilization, the sharp increase in labour costs, and the very severe credit squeeze, limited the real increase in industrial investment to less than 5%.

This was less than would have been expected from previous cyclical experience, but it will be seen from this example that business profits and forecasts of cash flow are of the utmost importance to successful forecasts of manufacturing industry investment. For both the short and the long term it is imperative to have sound forecasts of industrial costs, prices and profits, as well as an understanding of the political factors influencing such things as investment incentives and tax rates.

It will be apparent, therefore, that for forecasting both public-sector and private-sector investment a keen awareness of political factors is of paramount importance. The business cycle is to a great extent determined by political decision. Those decisions bear directly on investment by the public sector and indirectly on investment by the private sector. This factor is brought out yet again in the following chapter, in which building construction forecasts are considered.

CHAPTER 11

Forecasting Housing and Other Building Investment

BY R. B. MCDANIEL

To place building investment in its proper perspective, it should be stated that housing and other building comprised more than half the total fixed investment in the U.K. in 1969, and approximately one-seventh of total final expenditure at current prices. Accurate forecasting of future building demand is thus a problem facing numerous building and civil engineering companies as well as producers of building materials and building trades' merchants.

The purpose of this chapter is to outline what has happened in the past and to illustrate the problems and pitfalls associated with forecasting the future from the information available. The principal factors which influence demand and upon which most accurate prediction of building investment depends will be defined, and the importance of making the right forecasting assumptions in producing a forecast which is of genuine use to the firm will be emphasized.

One of the main problems facing the forecaster is the absence of the right kind of basic information. The eventual quality of the forecast depends heavily upon the availability and reliability of the historical statistical data, and it is the shrewd interpretation of past trends which forms the main basis of successful forecasting. Unlike most consumer and capital goods which serve a nation-wide or even world-wide market, construction is of a local, regional nature. Certainly as far as contractors and merchants are concerned, some estimate of the regional pattern of demand is one of the most important requirements at the level of the firm. Whereas it may be a relatively easy task to indicate broad trends, it is much more difficult to predict what the national trends mean for particular regions.

On the whole, statistics of housing are fairly prolific and reasonably accurate, but for other types of building statistics are less abundant and not so accurate. In both cases a considerable measure of individual judgement has to be exercised, not only to derive value from the past data, but also to place forecasts within likely limits of accuracy. It is appropriate to note that the actual patterns of output are not necessarily a true guide to the real trend, as they will have been affected from time to time by weather fluctuations, by capacity limitations of one kind or another, and perhaps by industrial unrest. Broadly speaking, there are two kinds of data which provide the basis for the estimates of building investment – expenditure and output data – but owing to their greater reliability it is the expenditure data that are primarily used by the Central Statistical Office, except for the private housing figures.

HOUSING

As housing appears to provide the more easily definable forecasting problems, it will be examined first. In the National Plan published in September 1965 it was estimated that 500,000 new houses a year would be built. Five years later the annual rate of completions in Great Britain was no higher than 340,000. Plans based on such inaccurate conceptions can have serious implications, so we shall attempt to establish criteria on which more realistic predictions can be made.

Some of the factors affecting house-building in England and Wales over a twenty-year period were discussed in the *National Institute Economic Review* of November 1961, under the title 'A Long Term View of Housing'. Looking ahead to 1980 the article drew attention to the problems facing, not only the forecaster, but also the authorities in the changing situation then becoming apparent. A deficit in the required housing stock was seen to be replaced by a system in which the rate of new house-building would primarily be influenced by the rate of demolition and replacement of existing houses.

A considerable volume of past and current data is readily available for this kind of analysis. The Ministry of Housing publishes statistics of housing starts, completions and numbers under construction for the public and private sectors, region by region. The Ministry of Public Building and Works produces a monthly series of figures of the value of new housing orders obtained by contractors and a quarterly series on work completed by contractors. Despite a wealth of basic housing statistics, there is still only limited information on the condition of the housing stock which is so important in determining the needs for slum clearance and redevelopment. Widely differing estimates of the number of substandard houses have been made at various times, but it is not really known how many of these houses are likely to be demolished and how many brought up to modern standards by their owners or occupants. It was partly to fill some of these gaps in the statistics that the Sample Census of 1966 was conducted and this has facilitated a more constructive analysis of the housing market and demand. Nevertheless, the effects upon investment of the steady improvements in quality of housing arising from the better overall standards of living – increasing average size of houses and more and better amenities – can only be estimated in broad terms.

Periodic White Papers, such as 'The Housing Programme 1965 to 1970' issued by the Ministry of Housing and Local Government and the Welsh Office and 'The Scottish Housing Programme 1965 to 1970' issued by the Scottish Development Department, help the forecaster from time to time, but the size of the future house-building programme remains a subject for wide differences of opinion. As recently as 1966 the government were strongly of the opinion that in order to solve the nation's serious housing problems, a rate of new house-building of 500,000 a year was essential. As it has turned out, the peak figure reached so far – in 1968 – was 426,000. Today it would be a bold forecaster who predicted an average rate of house-building in excess of 400,000 a year during the forthcoming decade, even though there are still considerable housing difficulties in certain areas. A building rate of 500,000 new houses a year is only feasible in the unlikely event of the average life of properties being severely reduced.

Public and Private House-building

In 1969, investment in dwellings amounted to £1,495 million at current prices and accounted for 36·1% of total investment in new building work and 18·9% of fixed investment as a whole. Of this total figure for investment in dwellings, 54·8% was in the public sector and 45·2% in the private sector. The pattern over the past twenty years, illustrated in Chart 32, has fluctuated considerably, but the evidence available indicates that in the broadest terms the gradual decline in housing as a proportion of total building investment is likely to continue. To some extent the relationship between public and private-sector house-building is likely to reflect the political colour of the day.

Chart 32

INVESTMENT IN DWELLINGS AND TOTAL BUILDING WORK

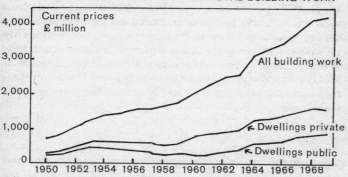

It is appropriate at this juncture to make clear what these investment figures comprise. Investment in dwellings as published by the Central Statistical Office includes all expenditure on the construction of new houses, bungalows, flats and maisonettes, including not only architects' and surveyors' fees, but also any other costs incurred by the purchaser. The estimates for public-sector dwelling investment include all expenditure on conversions and improvements, but owing to statistical difficulties the private-sector estimates include such expenditure only if grant-aided. Other expenditure on conversions and improvements is included in the housing item under consumers' expenditure.

The official statistics for private-sector fixed capital formation in dwellings are based primarily on the value of output figures collected since 1955 by the Ministry of Public Building and Works from a sample of builders. To this must be added an estimate for expenditure on dwellings in Northern Ireland, now collected and published on a comparable basis, an estimate of expenditure on architects' and surveyors' fees, an allowance for the cost of certain irremovable equipment, such as boilers, not installed by builders, and an estimate of expenditure by private housing associations.

Public-sector investment in dwellings is derived from returns and accounts of public corporations and public authorities, with the quarterly output figures used to assist in assessing short-term changes. All these estimates are based on current prices. The derivation of a price deflator to constant prices is particularly difficult in view of the variable nature of housing investment. Price indices are constructed in broad terms from an index of building material prices, an index of labour costs based on earnings and productivity, and an indicator of changes in overheads and profits.

Housing Forecasts

The starting point for predicting future investment in dwellings is a forecast of the level of house-building in physical terms, i.e. the actual numbers of starts and completions in both private and public sectors over the term of the forecast. The pattern of housing starts and completions and dwellings under construction at the end of each year is shown in Chart 33. The figures shown relate to Great Britain only and they demonstrate once again the changing relationship between public and private-sector house-building during the last twenty years.

There are three main elements of housing demand – the rate of

254

new household formation, the amount of the current housing shortage which has to be eliminated, and the rate of replacement of existing dwellings by reason of slum clearance or other re-development such as road-building. One ancillary factor which influences the housing shortage and about which little concrete statistical evidence is available is the extent of the demand for second homes. This may be in recreational areas for those who

Chart 33

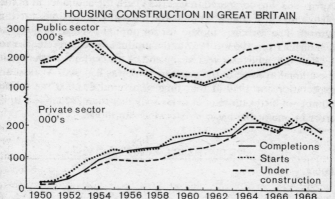

HOUSING CONSTRUCTION IN GREAT BRITAIN

live and work in urban communities, and perhaps in town centres for those who make their home in the country. Once we have estimated the size of the overall demand over a period of time, we can speculate on the influence of general economic factors, the availability of suitable building land and the flow of funds from building societies and other agencies upon the short-term pattern of future demand.

To begin with we shall consider the problems surrounding the future rate of new household formation. The Registrar General issues a periodic forecast of potential households in England, Wales and Scotland.[1] This basic information is continually sub-ject to revision and it is important to be aware of the basic assumptions used in deriving these predictions. For example, the

1. *Housing Statistics, Great Britain*, No. 16, February 1970.

forecast published in 1970 was based on 1968 population projections and headship rates (since revised) and migration projections – all prepared by the General Register Office.

One of the pitfalls of using such official population forecasts as raw material is illustrated by 'jobbing' back to the birth rate projections for England and Wales made only seven years ago. The projections published in the Registrar General's Quarterly Return for England and Wales for the fourth quarter of 1962, issued in April 1963, are compared in Chart 34 with the actual trend in the birth rate since that date (and the current assumptions for the future). The forecasts looked for an annual average of 870,000 live births from 1963 to 1967 and a gradual increase thereafter to 1,130,000 live births a year at the end of the century. In the event the annual average in the years to 1967 was 854,000. Against an expectation for 1969 at that time of around 895,000 the actual number of births turned out to be no higher than 798,000 – a 10% error in one of the basic statistical assumptions.

Chart 34

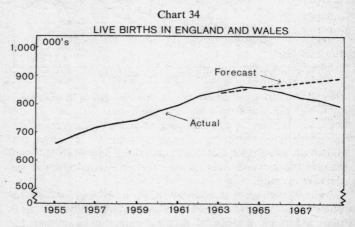

LIVE BIRTHS IN ENGLAND AND WALES

Potential households for the purpose of the Registrar General's projections are defined as families and other groups likely to want separate dwellings, and their number is estimated as the total of census-type households plus married couple families, with or without children, not forming or heading a household, less three-quarters of those one-person households who share dwellings with other households. The population forecasts are converted into potential households by means of the headship rates derived from the census of 1961 and the Sample Census of 1966. The rate of new household formation projection thus depends primarily on the projection of the population increase. A check on the feasibility of the projection of potential households can be made by considering what this means for changes in average household size, i.e. the average number of persons per household. Taking England and Wales, for example, Table 64 illustrates the pattern

Table 64

Forecast Number of Households

	1911	1951	1961	mid-1966	mid-1971	mid-1976	mid-1981
Private household population (000s)	34,606	41,840	44,273	46,622	48,686	50,212	51,747
Potential households (000s)	7.943	13,118	14,702	15,939	16,606	17,241	17,751
Average potential household size	4·36	3·19	3·01	2·97	2·93	2·91	2·91

of private household population (excluding population in absent potential households), the number of potential households and the average number of persons per household.

Such a forecast by the Registrar General implies an average rate of population increase of 0·7% a year from mid-1966 up to mid-1981 and a small reduction in average household size. The anticipated incremental household formation in England and Wales is approximately 130,000 a year up to 1976 and 100,000 a year from then up to 1981, compared with 190,000 a year in the 1961/71 decade.

There is an argument for assuming that average potential household size will be lower than implied by this forecast by 1981 in that a faster rate of reduction has taken place hitherto and that there could be a tendency for more older people to live as separate households rather than as dependents. This would result in a continuing gradual fall in average household size. If we were, therefore, to assume an average household size of 2·85 by 1981, the number of potential households would become about 18·15 million, or an extra 40,000 new households a year on average during the decade. This immediately demonstrates the considerable scope for an important variation in the resulting forecast arising from a relatively minor variation in a single assumption. Nonetheless, when the average potential household size stabilizes, and at whatever figure, the number of potential households will bear a direct relationship to population changes, resulting from both natural increase and migration, thus reducing the demand for housing from new household formations.

It is possible to carry out a similar exercise for each planning region and by this means to establish the likely requirements arising from new household formation region by region. To take two specific examples, we shall examine the situation in the north-west and in the south-east, including Greater London. These are the two most heavily populated economic planning regions. Using the Registrar General's projections for population and potential households, the demand arising from new households in the north-west will fall from 20,000 a year in 1966 to 1971, to 13,000 a year in 1971 to 1976, to only 9,500 a year in 1976 to 1981. It is a similar story in the south-east with the average annual incremental household formation falling from 48,000 in 1966 to 1971, to 41,000 in 1971 to 1976, and 34,000 in 1976 to 1981.

The Housing Shortage

Next, we turn to consider the extent of the housing shortage. There are frequent reports of housing shortage in specific areas and the hardship arising therefrom, mainly in the most densely populated conurbations. But what is the real housing need? The evidence is that the nationwide shortage of dwellings has already evaporated and there are only pockets of severe shortage. To begin with the Census of 1951: in that year in England and Wales there was a substantial statistical surplus exceeding one million of private households over the stock of dwellings, which was put at 12·08 million. By 1961, again a census year, this surplus had been reduced to 370,000; by 1966, at the time of the Sample Census, the surplus was down to 160,000. By 1968 this overall statistical surplus of households over dwellings had been eliminated, probably for all time.

In future the overall stock of dwellings seems certain to exceed the number of private households, and in assessing long-term demand it is thus important to take a broad view of the likely vacancy rates. The very existence of vacancies will undoubtedly create more scope for variations in demand from year to year according to changes in the general economic climate, and so there are likely to be greater periodic fluctuations in demand. What we are, therefore, concerned with is predicting the number of houses required at any moment of time to eliminate shortages throughout the country. In doing so we have to make assumptions about the average vacancy rate for the country as a whole and the number of householders that require second homes. In the long term an overall vacancy rate as high as 7% would seem likely to permit an adequate degree of inter-regional migration, and the number of houses required should therefore be adjusted accordingly. Making an estimate of the adjusted requirement at the end of 1969 and comparing it with the actual stock of dwellings reveals an overall apparent shortage in Great Britain of around 1 million dwellings at the close of 1969, indicating an average annual net construction rate of 100,000 dwellings during the 1970s. To this must be added a figure to allow for the number of second houses required, say 20,000 annually, making an average requirement arising from shortages of 120,000 dwellings a year. Ideally these estimates will be constructed by summing the requirements of the various regions.

Housing Replacement

Finally, we must consider the replacements of existing dwellings needed for purposes of slum clearance and for redevelopment, perhaps associated with new road-building or with comprehensive town-centre schemes. For years extravagant estimates have been made of the number of unfit dwellings in the British Isles, but the rate of demolition or closure of dwellings in recent years has scarcely changed, averaging approximately 70,000 to 90,000 a year. What is certain is that this rate of demolition needs to be accelerated to cope with the adequate modernization of the housing stock and to provide a housing programme commensurate with the resources available. The age analysis of the stock of dwellings according to the February 1967 House Condition Survey of England and Wales is shown in Table 65.

Table 65

Housing Age: England and Wales

	Thousand dwellings	%
Pre-1919	6,029	38·4
1919 to 1944	4,255	27·1
Post-1944	5,416	34·5
TOTAL	15,700	100·0

The number of unfit dwellings deemed to be not reasonably suitable for occupation within the basis of the Housing Act 1957 was put at 1·8 million out of the total of 15·7 million. Some of these houses will undoubtedly be made fit, and in assessing the future rate of replacement we have to take notice of the policy and steps taken by way of conversion and improvement grants to modernize older dwellings, and thus to eliminate their obsolescence. The past pattern of slum clearance and other losses, which shows only a gradual rise in most years, seems likely to set the broad trend for the future. The bigger problem facing the forecaster, however, is to assess the average life of dwellings. It is clear that errors in this assumption can make an enormous difference to the potential rate of replacement, and it is quite possible that the expected life of a house today might change in the future. In the medium term it seems imprudent to assume an average life of less than eighty years, and with this in mind, on average, all homes built in the nineteenth century would be assumed to be demolished during the course of the next ten years. This is a total of some 5·5 million dwellings in Great Britain, and it would imply a rate of replacement for obsolescence of up to 550,000 a year. When this figure is compared with the rate of demolition and closure in the recent past, it can be seen that a major change in policy would be required to eliminate most eighty-year-old properties by the end of the decade. If on the other hand, an average life of a hundred years is assumed, a much lower rate of replacement of about 180,000 a year would be implied. But the chances are that large areas of houses will become socially obsolete.

Using these methods it is possible to establish the broad requirement in terms of housing completions in the three main demand categories, region by region. For the decade as a whole the housing requirement in Great Britain, on best estimates, is between 350,000 and 375,000. We can then assess how realistic this overall demand forecast is in relation to what has gone before. As was illustrated in Chart 33, in the decade 1950 to 1959 2,769,000 houses were built in Great Britain, 881,000 in the private sector and 1,888,000 in the public sector. In the following decade 1960 to 1969 3,524,000 houses were completed, 1,937,000 private and 1,587,000 public. In the earlier years the average rate of new household formation was higher and the level of the housing shortage was greater, so a forecast of even 375,000 houses a year through to 1980 needs sound justification.

Government Policy

In ensuring that the overall forecast is reasonable we are faced with another problem which deserves attention. The swings between public-sector and private-sector housing demonstrate the importance of government policy in forecasting the future. To test the feasibility of the forecast it is necessary to study political statements of policy and overspill plans to re-house people from the overcrowded conurbations in agreed town development schemes. The Conservative manifesto *A Better Tomorrow* referred to the following main objectives of housing policy under Conservative party administration:

1) To house the homeless, to concentrate on slum clearance and to provide better housing for those many families living without modern amenities.

2) To bring about a great increase in home ownership so that the majority of our nation fulfil their wish to live in a home of their own.

3) To see that the tenant, whether of a private property or of a council house, receives a fair deal.

The forecaster must assess how far such aspirations are likely to be translated into action.

Regional Factors

Before turning to housing investment in value terms it is necessary to examine the regional pattern. A really useful user forecast must analyse the pattern of housing completions, region by region, and even by statistical sub-divisions of regions. There are significant differences in completions per thousand of population and in the number of private dwellings completed as compared with public-sector completions. Table 66 demonstrates the range of difference for certain specific regions and sub-divisions of regions in England and Wales during the last four years.

Another problem to be noted is the effect of the changing proportion of flats in the total of all dwellings. For England and Wales these figures are published in *Housing Statistics, Great Britain*. In general terms the proportion of flats in total completions is only $7\frac{1}{2}\%$ in the private sector, but a significant 50% in the public sector.

Table 66

Housing Completions by Region

	mid-1969 population	Completions per 1,000 population				% in private sector
	000s	1966	1967	1968	1969	1966–9
England and Wales	48,827	7·3	7·5	7·6	6·6	55
East Anglia	1,657	11·2	10·5	10·3	9·1	66
Outer South-East	4,236	10·3	9·6	9·8	7·9	64
South-West	3,832	8·2	8·4	8·8	7·1	69
Wales	2,725	7·2	7·4	7·1	6·3	50
Manchester	2,503	6·7	6·0	5·7	5·7	46
Inner London	4,721	4·0	4·1	4·2	4·1	17

Investment in Dwellings

Having made an attempt to determine a realistic forecast for the rate of house-building for a decade in terms of the housing requirement, we are in a position to estimate the value of investment in dwellings year by year. Forecasts of future housing investment are best based on house-building data as opposed to the compromise between output and expenditure data used for the official statistics. The first step to be taken is the conversion of the longer-term housing requirement into the annual/quarterly pattern, having regard to all the factors which can affect investment in housing in the short term. The factors which have to be brought into consideration, especially in respect of private housing, are the general economic climate, government and local authority policy and practice, personal incomes and savings, the supply of land, the flow of funds into building societies, the availability of funds from other financial institutions, the state of the stock market, the cost of money and the price of houses and immediate trends. A useful note by A. R. Nobay, 'Short-Term Forecasting of Housing Investment', was published in the *National Institute Economic Review* (August 1967). The author presented some exploratory results but drew attention to the difficulty of finding satisfactory relationships when so many factors have to be taken into consideration.

Estimates of housing starts are converted into investment by using the concept of 'equivalent completions'. This is derived from a forecast of housing starts, quarter by quarter, by applying a factor for time taken for building. Figures for the estimated time-lag from start to completion are published quarterly in *Housing Statistics in Britain*, and the general pattern during the last decade is illustrated in Chart 35. Although there has been a general long-term tendency for the time-lag to increase, it is considered that the peak might now have passed during 1970 and that the broad trend may now be a modest acceleration in the

Chart 35

CONSTRUCTION TIME-LAGS

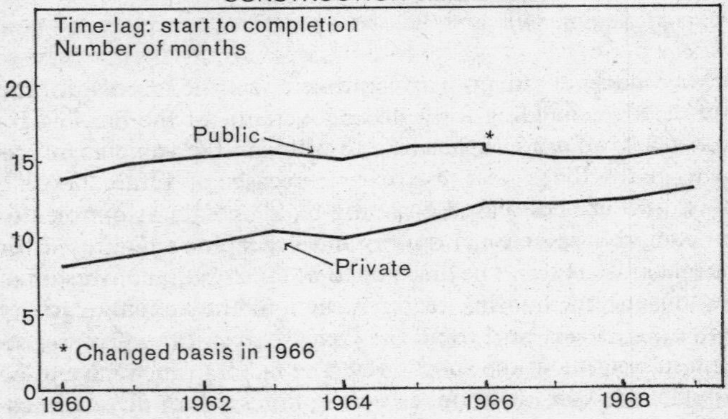

apparent rate of building with more efficient building methods being more widely employed to make the more productive use of labour.

The relationship between equivalent completions in the United Kingdom and investment at constant prices provides us with a variable factor which must be calculated and predicted to derive future investment figures. This key factor is not only a quality and size factor, but it also includes all the items entering into the investment figures which are not directly attributable to new house-building, such as fees and certain expenditure on conversions, improvements and irremovable equipment. Moreover, it is dependent upon the correct price assumptions having been made in the official adjustment of the investment figures from current to constant prices. Some doubts have been expressed about the validity of the price factor used, especially for the public sector.

The derivation of suitable factors for public and private dwellings presents additional problems in that further assumptions have to be made. For example, is the average quality of dwelling likely to improve with a demand for better standards and amenities, such as central heating, more bathrooms/toilets and built-in cupboards? Is the average size of dwelling likely to alter in response to increasing incomes or changes in average family size, or changes in the proportions of houses and flats? On the whole, in converting equivalent completions into investment, it seems most prudent to project into the future the past upward trends in these variable factors. Thus, the investment forecast for dwellings can be devised, having made numerous assumptions within the considerable limitations of the basic data from which the figures are produced.

Finally, what is the interpretation of these figures for the private house-builder? The estate developer was severely hit by the decline in demand during 1969 and 1970 and he faces a considerable problem for the future. With trends now apparently unfavourable, his heyday may well have passed. It is likely that future demand will show little tendency to rise, and, as a consequence, a buyers' market will develop in which the location and manner of building become much more important than in the past. The closer the U.K. comes to having a sufficient stock of dwellings in relation to the population requirements the more likely will be the risk of sharper fluctuations in future demand. With house-building an extremely fragmented industry in Britain, it is almost certain that a number of the companies involved will be unable to survive in a more competitive trading environment.

BUILDING INVESTMENT OTHER THAN HOUSING

So far as civil engineering and constructional work is concerned, the problem has to be assessed in a different way. Whereas in the case of housing it is possible to make a plausible estimate of the requirement over a whole decade on the basis of agreed assumptions of household formation, housing shortage, slum clearance and redevelopment, this is not possible with other building investment. The nature of the expenditure is much more diverse than with dwellings, and the statistics available are neither so prolific nor so precise. The requirement for building and constructional work is open-sided, depending much more on the general rate of economic growth and what the nation can afford.

It is appropriate to start by outlining what is included in building investment in this context. Expenditure on 'other new buildings and works' is the gross domestic fixed capital formation representing an addition to the stock of physical assets. The only contribution of land in the figures are the costs of transfer from one owner to another – a relatively small but continually rising component. The estimates made by the Central Statistical Office represent the value of work done during the period. Repairs and maintenance are not included in investment, as this expenditure is regarded as current spending and not capital. However, building investment other than housing does include such items of equipment as lifts, heating, ventilating and air-conditioning plant, railway track and gas and water mains, as well as all extensions and structural alterations to existing buildings. It also includes all costs, such as stamp duties and fees for the services of agents, solicitors, architects, surveyors and consulting engineers. Finally, amounts realized from the sale of fixed assets are deducted in deriving the total gross domestic fixed capital formation.

About two-thirds of the total expenditure under consideration is incurred in the public sector, and there was a tendency for this proportion to rise during the period of Labour government, as illustrated in Chart 36. The major categories of expenditure are schools and universities, roads, water and sewerage, gas, health and welfare services and electricity. In the private sector, the main investment is made in insurance, banking, finance and other services, including distribution, and in manufacturing industry, mainly factory buildings.

The principal statistical raw materials are provided by three main series of data, to which must be added information extracted from periodic White Papers setting down programmes for public-sector work. First of all, investment in new buildings and works is

Chart 36
INVESTMENT IN OTHER NEW BUILDINGS AND WORKS

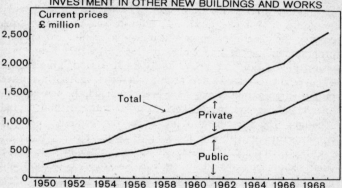

published under thirty-eight categories in the annual National Income and Expenditure Blue Book, but the figures given are on an annual basis only and are always historic and subject to later revision. However, for each of the headings shown we can calculate the proportion of total investment comprised by new building work for which it is helpful to establish the past pattern and trends. Secondly, output data for work done is collected by the Ministry of Public Buildings and Works from a sample of contractors, and published quarterly on exactly the same basis as the housing output data. Finally, similar data on orders are also published by the Ministry; at monthly and quarterly intervals, the quarterly series covering eighteen different types of work and the monthly series showing rather less detail. For the short-term forecaster the orders data are particularly useful in that they are also published by planning region. Both the quarterly output and order series are available in current prices and also, with less accuracy, at constant prices seasonally adjusted. All these Ministry figures cover Great Britain only, and an appropriate allowance must be made for Northern Ireland when converting to United Kingdom figures.

Public expenditure White Papers, referred to above, are published by the government from time to time and provide particularly useful raw material for certain categories of public-sector expenditure in the medium term. The White Paper 'Public Expenditure 1968/69 to 1973/74', published in December 1969, covered the general prospect and individual capital expenditure programmes for the financial years 1968/9 to 1971/2 and provisional allocations for 1972/3 and 1973/4. Although the change of government created a new problem in the extent to which these published programmes may have been amended, the new government's policies are more likely to affect current than capital spending. The subsequent White Paper on spending to 1974/5 confirms this view, though less detail was provided.

Other periodic publications set down programmes for particular sectors of expenditure, such as for roads, education and hospitals. The continual problem is to forecast what effects subsequent economic developments are likely to have upon these programmes – more often deferring than accelerating them. It appears that the latest policy is to publish a programme which may cover a variable number of years. For example, the White Paper 'Roads for the Future', published in May 1970, lays down a new road programme for England over fifteen to twenty years, having first appeared as a 'green paper' for discussion in May 1969.

Forecasting Method

The techniques to be used in making forecasts of new buildings and works are as follows. The most reliable procedure is to develop the forecast from the whole economy to the sector – 'macro' to 'micro'. The starting point is thus a forecast of Gross Domestic

Product and an endeavour to predict from past trends and known changes in the broadest terms the proportion which will be comprised by new building work. As mentioned above this proportion rose from $5\frac{1}{4}\%$ in 1959 to $6\cdot9\%$ in 1969, and there is every reason to believe that this percentage will continue to rise, perhaps to about $7\cdot5\%$ during the decade. Expenditure has been growing fast in such fields as roads, education, gas, health and welfare, and sewerage and land drainage, where building comprises a high proportion of total expenditure. Further heavy investment programmes have been published for fields of activity such as roads and hospitals.

It is then possible to allocate this forecast of expenditure between public and private sectors. The government has a very substantial influence both upon the general level of building activity and upon the distribution between public and private sector. Not only are there incentives to building, such as investment grants, but there are also disincentives, such as industrial development certificates and restrictions on the availability and cost of finance. One of the effects of the Labour government's term of office was to create a virtually static expenditure in the private sector, while public-sector investment continued to increase. The problem for the forecaster is to assess how far the Conservative administration will reverse this trend.

The first stage in forecasting other building investment is, therefore, to answer certain general questions. What is the relationship between expenditure on new buildings and Gross Domestic Product? What is the relationship between building and total fixed investment? What is the relationship between public-sector and private-sector expenditure within the total expenditure on new buildings and works? That past trends alone, however, cannot be used in predicting the future for individual programmes is demonstrated by examining the gas and electricity industries' expenditure on fixed assets. The medium-term programmes bear small relationship to the experience in the past, as is shown in Chart 37, and the changes in trend make longer-term prediction hazardous.

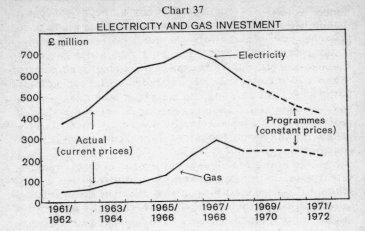

Chart 37

ELECTRICITY AND GAS INVESTMENT

The Public Sector

The major investment categories must be examined in greater detail and we begin by looking into the problems of forecasting public-sector investment. Within the public sector, road-building investment by the central government and local authorities is running at a rate of over £400 million a year and is perhaps the most important programme for the construction industry. This expenditure comprises the cost of construction and major improvement of motorways, trunk roads and other roads, including purchase of land, and capital expenditure on car parks and public lighting. Most of this expenditure enters into the figure for investment in new buildings and works, which, for roads, has increased at a rate of 19% a year from 1959 to 1964, and 14% from 1964 to 1969. Such is the need for new roads, created by ever-increasing traffic throughout the country in both urban and inter-urban areas, that a similar rate of growth is inevitable. The annual pattern of orders has not always been consistently upwards however. There were deferments in July 1965 and further cuts in planned expenditure in January 1968, affecting both new construction work and maintenance. However, 'Roads for the

270

Future' envisages expenditure of £3,400 million at 1970 prices merely on improved trunk roads between cities in England over the next fifteen to twenty years as future economic circumstances allow.

From 1959 to 1969 road expenditure as a proportion of total investment in new buildings and works increased from 4·4% to 8·8%, and all the indications are that this trend is certain to continue. The first requirement is to complete throughout the country the motorway and dual-carriageway trunk road pattern which was commenced in 1958. However, more attention will be paid in future to urban motorways, with their flyovers and under-passes. This will affect the investment picture because a lower proportion of the total expenditure will be incurred in the road construction itself as a result of the higher costs of land acquisitions and demolition of existing buildings. Although the future trend will undoubtedly be strongly upwards, the problem is to predict the effects of government policy and the economic climate upon this underlying pattern. The most reliable indicators are the relationships with the overall level of investment in new buildings and works and gross domestic fixed capital formation as a whole.

Educational capital expenditure is another category with strong underlying growth. It includes expenditure on schools, technical institutions and universities and is now running at an annual rate in excess of £350 million. This expenditure is based on estimates of the likely numbers of students in full-time education. The upward trend of expenditure in the past – 11% a year from 1959 to 1964 and 7% a year from 1964 to 1969 – has been associated partly with the high birth rate after the Second World War, partly with the periodic raising of the school-leaving age, which increases the number of children and young people in full-time education, and partly with the need for better facilities for higher education. Looking to the future, a declining birth rate and lower numbers reaching school age will tend to eliminate the first element in this growth, while raising the school-leaving age to sixteen in 1972 should remove the second element of growth. The demand caused by the inadequacy of educational facilities which has resulted in too many pupils in each class and the perpetuation of archaic buildings will remain. Many temporary structures, erected in times of the severest need, may also be replaced by permanent buildings.

Over 75% of fixed investment in education comprises expenditure on new buildings and works, and from 1959 to 1969 educational expenditure as a percentage of total investment in new buildings and works was a fairly steady 7–8%. It is clear that expenditure on new schools will increase at a high rate up to 1972/3, but a more modest requirement thereafter seems appropriate. Expenditure on further education and universities will also continue to rise, but this item forms a much smaller proportion of the total.

Health and welfare services provide yet another strongly rising category of investment in the public sector at the present time. An ambitious new hospital programme set out in the White Paper 'Hospital Building Programme', published in May 1966, contained plans to spend £1,000 million in England and Wales in the ten years up to 1975. Most of the expenditure is for new buildings. This requirement is created not so much by growth in pure demand as by shortages resulting from the inadequacy and obsolescence of a great many of the existing buildings. Once this shortage of adequate facilities has been dealt with, the rate of new hospital building will slow down, but this is unlikely to occur before the end of the 1970s. Health and welfare services also include expenditure incurred by local authorities on homes for the elderly, health centres and any special facilities needed for mentally and physically handicapped patients.

Altogether, expenditure on new buildings and works under the heading health and welfare increased by $26\frac{1}{2}$% a year from 1959 to 1964 and $10\frac{1}{2}$% a year from 1964 to 1969. During this period the proportion of total expenditure on new buildings and works increased from 1·5% to 3·4%. All the available evidence points to the need for continued heavy expenditure and a high level of priority on health and welfare services in modern society, at least for the next ten years, with some possible slowing-up in the need for new building work thereafter.

Local environmental services are becoming another significant category of expenditure, with an important element of new building work. It covers spending on water supply, sewerage, refuse disposal and clean air, playing fields, swimming baths, other recreational areas and industrial and commercial development by new town development corporations. However, only water supply and sewerage and land drainage are treated separately in the Blue Book fixed investment figures. Other spending on local environmental services is included under the item 'other public services', with each expenditure on the police, parks, the fire service, libraries and other local government services.

From 1959 to 1969 the expenditure on such new buildings and works as a percentage of total expenditure on new buildings and works declined from 2·2% to 1·9% for water and increased from 2·5% to 3·1% for sewerage and land drainage. The average annual rates of increase from 1959 to 1964 were 8% for water and 11¼% for sewerage, and from 1964 to 1969 6½% for water and 11% for sewerage. With increasing problems of water supply to meet the rising demand and greater attention towards anti-pollution, a high rate of growth is assured. Similar considerations apply to other local environmental services, but these have less impact upon the total level of new building.

The only other principal category of public-sector expenditure on new buildings and works is the spending (discussed in the previous chapter) of the nationalized industries – mainly gas, electricity, railways, the Post Office, air transport, steel and coal mining. For some of these industries a high proportion of capital spending is on new building and works, including such items as gas pipelines and replacement of railway track. For example, in 1968 the percentages for gas and railways were about 60%. Otherwise the capital expenditure is mainly on plant and vehicles. The main problem is the cyclical nature of nationalized industries' capital spending, as illustrated in Chart 37 for gas and electricity. The result is likely to be that overall spending on fixed assets by the nationalized industries will remain fairly static in the short term, rising again only in 1972/3 and 1973/4. This is mainly because electricity investment is falling to the bottom of its cycle and gas industry investment is reaching its peak following the completion of the new natural-gas pipeline network. The trends in coal mining and railways are likely to remain static, and may even decline. This leaves the main elements of growth as the plant and equipment for Post Office and telecommunications, steel, where investment has been at a low ebb since the establishment of the British Steel Corporation, and air transport, where, apart from proposals for the third London airport, investment is principally in aircraft.

Although public expenditure White Papers are of some value in predicting the pattern of investment in the public sector, experienced interpretation of all the available data can lead to substantial discrepancies between forecasts by different individual forecasters.

The Private Sector

Turning to the private sector, which is responsible for approximately one-third of capital expenditure on new buildings and works other than housing, the main categories are insurance, banking, finance and other services, manufacturing industry and retail and wholesale distribution. Unlike the public sector, where relatively few decisions create the various programmes of capital spending, in the private sector the overall pattern arises from numerous much smaller individual decisions. Short-term economic circumstances can often be more important in determining the pattern of investment than longer-term trends.

The services sector as a whole, which includes offices, property developments, hotels, recreational buildings, shops and warehouses, accounted for $12\frac{1}{4}\%$ of total spending on new buildings and works in 1959 and 13% in 1969. The average annual growth rates were 14% from 1959 to 1964 and $5\frac{1}{2}\%$ from 1964 to 1969, reflecting a deliberate government policy to contain the capital expenditure of the services sector. Provided that the general economic climate allows, the rate of spending on fixed assets by the services industries under a Conservative administration is likely to accelerate once again, probably raising further the proportion of total spending on new buildings and works.

Expenditure by manufacturing industry on new buildings and

works was $12\frac{1}{2}\%$ of total new building work in 1959 and only just over 9% in 1967 and 1969. New building formed a reducing proportion of total fixed investment by manufacturing industry, falling from $25\frac{1}{4}\%$ in 1959 to $21\frac{3}{4}\%$ in 1969, while expenditure on plant and machinery has risen correspondingly. This trend is associated with the greater mechanization of industry. Sophisticated new machinery tends to require less of both space and labour.

While it is a relatively straightforward task to make a plausible forecast of investment in new buildings and works by manufacturing industry as a whole, industry by industry it is hazardous, one of the principal difficulties being the varying cyclicality of the individual industries. An expansion programme created by shortage of supply and resulting in a substantial accretion to capacity inevitably brings in its wake a situation of surplus. The larger the individual companies in an industry, the more pronounced the peaks and troughs are likely to be.

If a faster rate of economic growth can be achieved in the years to come, private-sector capital spending might increase at a more healthy rate than in the recent past, but although there is scope for a great deal of industrial renovation and refurbishing, the services sector seems likely to become responsible for an increasing proportion of total private expenditure on new buildings and works.

Regional Patterns

The only published evidence of the regional pattern of building work other than housing is provided by the Ministry of Public Building and Works' statistics of the value of new orders obtained by contractors. These figures demonstrate substantial fluctuations under the various categories quarter by quarter and year by year, and are unlikely to be a particularly reliable indicator of the pattern of work done. However, the series dates back to 1965 and it is thus possible to analyse in the broadest terms changes in the proportions of total orders for public-sector work other than housing, and for private industrial and other work by each economic planning region. For the future it must be assumed that government regional policies will ensure that an adequate volume of work will be directed into the development districts. In addition general predictions of population movements are likely to provide some indication of where new work will arise.

The Need for Judgement

As the scale of building operations becomes even larger so the risks associated with building and civil engineering become greater, with additional importance attaching to shrewd prediction of future trends. There will always be opportunities for the most efficient companies which are able to take advantage of them, but an increasing degree of specialization is likely to become desirable, with a rising trend towards negotiated contracts as opposed to pure tendering.

To sum up, it can be concluded that the prime problem in forecasting housing and other building investment is concerned not so much with statistical techniques as with making the right assumptions in the light of all the statistical data available to the forecaster. Forecasting in this field is more than a question of searching for relationships and using sophisticated econometric models.

CHAPTER 12

Forecasting Sales and Output by Sectors

BY ALLAN F. HODGSON
AND MELVYN ROWE

Preceding chapters have outlined the method by which the central
forecast of Gross Domestic Product (G.D.P.) is determined. In
constant prices, the exogenous factors such as exports are forecast, and to these are added estimates which have been constructed of the other items of final expenditure, such as consumers' expenditure. This chapter will examine a means of translating these macro-economic features of output into a form more
meaningful to the businessman.

The future level of domestic activity, most suitably described in
terms of a G.D.P. measurement, is best arrived at by the methods
outlined in Chapter 2. Government forecasts are made along
somewhat different lines, although similar principles underline
the methods. Under the government's method constant price
forecasts are made of the components of final expenditure, with
the aim of determining the level of activity at the end of the forecast period, while at the same time an attempt is made to identify
cyclical or secular movements during the period.[1] Table 67 shows
the estimated relative weighting of the various components of
final expenditure in 1969 at constant prices, from which the
broad estimates and forecasts are compiled.

Up to this point, the forecasting model has run along macro-
economic lines, by projecting the future course of the economy
in the broadest possible terms. An alternative method of forecasting would be to aggregate individual forecasts of the separate
parts of the economy in some detail, and thus arrive at what
might be termed a composite estimate of G.D.P. However, in

1. 'Short term economic forecasting in the U.K.', *Economic Trends*,
August 1964; and 'Short term forecasts of income, expenditure and saving',
Economic Trends, February 1968.

practice, it has been found by the forecasting team in which we collaborate that the best results have been obtained by forecasting the total macro-economic features first, then breaking down into the appropriate sub-totals, and reconciling the parts so that they fit within the agreed totals.

Table 67

Expenditure on G.D.P., 1963 Prices

	£m	% of total
Consumers' expenditure	22·6	52·2
Public authorities' current expenditure	5·8	13·4
Fixed investment	6·6	15·2
Investment in stocks	0·3	0·7
Exports of goods and services	8·0	18·5
Total final expenditure	43·3	100·0
Less:		
Imports of goods and services	−7·8	
Net indirect taxes	−4·2	
	31·3	

This stage could thus represent an important policy decision for the forecaster of sector sales and output. Individual sector forecasts made in isolation tend to be over-optimistic. A similar forecasting weakness can be identified at the company level, when divisional sales forecasts are added together, and at the equity investment level, when analysts' forecasts of companies' earnings are aggregated. The general tendency is for the business analyst to assume an increasing share of the market, and for the investment analyst to assume unimpeded profit growth for each individual stock.

To return to the macro-economic features of the table above, forecasts of these items can be used to provide a very general guide to the environment in which industries and companies operate and to the nature of the constraints placed upon them. But because of the enormous size of the major constituents of demand and their complexity, the relevance and efficiency of their use as indicators may be questioned. For example, the information that consumers' expenditure in a particular year was forecast to be substantially higher than in that preceding is probably of little use to companies in the footwear industry, whose sales amount to only a very small percentage of total consumer spending. Similarly, if it is forecast that fixed investment is likely to be sharply lower next year, what is the relevance of this important piece of news for a company manufacturing pumps and valves?

The problem is that growth rates differ. In terms of volume or in terms of value, marked disparities occur within each of the categories of total home demand. Table 68 illustrates this point

Table 68

Changes in Consumption and Investments

	1964–9 % change p.a., 1963 prices
Consumers' expenditure – total	1·6
Food	0·6
Housing	3·5
Footwear	0·7
Cars and motor cycles	−0·4
Fixed investment – total	2·9
Mining and quarrying	2·5
Gas, electricity and water	−2·7
Transport and communications	6·0
Dwellings	1·0
Public services	7·0

with examples drawn from the totals of consumers' expenditure and fixed investment.

Explanations of these disparities are numerous. Perhaps the most severe are those determined by the demographic and geographic factors of a particular sub-group. Housing probably falls into this category, for, as discussed in the previous chapter, it now appears there is a surplus of housing. With regard to the birth rate, the latest estimates[1] by the Government Actuary's

1. *Monthly Digest of Statistics*, May 1970.

Department of the future total population of the U.K. include a lower assumption for births than in the previous years' estimates. In fact, 1969 was the fifth successive year in which births were fewer than in the previous year.

Changes in consumer tastes and preferences are another obvious source of distortion. On a small scale the conflict between the 'mini' and the 'maxi' is typical of the swings in preferences. Although of a different order, changes in government policy are also important. The effect of the taxes levied on commodities for which demand is broadly inelastic can be clearly seen. Public spending too is an additional powerful source of growth and decline (see Chapter 6).

In the larger industries, management is a factor which may have only a very marginal effect on an industry's performance. However, there are instances where it has been significant – favourably in textiles; possibly adversely in shipbuilding. Similarly, marketing and technological development can be responsible for marked departures from the norm. The marketing of imported cars has undoubtedly played an important part in winning a growing share of the domestic market, while the technological impact of John Logie Baird or Sir Alexander Fleming was such as to create entirely new industries.

Finally, overseas influences can play an important part. Where an industry is heavily dependent on exports, any fluctuations in foreign markets or increased competition may have a disproportional effect – as was seen in the recent experience of the toy industry. In foreign markets, a change in legal requirements can disrupt production – the recent tightening of car safety legislation in the U.S.A. being a case in point.

Thus growth rates of sectors can and do differ, making meaningful application of the macro-economic features a difficult, and often impossible, task for the businessman. To produce forecasts of any practical significance for business it is, therefore, necessary to disaggregate the totals into their component parts, reconciling individual items in the process.

FIXED INVESTMENT

Disaggregation of the fixed investment figure can be tackled in several ways. The Central Statistical Office publication *Monthly Digest of Statistics* analyses investment by sector, by type of asset and by industry group.

The private sector accounts for about 55% of total fixed investment at 1963 prices, public authorities for 27% and the public corporations the remaining 18%. By type of asset, plant and machinery is the largest single component, followed by other new buildings and works. Then come public dwellings, private dwellings and vehicles, ships and aircraft.

Perhaps most business interest in investment centres around the industry break-up, where manufacturing is responsible for some 22%. This is the sensitive indicator for total investment, which is the regular subject of the government and C.B.I. intentious surveys. Broadly speaking, the manufacturing investment cycle tends to exaggerate that of total investment and thus any marked change in survey responses can be taken as likely to apply to investment as a whole. Dwellings again appear as a sub-sector, while other significant categories include the utilities, distribution, transport, and communication.

A more detailed industry group analysis, on the lines of the index of production classification, is available for manufacturing investment. The engineering and shipbuilding group accounts for more than 21% of the total. Chemicals and food, drink and tobacco are the next most important categories. An industry group analysis is also provided for investment in the distributive and service industries, and here, of the identifiable sectors, retail distribution is the largest, followed by the extremely volatile shipping sector, and by the relatively stable wholesale distribution group. An additional category for 'other industries' is given which includes the remaining service industries ranging from insurance to scientific services.

CONSUMERS' SPENDING

A very detailed analysis of consumers' expenditure is to be found in both the National Income Blue Book and the *Annual Abstract of Statistics*. It is worth noting that the value of consumers' expenditure at 1963 prices is between three and four times as great as total fixed investment. Table 69 shows the magnitude of the

Table 69

Consumers' Expenditure in 1969

	£m. 1963 prices	%
Food	4,921	21·7
Alcoholic drink	1,346	6·0
Tobacco	1,246	5·5
Housing	2,613	11·6
Fuel and light	1,226	5·4
Clothing	2,053	9·1
Durable goods	1,818	8·0
Other goods and services	7,397	32·7
TOTAL	22,620	100·0

chief sub-headings. The detailed breakdown divides spending on food into ten categories, of which meat and bacon is easily the largest, followed by dairy products and bread and cereals. Alcoholic drink is split into beer (60% of the total) and wines, spirits, cider, etc. Housing is very largely rent, rates and water charges, with maintenance, repairs and improvements accounting for the remainder. Fuel and light is conventionally divided into electricity, coal and coke, and gas, with other fuels taking only a very small share.

Clothing expenditure is divided into men's wear, women's wear and footwear. The sensitive durable goods sector consists of motor cars and motor cycles, furniture and floor coverings, and radio, electrical and other durables. Just as manufacturing investment is very much the bellwether for changes in total investment, durable goods spending similarly shows a marked exaggeration of the swings in total expenditure.

'Other household goods' is a minor but awkward category, its constituents ranging from matches to soap; while books, newspapers and magazines, an even smaller sub-section, is rather more identifiable. Chemists' goods, miscellaneous recreational goods and other miscellaneous goods complete the hardware side of consumer spending. It is interesting to observe that the 'other goods' miscellany falls next in size to food and 'other services' in any group ranking. This rapidly growing services element of consumers' expenditure accounts for almost 19% of the total. Its constituents range from running costs of motor vehicles to domestic service and to insurance.

Finally, total consumers' expenditure is obtained by deducting from the sum of the above items expenditure by foreign tourists in the U.K. and then adding consumers' expenditure abroad – both of which are estimated in the fullest sense of the word!

Thus for these two categories, investment and consumers' expenditure, it is possible to obtain a fair degree of detail on the composition of the totals. Similar disaggregation is available for the other macro-economic features of total spending discussed earlier.

ESTABLISHING RELATIONSHIPS

It is possible, therefore, to establish relationships between, say, total consumer spending and spending on food, and to interpret the implications of changes in the macro-economic items. Furthermore, it will now be possible, given this disaggregation, to relate the detailed series to index of production data and other volume indicators which are available on a monthly or quarterly basis in the *Monthly Digest of Statistics* and *Business Monitor* series. Similarly, the index numbers available for both material and fuel prices and sales prices of a wide range of commodities, published in the *Board of Trade Journal* and the *Monthly Digest of Statistics*, may also be linked to the disaggregated items.

At this state, it is possible in theory to break down the main macro-economic features of the model, relating the detail to prices and production indicators, and so to produce meaningful information of considerable business application. There are, however, problems, some of which apply to past data and some to projections of the future.

THE PROBLEM OF DEFINITION

One central problem which bears heavily on the business fore-caster is the definition of an industry. On the one hand Index of Production data tends towards an excessively broad coverage, so that any clear-cut definition is often difficult. On the other, many firms operate in a number of industries so that analysis based on aggregates of companies can be misleading. Similarly, the broad industrial classification used in the *Financial Times/ Actuaries* share indices tends to bracket diverse companies within some of the industrial categories. This particular weakness has, to a great extent, been eliminated by the recent Actuaries/Stock Exchange 'Classification of Quoted Securities', which not only disaggregates sectors such as engineering (non-electrical) into eight sub-groups, but also provides a definition of each sub-group!

Past data falls victim to the ever-present hazard of revisions. Residual items, such as personal saving and trading profits of companies, tend to suffer most. Progress in the official collection of statistics has thrown up new areas of consumer expenditure, which necessitates probing backwards in existing series. A further example was the discovery of the under-recording of exports and thus one must guard against accepting statistics at face value without questioning the methods of collection and the nature of the data obtained.[1]

Changes in the weights allotted to industries can lead to quite substantial revisions to published series. The recent rebasing of the index of production on 1963 Census data, compared with the previous basing on 1958 Census data, made a number of sig-

1. C.S.O. publication *Sources and Methods* is extremely useful in this respect.

nificant changes to 1968 output indices, as Table 70 shows. Classification switching has been partly responsible, but more important have been the changes which have taken place in industrial structure and the composition of output. Thus, a number

Table 70

Rebasing the Index of Production

	1968	
	Old index	New index
All industries	117·0	119·7
Chemicals and allied	131·9	139·8
Shipbuilding and marine engineering	91·7	86·8
Vehicles	109·2	116·5

Source: *Economic Trends*, August 1969, p.x.

of old indicators have been scrapped – for example, the relatively meaningless aircraft engine series – and new ones introduced which should prove more suitable guides to movements in output at constant prices.

KEY RATIOS

What are the problems to be faced in forecasting, given that we can to some extent determine past trends? Firstly, the danger must be avoided, where possible, of simply extrapolating past trends, for, as a distinguished government economic adviser put it, the economy can rarely be described as 'A creature that moves in determinate grooves'.[1] Yet in several cases this is the technique used by the Treasury in forecasting certain residual items, while their forecasts of the rents and rates index and of the trend element in wages and salaries are also extrapolations of past data.[2] One simple method of forecasting which avoids some of the traps of extrapolation is the use of key ratios, which firstly identify

1. Sir Alec Cairncross, *Economic Journal*, December 1969, p. 806.
2. *Economic Trends*, August 1964.

growth rates for G.D.P. (or whichever macro-economic feature is applicable) and for a particular industry indicator over the cycles of the past ten and five years. The relationship between the growth rates of the two factors is then established, and, given a forecast of the macro-economic feature, it is possible to make an estimate of the appropriate relationship for the next five years (or cycle). From the forecast ratios the appropriate rates of change can be estimated for the sector and thus a horizon level of output or price can be determined for the end of the forecast period. Performance in the intervening period can then be resolved by reference to the cyclical pattern of the macro-economic feature.

We must also ensure that the assumptions underlying the macro-economic model are consistent with those for the industrial forecast; and should they conflict, then it must be established that the reasons for the differences are soundly based. This point of difference between the macro-economic forecast and the industrial forecast extends also to actual projections. If we expect consumer expenditure as a whole to rise sharply in a particular year, then a forecast for, say, spending on footwear, which shows an opposite movement, must be critically re-examined to ensure that there are really valid reasons for such a change. Similarly, any projected marked change in what had been a firm trend must also be checked, for as a general rule major trends change only gradually. Against this it can be said that there is little constancy in most economic relationships and that chance factors such as wars or industrial disputes can entirely disrupt an attractively packaged set of equations. But if this argument is given undue weight then forecasting and planning have to be abandoned. It should be recognized, therefore, that there must exist a framework of inter-relationships which enable projections of variables to be made, given past data and given estimates of major exogenous items. Thus we can make useful forecasts providing the limits of the data and techniques are recognized and admitted with varying degrees of confidence.

If industrial forecasts are to have any meaningful application for business, they cannot be compiled on the assumption that government policies are unchanged. Thus it is necessary to maintain a flexible approach to changes in taxation, to exchange rate parity adjustments and other key developments – a vital difference from most other forecasts. In this respect, industrial forecasting falls clearly within the realm of political economy – and, as such, possesses an appropriately greater degree of relevance to those in the business community asking the key question: what is most likely to happen?

A further danger which should be scrupulously avoided is that of 'relating the unrelated'. There may, for example, be a close correlation over a long period between the number of civil servants and the size of the G.D.P. But economic forecasts should not be made on the basis of Parkinson's Law! It is, therefore, important to establish the logic of the relationship between variables and to ensure *a priori* that there is no more intellectually satisfactory pair of items available. With the increasing availability of computer time, there is a strong risk – and indeed, some limited attraction – in churning a data bank to produce what have been described as 'dustbin' relationships. This is especially applicable to predictions of the stock market. Financial forecasters no doubt dream of uncovering an equation in which the *F.T./Actuaries* index lags some weekly statistics by three or six months, but unless there is an obvious logical connection between the two variables, their discovery may prove to be expensive. All relationships must stand the test of common sense.

Finally, we come to the problems of reconciliation – of ensuring that the sum of the parts does not exceed the whole. Clearly it is impossible to reconcile sales for the whole economy, since one firm's sales are another firm's costs. National income accounting – the principles of which frame the model – is concerned with the measurement of added value, that is the difference between purchases and sales. The surplus, or added value, accrues to the owners of the business in the shape of gross trading profits, and to the employees in wages and salaries. Thus the added value can be measured and analysed in some meaningful way, and a complete set of industrial sector forecasts for the whole economy be reconciled. The labour bills for each industry should add to the total for the whole economy, while the sum of each industry's gross trading profits should equate with the national profit total in the same way.

The problem of reconciling material costs is similar to that for sales since, again, one firm's material costs are another's sales. The overall constraint which ensures that sales and material costs conform to the features of the central model is, of course, the use of key ratios, which, as noted above, relate the sector's growth performance to whichever macro-economic feature is applicable.

THE CENSUS OF PRODUCTION

Having discussed the features and the problems of industrial-sector forecasting at the macro level, we can turn now to the individual-industry approach. The specific methodology of forecasting profits by industry groups from Census of Production and other data is straightforward. The Census of Production data supply for one year the total amounts that an industry receives for its sales, and the total amounts that that industry pays out for purchasing raw materials and fuel, for paying for labour and for other charges such as rates, repair and maintenance, insurance etc. By applying the appropriate volume and price changes to these base figures it is possible to trace out the trends in sales and costs from year to year, and, by subtracting total costs from total sales, trends in profits can be assessed.

Before going on to describe the methodology in more detail, it is worthwhile recognizing certain limitations in the basic data provided in the Census of Production. The time period covered is not common to all firms contributing to the Census, since firms were required only to supply data in respect of a financial year ending anywhere from April 1963 to 5 April 1964. Thus disruption caused by weather conditions or fluctuations in commodity prices, for example, anywhere in the period from May 1962 to early April 1964 could affect what is assumed to be the economic situation of the industry in calendar year 1963. In this connection, a recent survey conducted by the Institute of Chartered Accountants of a large number of published accounts of major industrial companies established that less than half of these companies had December year ends, so that it seems likely that less than half of the Census returns were actually in respect of calendar year 1963. The precise position of any industry as regards the period covered is analysed in the respective Census.

There are the usual difficulties associated with the various conventions of what constitutes sales (or purchases). Some firms record as sales only those cash payments received in a twelve-month period, some of which payments may be in respect of deliveries in a prior period. Some other firms might record in sales progress payments received for work to be delivered in a subsequent period. The treatment of credit sales is yet another area where differing assumptions can be made. Against these problems of the treatment of sales one can expect that there will be fewer discrepancies of treatment within a given industry than between different industries, but nevertheless the limitation does exist. Contrary to practice in business, in the Census the sales and material figures are all adjusted to allow for changes in stocks by subtracting stocks at the beginning of the year and adding year-end stocks to the figure for sales receipts and material costs for the year in question. Thus an industry that builds up stocks during the year will register a better economic performance in terms of sales at least than a firm which runs down its stocks. This bias towards output rather than sales is an appropriate reflection of economic activity in the Census year, but it is not the most helpful way to present figures for use in a continuous year-on-year survey. In addition to this bias there are further problems associated with price changes and obsolescence in stock valuations and with secular trends in the stock/output ratio.

The final, and probably the most important, limitation of the base data lies in the definition of gross output used in the Census of Production. It is the gross output figure that is used as the base sales figure for each industry, but this figure includes sales made by firms to other firms in the same industry. The proportion of inter-industry sales to gross output, thus defined, can vary from year to year within an industry, depending upon capacity utilization and the state of the trade cycle. This situation is quite common in, for example, the textile industry when in busy times small-treatment firms get a lot of business which disappears after the peak of the cycle. It also happens that in certain industries the proportion of inter-industry sales to gross output, thus defined, can go up or down as a secular trend over a number of years. Thus in any industry where any such trends are present the base data is likely to be less useful than in those industries where none of these trends are present. Happily, the 128 industries covered by the 1963 Census of Production have been compressed into seventy industries where it is possible to obtain gross output free of duplication from inter-industry sales by reference to the expanded input–output tables published by the Central Statistical Office in January 1970.

INPUT–OUTPUT TABLES

These expanded input–output tables are a very valuable development of the Census of Production data. They are designed to make the various industry reports of the overall Census mutually consistent. Although many assumptions must be made to achieve this consistency the input–output tables do ensure that no individual industry report reflects an untenable situation with regard to the rest of the economy.

The input–output tables do, of course, provide non-duplicative totals for the value of materials purchased and for labour costs, as well as for the value of overall sales. There are other sources for obtaining overall sales figures for industries, and for some of the cost components. The Board of Trade follows many important industries on this basis, publishing the results in the *Monthly Digest of Statistics* or in the *Business Monitor* series. The Ministry of Technology, the Ministry of Public Buildings and Works, the Ministry of Power and the Ministry of Agriculture also provide information on aggregate sales by industry. Much of the data is provided to government departments by trade associations and the flow of information has increased since the advent of the Prices and Incomes Board, and the consequent necessity to have available the precise economic situation of any given industry.

DATA PROBLEMS

Although these supplementary sources of information are useful they are not altogether without associated problems. The definition of the industry may not correspond exactly to the Standard Industrial Classification, nor will the method of sales valuation necessarily be consistent as between surveys. The real value of these other sources of sales information lies in the fact that they are published on a continuous year-on-year basis, and are also often available on a quarterly basis.

If it is possible to relate these other sources of aggregate sales information to the base data of the Census of Production and the expanded input–output tables, another drawback of these latter two sources can, to a large extent, be overcome. This problem is the long time-lag between the date of the Census and the publication of the results. The 1963 results of the Census were not published until 1968, which was also the year in which a twenty-seven industry input–output table for 1963 was published. Strenuous efforts were made to speed up the compilation process of the 1968 Census of Production, so that the preliminary results of that Census for 153 industries were available by the end of 1969. The importance of speeding up the compilation and publishing process lies, of course, in the fact that the reliability of any projections decreases the longer the elapsed time from firm base data, whereas the usefulness of the whole estimating and forecasting process is primarily concentrated in the evaluation of the short-term contemporary situation and outlook. The use of sources of continuous sales information, in conjunction with a speeded-up dissemination of Census of Production data, provides a very valuable check on the projection technique now to be examined.

DEFINING THE OBJECTIVE

Before setting out to trace an industry's record and to project its future, it is vitally important first of all to establish what is required of the survey. If some indication of the prosperity of the companies operating in the industry in question is needed it may be advisable to adopt a different approach from that which would be used to assess the record of and the outlook for the product of the industry. This is because very few quoted public companies are now 'one-product' companies, and by the same token very few industries produce one homogeneous product. Thus for example, in the building material industry the gross output of miscellaneous building materials in 1968 was greater than the combined gross outputs of the two major individual building materials, bricks and cement. And taking the brick industry alone, the gross output covers both building bricks and refractory bricks, the demand cycles for which do not necessarily coincide. The problem, therefore, is whether the survey should be narrowly defined and run the risk of excluding from the calculations major areas of activity in which constituent firms will be engaged, or whether a broader survey should be attempted which will include some rather unrelated areas of activity. The choice that is made will depend on what is required of the survey.

If the report is to be narrowly defined, it will probably be based on one Census of Production report. Most Census reports are sub-divided into more detailed industries, but only in respect of those firms engaged in the industry which employ more than twenty-five people. If it is required to include all firms irrespective of size, it is possible to gross up the sub-divisions by assuming that the sub-divided industries all have the same proportion of gross output contributed by firms with fewer than twenty-five employees. However, for most industries there is probably no need to get involved with the sub-divisions at all. Where the sub-divisions have to be considered, and because of a broad definition of the industry group, it will probably be an unnecessary sophistication to gross up to avoid the exclusion of small firms.

If the report is to be broadly defined, it will probably be based on a return in the expanded input–output tables. From these tables it is possible to assess some of the characteristics of the chosen industry. In the table laying out the commodity analysis of domestic output in 1963, the columns indicate the extent to which an industry has by-products which are really the principal products of another industry altogether, and also the extent to which a given product or commodity is processed by industries other than one whose principal concern it is to process that product.

One further factor to be borne in mind in deciding on the scope of the survey is that the more narrowly defined the survey is, the more difficult it becomes to get information on the whole range of the industry's activity. This is particularly so in respect of indices of production and price series for output and material input. Where the industry is involved in export markets to a significant extent, the fact that the Standard International Trade Classification is different from the Standard Industrial Classification is a further drawback to the use of narrowly defined surveys. And finally, in those small industries undergoing either rapid expansion or decline, there is a greater possibility of reclassification of and discontinuity in their statistics.

A vital part of the construction of any survey is the preliminary work of determining what is required of it, and the evaluation of just what the base data is setting out and, as importantly, what it is not setting out. The first part of the exercise, therefore, is a reconstruction of the past, filling in gaps in the published data. Having done this the remainder of the survey construction is fairly straightforward. The survey will trace out over time the trends in sales, material costs, labour costs and other 'overhead' costs, and each of these will now be examined in some detail, leaving as a residual the profit trend. Once this stage is complete then forecasts can be constructed by marrying the evidence of the trends and key ratios with the special factors surrounding the industry.

VOLUME CHANGES

Given base year sales from the selected information source, the year-on-year changes are established by compounding onto the base figure the changes both in output volumes and in product selling prices. In a broadly based survey, the Board of Trade indices of industrial production are probably the best means of establishing volume changes. Of course, by their very nature these indices are non-specific as regards individual products, and as such are liable to error over a period of time as the component weights change. The great advantage of a narrowly based survey is that it is possible to use as the volume indicator the number of articles or the weight of the commodity produced. Thus the number of building bricks produced, or the weight of cement, can be used as volume indicators, and this statistic is both highly reliable and readily available.

It is also usual to have some indication of stock levels in specific commodities, whereas this is not so when indices of production are used. Nevertheless, it is quite common to have quality variations in commodities and products, and in these circumstances an overall physical total must be used with care. Thus, there are fletton and non-fletton bricks, and there are 'minis' and Rolls Royces in the car market; simply using the aggregate total for all these products can be strictly correct only if there are precisely similar proportionate trends in each of the quality groups of the commodity or product.

Possibly the most troublesome aspect of the whole procedure of describing industry trends is the selection and applicability of the selling price indicator. For most industries the price index that is to be used should be the wholesale price index, and the Board of Trade publishes a wide range of such indices. For broad sectors of industry, these are available on a monthly basis in the *Monthly Digest of Statistics*, and some of the more detailed indices are published regularly in the *Board of Trade Journal*, although in a less useful manner of publication than in the *Digest*. The entire range of indices, on an annual basis, is published in the *Annual Abstract of Statistics*.

294

The problem that is common to all wholesale price indices is that of discrimination amongst customers. As industry becomes more and more concentrated this problem will probably become more severe still. The discounts that are given from wholesale list price can make the nominal price index somewhat less than ideal. Even in industries where price agreements are in operation, there are often provisions for non-price competition, and these provisions can upset the analysis. Furthermore, if an industry enters into a highly competitive phase of a cycle, it is possible that discounts from list price become universally available, leaving the nominal price index in a very unrealistic situation altogether.

PRICING PROBLEMS

There are also the usual problems of price indices associated with changing component weights, and for some industries in rapid expansion or decline there is the further problem of innovation and obsolescence in products. In certain instances it might be possible to use retail price indices as an indication of wholesale price trends, but where there have been changes in indirect taxation as sweeping and irregular as in the U.K. in recent years (particularly as regards Selective Employment Tax) the retail price trends can have only very limited application.

One final point on pricing problems is worth making. In industries that are to a great extent vertically integrated and concentrated into the control of a handful of large companies, it becomes very difficult to value objectively the economic condition of one stage of the production and marketing sequence. The answers that are obtained depend vitally on the assumptions made, and these assumptions, set out in the Census report, should be closely examined.

MATERIAL COSTS

In forecasting material cost trends, the analytical procedure is much the same as for trends in aggregate sales. For most industries, the Leontief assumption of constant returns to scale (i.e. constant input/output coefficients) over the short term should suffice to give an adequate description of trends. Thus the volume of raw materials required will move precisely in line with the volume of aggregate sales. Of course, where it is known from other sources that economies or dis-economies of scale in raw materials have occurred, or will occur, this assumption must be modified. This sort of situation arises when an industry, usually with a below-average growth record or outlook, seeks in effect to raise selling prices by maintaining unit output volume while at the same time reducing the weight of the unit that is sold. The effect of such an operation will show up in the material cost total rather than in the aggregate sales total. When such tactics are in use, special care must be taken in the evaluation of the output volume indicator.

Details of material cost trends by industry are not available for as wide a range of industries as for wholesale selling prices. While this state of affairs is hardly helpful, it is nevertheless not a crippling handicap. Many material inputs (which in this instance are taken to include fuel usage as well) are common to most industries, and therefore to a certain extent many cost pressures are common to all industries. This, of course, is even more the case as between the sub-sectors of the industry groupings for which material cost indices are available. In the case of an industry using a significant amount of a raw material peculiar to that industry alone, it is quite often the case that trends in the price of that raw material can be established in the commodity markets. It is then possible to estimate total material costs as the sum of two or more components, one or more derived from commodity price trends and the other from the close applicable index of material costs, with the volume trend being common to both or all components.

LABOUR COSTS

The estimation of labour costs is, perhaps, the easiest component of all to establish. There is probably not a great deal of variation in labour price trends throughout the economy, other than in the short term, and trends in labour costs and usage are well documented.

The Blue Book on National Income and Expenditure lists separately the wage bill and the salary bill for major industry groupings. To these components of the total labour cost bill must be added an allowance for employers' contributions to the social security system, and to private pension and health schemes, the trends of which are also set out in the Blue Book. The individual Census reports also set out these totals, so that trends in labour costs for individual sub-sectors of industry can be established by relating the employment trends in the sub-sector to the employment trends in the industry group in question. Employment trends can readily be followed in the statistics of the Department of Employment and Productivity, the only problem here being that there have recently been some reclassifications of workers between industries. This does lead to some discontinuity in the employment series, but it is not difficult to adjust backwards for these usually slight alterations. Having established this historical record, one can deduce from it trends in productivity and hence in labour costs per unit. These trends then form the basis for future projection.

The third component of the overall cost bill is made up of various miscellaneous items, and as such is rather difficult to estimate. It consists of two main items: certain 'overhead' charges and taxes less subsidies on expenditure. The 'overhead' charges consist of repair and maintenance on plants, machinery and vehicles, the insurance, licensing and depreciation of road goods vehicles, rates excluding water rates, hire of plant and machinery, and postage, telephone, telegram and cable charges. These charges are separately indentified in the Census reports, not being charged as material purchases. From their nature it seems likely that these items have increased in cost more rapidly than most other material cost items, and therefore this is allowed for in assessing the trend over recent years.

Taxes less subsidies on expenditure are identified by major industry group in the expanded input–output tables, and it is possible to assess to sub-sectors of these major groups their proportion of this item by relating the gross output of the sub-sector to the gross output of the major group. The gross output of the major group in this case should be that shown in appropriately combined Census reports rather than that shown in the expanded input–output tables, since, as was pointed out above, the definitions of gross output differ slightly between the Census and the input–output tables. Given base year levels for taxes less subsidies on expenditure, trends over time can be established by relating the base year figure to trends in overall taxes less subsidies shown in a table in the Blue Book. It may seem rather strange to regard this item as a cost, but nevertheless it is an item that must be deducted from gross output to establish profits available to business.

AN EXAMPLE FROM THE CHEMICAL INDUSTRIES

The general approach towards the construction of industry surveys from input–output data has now been set out. With the recent publication of the results of the 1968 Census of Production one can now examine how well the 'reconstruction' technique has operated over the period 1963 to 1968. The industry taken as an example is that concerned with the production of inorganic, organic and miscellaneous chemicals, and the data used for comparative purposes in both 1963 and 1968 is that published in the *Board of Trade Journal* of 31 December 1969. This approach is necessary in this case because the chemical industry has been reclassified between the construction of the Standard Industrial Classification in 1963 and 1968.

The inorganic, organic and miscellaneous chemicals sector, responsible in 1963 for some 36% of the gross output of the whole chemical industry, is much the largest single sector, and should be broadly representative of trends in the industry as a whole. Gross output in the sub-sector amounted to £783·4 million in 1963. The index of output for chemicals and allied industries stood at 140 in 1968, compared with the 1963 base of 100. The wholesale selling price index for general chemicals stood at 102·9 in 1968, again compared with the 1963 base of 100. A 40% increase in output with a 2·9% increase in selling prices gives a 43·6% increase in sales, suggesting gross output of £1,126 million in 1968. The actual gross output in 1968 shown in the preliminary results is £1,143 million, so that estimated gross output was 1·3% lower than actual gross output.

Total purchases of materials in 1963 were £404·6 million. The index of the cost of materials and fuel used in chemicals and allied industries stood at 115·1 in 1968 against the 1963 base of 100. The 15·1% increase in material price allied to the 40% increase in output implies a 61·2% increase in materials costs, suggesting total costs of £651·9 million in 1968. Actual material costs in 1968 came to £664·3 million, so that estimated material costs were 1·9% less than actual material costs.

To establish wage and salary trends by the use of the Blue Book wage and salary trends, it is necessary to enlarge the definition of the chemical industry to include the mineral-oil refining industry, which was part of the chemical industry in the 1963 Standard Industrial Classification, but is a separate industry in the 1968 Classification. The 1969 Blue Book tables were based on the 1963 Classification.

On the basis of the employment data for the average total number of people employed, including working proprietors, the organic, inorganic and miscellaneous sector was responsible for 25·6% of total chemical industry employment in 1963 and for 24·7% in 1968. The fall in share over the period was some 3½%. The 1963 wage and salary bill at £112 million, was 29·2% of the total chemical industry bill of £384 million. A 3½% fall in this share, reflecting an identical fall in employment share, suggests a 28·2% share of the whole wage and salary bill of £528 million in 1968. Thus estimated wages and salaries come to £149 million, which is identical to the actual figure for 1968.

The relationship of the past figures to the forecast figures is not obtained by extrapolation alone, but rather by informed judgement constrained by the macro-economic trends. The technique is illustrated in Table 71 for the sales component of the forecast, and is broadly similar to that for the other components.

Table 71

Chemical Output and Prices

% change per annum

	1958–68 Actual	1963–8 Actual	1968–75 Forecast
1) Output of chemicals:	6·8	6·9	5·1
2) G.D.P. in constant prices:	3·3	3·8	3·0
Ratio of 1) to 2):	206%	182%	170%
1) Wholesale chemical prices:	0·6	1·0	1·4
2) All prices:	2·9	3·3	4·0
Ratio of 1) to 2):	21%	30%	35%

This sector of the chemical industry clearly has grown much more rapidly than the whole economy, and since basic relationships change only slowly, the industry is likely to continue to grow more rapidly than the national average. A good deal of its past growth, however, can be attributed to growth in exports, where the scope for increasing market penetration is diminishing; and so a lessening in the ratio of the growth in chemical output to the growth in G.D.P. in constant prices seems likely. Given as a constraint the previously determined estimated growth in G.D.P. in constant prices, the growth rate in chemical output of 5·1% is determined by multiplying the ratio of 170 by the G.D.P. growth rate of 3·0%.

Devaluation has lessened the threat from foreign firms in the home market and given better margins in the important export markets. Since the chemical industry is one of the U.K.'s major trading industries, it seems likely that it will be able to use this position to raise prices more rapidly than many other sectors of

U.K. industry. Thus it seems reasonable to expect the ratio of wholesale chemical price increases to all price increases to increase in relation to past experience, and thus future trends are established.

It is, of course, possible to argue that the relative trends in output and selling price will be different from those suggested above. Devaluation could lead to still faster export growth than in the past, and allow U.K. manufacturers to cut selling prices in foreign markets, maintain them in the home markets and still operate on much the same profit margins as obtained before devaluation. The choice between the alternatives depends on judgement based on knowledge of the industry.

The basic principles of this technique are straightforward, as can be seen above, and work well for major industry groupings. There are, however, considerable complexities involved when the assessment of particular narrowly specified industries is required, although no fundamental change in principle is involved. This can be overcome mainly by close study of the base statistics, and in this the expanded input–output tables are particularly useful. One particular problem not so far mentioned is the distortion caused by devaluation, since many sub-divisions of major industry groupings differ in their imported raw-material content. The input–output tables are of great assistance in determining exposure to this possible source of distortion. It is possibly appropriate to end on this note of caution, and to draw attention to the necessity to treat each industry as an individual case, requiring considerable background inquiry. Knowledge of the method of statistical compilation is indispensable, but probably the most important requirement in analysis and forecasting is the capacity to prefer common sense when it conflicts with strict formulae.

CHAPTER 13

Interest Rates and Security Prices

BY JAMES MORRELL

The question of forecasting monetary policy and the separate problems of forecasting profits in aggregate and for individual industries have been discussed in previous chapters. It now remains to link the three analyses so as to arrive at a basis of forecasting both interest rates and security prices.

Interest is a cost to business and short-term borrowings will result in a variable cost, since rates will fluctuate over time. In addition, given the much higher spectrum of interest rates at the end of the 1960s, the level of rates poses problems for certain business situations. Whether or not equity capital financing is preferred to fixed interest financing will depend upon the overall return on capital employed, the degree of risk and the market rate of interest. Since a present decision to borrow must rest on forecasts of future business operating results in relation to future rates of interest, a view of prospective interest rate levels is required.

Moreover, where a firm wishes to raise new capital and is able to be flexible in the timing of a new issue, it must be in a position to assess the level of the market and to form a judgement as regards the timing of the issue. If it appears likely that interest rates will fall in the short run it will pay the firm to defer the issue.

Similar considerations apply with respect to equity financing and issues. Not only is a short-term view of interest rate movements required, but a sophisticated analysis of profit movements, market levels, the basis of evaluation and of the individual share price in relation to the market as a whole is essential. This form of analysis becomes even more critical in the case of merger or acquisition projects. Management, therefore, has a need to understand the forces dictating movements in money and security markets, and will, on occasions, require forecasts of both interest rate and share price movements. This is probably the most difficult and hazardous forecasting problem discussed in this volume, with the possible exception of the balance of payments.

WHAT DETERMINES INTEREST RATES?

A rate of interest is a price of money. It is a price charged for the sacrifice of purchasing power and liquidity on the one side, and the price paid to acquire such resources on the other. If funds are plentiful in relation to demand, rates will tend to be low, and vice versa. As a general rule, therefore, the overall level of the stock of money in the community will be of very great importance with regard to the level of interest rates.

Yet this factor, taken in isolation, tells only part of the tale. The demand for funds is of equal importance and money is required not only to facilitate normal, every-day transactions, such as the housewife's shopping, but business and commercial transactions, for both home and overseas trade, purchase of capital plant and buildings, payment of wages, payment of taxes, for house purchase, dealings in the stock-market and so on.

The break-down of the money supply and the operation of monetary policy was discussed in Chapter 5. Suffice it to say here that if the national income and spending rises faster than the supply of money, then the stock of money has to be turned over more rapidly to satisfy the higher volume of transactions. In other words the velocity of circulation is forced up and some sectors of the community may have to struggle hard to get the funds they require. In this kind of situation the price of money tends to be bid up. In other words, interest rates rise.

This has been the prevailing tendency since the Second World War and is illustrated in Chart 38. It will be noted that from 1945 to 1964 the velocity of circulation rose, while the long-term rate of interest – as represented by the irredeemable government bond, 2½% Consols – rose in parallel, but with cyclical fluctuations. The break in this relationship since 1964 requires a detailed explanation and is bound up with a major change in investors' expectations.

Chart 38

VELOCITY AND THE LONG-TERM RATE OF INTEREST

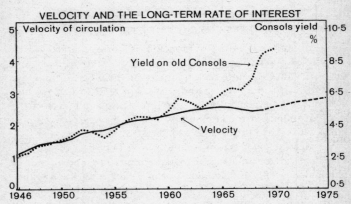

Given the large and much publicized balance of payments deficit, the accession of a Labour government and the strong possibility of devaluation, investors surmised (correctly) that the chances were for a faster rate of price inflation. From that point on, therefore, a shift in preference developed in favour of all forms of equity investment. In effect, the investing community began to switch from bonds to equities, with the result shown in Chart 38, namely that bond yields rose out of line with the normal monetary considerations. Ultimately, after devaluation, there was a sharp upward movement in equity prices, while bond prices fell and gilt-edge yields were forced up to all-time highs in 1969.

THE SIGNIFICANCE OF THE VALUE OF MONEY

This movement marked the pronounced change in investors' expectations. The illustration is important in that it draws attention to another facet of interest rates. Since money has a function as a store of value, the erosion of purchasing power through inflation has some relevance for the level of interest rates. Since the rate of interest is regarded as the price for money and for sacrifice of liquidity and immediate purchasing power, then any erosion in money values must be compensated in some fashion through the price of money, i.e. rates of interest.

The normal tendency, therefore, is for interest rates to rise as the price of commodities rises. Such a tendency will be distorted from time to time depending upon the methods employed to manage the monetary situation. For example, during the Second World War the economy was deliberately flooded with money in order to keep interest rates down. Even so, retail prices rose fairly rapidly. Over long periods, however, it is more likely that interest rates and retail prices will tend to move in the same direction. Whether or not investors have some predetermined notion of the acceptable real rate of interest, i.e. the rate of interest adjusted for changing purchasing power of money, is impossible to say. In any case, if such views are held they are unlikely to be formalized. Suffice it to say that over the past 150 years the real rate of interest on long-term government bonds has averaged less than 3%. Table 72 illustrates the movements for recent years. The returns, after allowing for the change in retail prices, have in fact been higher since devaluation in 1967. The average shows a real return of almost 3% for the seven-year period from 1964 to 1970 and is, if anything, slightly in excess of the long-term performance.

SHORT-TERM FLUCTUATIONS

Whether or not long-term rates of interest can be forecast for more than a relatively short period is debatable. Unless the assumptions concerning government policy, and monetary policy in particular, can be successfully predicted, it will not be possible to gauge the rough movements of interest rates. But even assuming that the forecaster has good ability to anticipate policy changes and to gauge the overall direction of economic management, it is by no means sure that changes in investors' expectations will be forecast with any practical degree of precision.

Table 72

The Real Rate of Interest

	Gross yield on $2\frac{1}{2}\%$ Consols	Change in retail prices	Real rate interest
	%	%	%
1964	6·0	+3·3	2·7
1965	6·4	+4·8	1·6
1966	6·8	+3·9	2·9
1967	6·7	+2·5	4·2
1968	7·4	+4·7	2·7
1969	8·9	+5·5	3·4
1970	9·2	+6·0	3·2
Averages	7·3	+4·4	2·9

It is necessary, therefore, to pay particular attention to short-term factors and short-term rates. Since Britain has a relatively open economy and is influenced to a great extent by developments in overseas trade, the balance of payments will always remain a sensitive area for economic policy. In practice the U.K. authorities have been obliged to pay the greatest attention to business developments in the United States. This is for two reasons: firstly, to take due account of the effects of the American business cycle on British export prospects, and secondly, because changes in the business climate in the U.S.A. will produce changes in interest rates which subsequently affect other capital markets. A rise in short-term rates in the United States will tend to pull up interest rates in other centres. This is particularly true in the case of London. During the 1960s the system has become even more sensitive through the development of the Eurodollar market. This market is truly international and has grown into a major world money system. A shortage of funds in the U.S.A. has resulted, in recent years, in American business looking for funds in the Eurodollar market. Eurodollar rates have thus been raised to higher levels and this market in turn has influenced rates in domestic markets.

To forecast interest rates, therefore, the analyst must have a view of developments in the United States. It would be unwise to assume that the magnitude of the changes can be forecast at all closely, but it should be feasible to gauge the changes in direction and to anticipate, with some success, whether rates are likely to move upwards or downwards and to assess the probable timing of turning points. From the British angle it will still be necessary to work from the balance of payments situation in order to identify the major influence affecting rates policy.

BANK RATE

The key rate in the past was Bank Rate. Bank Rate is a rate of re-discount of bills. The central bank in the leading economic systems helps to regulate monetary conditions and to maintain orderly markets by acting as the lender of last resort. In other words, the Bank of England (to take the British case) is available to make cash available to the banking and monetary system when all other normal sources have failed. The rate of interest at which the Bank is prepared to operate is linked to the re-discount rate, i.e. Bank Rate. This rate is published and is changed relatively infrequently. Other lending rates tend to be tied to Bank Rate and the clearing banks, for example, have operated a system whereby the rate of interest charged on overdrafts, and the rate paid for money on deposit, has varied directly with Bank Rate.

This pattern is no longer so powerful and important as in the past, and Bank Rate is no longer the key indicator for short-term money rates that it was for most of the nineteenth and twentieth centuries. Nevertheless, Bank Rate changes form an important part of the Bank of England's signalling mechanism so far as changes in monetary policy are concerned. For example, where the Bank is obliged to operate in such a way as to protect the balance of payments, then it may be necessary to tighten the money supply, make credit scarce and force interest rates higher. An increase in Bank Rate will be recognized, both at home and abroad, as a signal of the authorities' intentions so far as economic policy is concerned.

SHORT AND LONG RATES

Because of the central position accorded to short-term interest rates in the management of the business cycle it will be seen that changes in short-term rates must exercise a powerful influence on long-term rates. In so far as a change in short-term rates is associated with a change in credit policy, change in the money stock resulting from credit policy will, after a time-lag, influence the long-term rate of interest. In practice the market will move fairly quickly in response to such monetary changes, and where Bank Rate has been raised, for example, the prices of all bonds will tend to fall regardless of whether they are short or long.

The magnitude of changes in the rates will depend to some extent on how successful the market has been in the preceding period in anticipating the likely course of events. The difference between the short-term yields and the long-term bond yields tends to be either wide or narrow at the approach of turning points. If the yield differential is small then the chances are that the market is signalling a rise in long-term yields. Conversely, if the gap is particularly wide, the implication is probably that long-term yields are about to decline. Since money invested for longer periods and locked up in long-term bonds represents a greater sacrifice of liquidity or purchasing power than money invested in short-dated bonds, then the normal market prices will reflect the difference in a higher yield for long-term investment. The bond market generally displays a highly rational pattern of behaviour, and a careful scrutiny of the yield curve (i.e. the pattern of yields for the varying maturities of length of life of government stocks) will give guidance as to the general direction of interest rates.

The history of yields in isolation will give only an imperfect view of interest rates movements and influences. The pure theory cannot be abstracted from the yield histories unless the relevant changes in taxation are also known and understood. During the nineteenth century, for example, income tax was a negligible factor so far as interest yields were concerned. From the First World War in particular, the level of income tax has exerted a powerful influence on the bond market. This has become increasingly so since some classes of investors have been granted total, or partial, exemption from income tax on investment income. Pension Funds, for example, are not liable to tax, and gilt-edged investment has a very different appeal to the Pension Fund compared with the high surtax payer. In the latter case the erosion of income through tax and the virtual absence of capital gain makes bonds relatively unattractive as against equity investment. Other changes in the tax regulations, such as the exemption of capital gains on government bonds from long-term gains tax, have created a differential in favour of the gilt-edge market. Industrial debentures, for example, have not been accorded such favourable treatment.

INTEREST RATES AND EQUITIES

From what has been said about the influences affecting interest rates, there can be little doubt of the difficulties in constructing accurate forecasts. Yet an attempt to forecast is still of value, for on questions such as the timing of new issues of fixed-interest securities, a short-term forecast of interest rate movements and the behaviour of the bond market will be a useful guideline. What is abundantly clear is that both the balance of payments and a reading of changes in money supply will be indispensable for this exercise. The same will be true for forecasting share prices. This is so because the rate of interest is one of the two major considerations affecting the level of the equity market. The purchaser of a share in effect buys a future stream of income, namely the profits and earnings attributable to that share. In evaluating this future stream of income the buyer values the income at a certain rate of interest. None, or very little, of this evaluation is formalized and very few investors will have taken the trouble either to have assessed the likely flow of future income with any precision or to have calculated the appropriate rate of interest required for risk investment. Yet, although the individual investor may have analysed the share price in a purely subjective fashion, the market as a whole can be seen to have behaved, over long periods of time, in a consistent way.

Chart 39

GROWTH IN DIVIDENDS AND SHARE PRICES

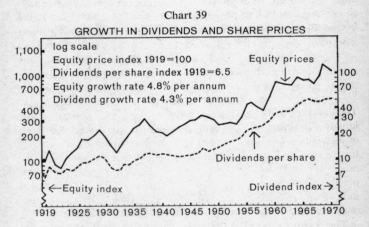

This is illustrated in Chart 39, showing the growth in both dividends and share prices since the First World War. Over this fifty-year period, dividends per share have grown at an average rate of 4·3% per annum. Share prices as a whole have grown by virtually the same amount at 4·7% per annum. The trend in both lines over the period is virtually identical and over specific cyclical periods the two lines can be seen to move in the same direction. This tendency is hardly surprising and when major movements occur the relationship between money factors and equity prices can be discerned. Thus in the great slump in the early 1930s the fall in profits associated with the difficult economic conditions was mirrored by a fall in dividends. The lower level of dividends and the difficult monetary conditions led inevitably to a sharp fall in share prices.

In more normal cyclical movements the change in interest rates and the level of the gilt-edged market can be seen to act as a leading indicator so far as the share market is concerned. In a recovery period, for example, the improvement in credit supply will bring about lower interest rates. After an interval the easier credit conditions will act as a spur to business, and a business recovery will set in. When the signs of recovery in profits begin to become apparent, then share prices rise, but there will have been a time-lag between the rise in bond prices and the rise in equities.

EQUITY GROWTH

The long-term movements in equity prices can be explained largely in terms of dividend growth. In a sense dividend movements are of greater significance than earnings per share, for the reason that earnings are frequently difficult to define with exactitude and precision. Dividends, on the other hand, are known precisely. Moreover, a change in a company's dividend rate is an indicator of the directors' assessment of the company's prospects, and therefore of the quality of the underlying earnings.

The illustration of growth over fifty years can be used as a means of determining the acceptable rate of interest on industrial equity investment. The argument can be illustrated more simply in relation to one single year. Thus, if it were known that the income from an investment was to grow indefinitely at a given rate, say $4\frac{1}{2}\%$ per annum, then, if all other monetary factors and preferences remained unchanged, the value of the income in one year's time would have risen by $4\frac{1}{2}\%$. In consequence the capital value of the security would have risen by a similar amount in a perfect market. This illustration is shown in Table 73. The sum of the capital yield and income yield is $9\frac{1}{2}\%$ before tax and this figure will be the appropriate rate of interest at which to discount a future stream of income in specific cases. The value of this approach is that some degree of certainty is attainable over a

Table 73

Equity Yield

Expected rate of growth	$4\frac{1}{2}\%$ per annum to infinity
Capital value at beginning of year	100
Capital value at end of year	$104\frac{1}{2}$
Capital yield (capital gain)	$4\frac{1}{2}\%$
Dividend yield – say	5% (gross)
TOTAL YIELD = Rate of Interest	$9\frac{1}{2}\%$

highly conjectural field. The fact that such a rate of interest on equity investment has obtained over a fifty-year period may be taken as a guide to the expectations of investors in general for this particular form of investment.

RISK

In practice it will be recognized that the degree of risk will vary considerably between investments, and that the appropriate rate of interest, for discounting purposes, must take account of the relative risk factors. In addition variations in the rate of interest in the bond market will influence the price of equities. If, for example, the bond yield rises then the rate of interest used to discount equity income must also be raised. In other words, a rough and ready equilibrium is established in markets, and some plausible relationship can be observed between bonds and equities.

The relationships can be seen in Table 74. It has been assumed that interest rates will remain unchanged, and therefore the price of bonds will be stable. In the example the total yield from equity is in excess of the yield on bonds. This would be appropriate where allowance is made for the additional riskiness of equities by comparison to bonds, and where bonds have a greater marketability than shares.

In the past, however, the relationship between bond and equity yields does not appear to have been particularly rational. The yield gap between the two classes of investment has varied considerably without any measurable and convincing pattern of

Table 74

Growth and Yields

	Bond yield	Equity yield
	%	%
Income yield, before tax	7½	5
Capital yield, before tax	nil	4½
Total yield, before tax	7½	9½
Income yield after, say, 40% income tax	4½	3
Capital yield after, say 30% gains tax	nil	3
TOTAL YIELD, AFTER TAX	4½	6

regard for risk. Yet the situation has improved, particularly since there is now far more knowledge and information concerning all classes of investment. Equity investment ought, in the future, to be far better informed than at any time in the past, and it is probable that persistent and rational relationships between bonds and equities will become apparent. In practice the market will probably make only minor allowance for the additional risk of equity investment, in which case the yield gap between bonds and equities will approximate to the potential growth rate from equity investment.

The position as it was in 1970 may well prove to be realistic so far as equity growth rates and the long-term rates of interest are concerned and the 1970 yield gap is appropriate on these grounds. The position is illustrated in Table 75. However, the fact that the equity yield after tax appears, on the assumptions, to be only slightly higher than the net bond yield suggests that equities are too highly priced in relation to bonds if allowance has to be made for the inferior marketability of equities, and that the initial yield gap between bonds and equities may well close to some extent in subsequent years.

Table 75

The Yield Gap

Long-term growth in equity dividends	$4\frac{1}{2}\%$ p.a.
Initial equity dividend income, before tax	$4\frac{3}{4}\%$
Capital growth, before tax	$4\frac{1}{2}\%$
Total yield, before tax	$9\frac{1}{4}\%$
Long-term rate of interest (yield on 2% Consols)	$9\frac{1}{4}\%$
Equity yield, after tax	$5\frac{3}{4}\%$
Bond yield, after tax	$5\frac{1}{2}\%$

RISK AND INDIVIDUAL SHARES

Although it is necessary to have some understanding of the factors determining market levels overall, the individual business will be more concerned with individual shares rather than market averages. Even so the principles discussed above with respect to equity prices as a whole must equally apply to the individual company shares. In Chart 39 the growth in share prices over a fifty-year period was shown to have mirrored the growth in dividends per share. In other words, share prices tend to reflect growth. In addition a share price must reflect the riskiness of the business in question, and it may be taken as a general rule that the higher the risk then the higher the rate of return required from such an investment.

Although there are several factors contributing to risk, the largest element appears to be volatility in profits. All businesses display cyclical characteristics, or to be more exact a company's profit record will, in nearly every case, show the effects of changing government policy and the resultant movement in the business cycle. Industries dependent upon credit, for example, will be more severely affected by changes in government regulation of the monetary system, and will tend to show more severe fluctuations in profits than the average. This factor is fully reflected in individual share prices.

Other risks, such as political uncertainty depending upon the country or the region in which the firm is operating, will also be reflected in the share price. In addition, the structure of management, over-dependence upon an important individual, dominant family shareholdings or uncertain prospects for the products in question will all be reflected in the individual share price. The point is worth making, since risk will be just as important as growth in many share price evaluations. As a general rule, the analyst should concentrate on these two factors of growth and risk in assessing the price to be paid for a share in relation to the market as a whole.

If the discounted cash flow principle was applied to the potential stream of equity income and no other factors were taken into account, the respective growth rates of earnings and dividends per share of individual companies would be the determinant of share prices. In practice it will be observed that two securities with the same long-term average rate of growth in dividends per share can be valued quite differently in the market because of a different degree of risk and volatility. Thus, it will be found, for example, that capital goods producers are valued on a higher uncertainty and risk basis than retailers.

THE PRICE OF AN ASSET

For the purposes of acquisition and mergers the business will need to take a whole range of factors into account in assessing the relative share prices. Not only must the growth risk and volatility factors be considered of the two companies in question, but the management factors must be assessed, as well as political influences. In addition some regard will need to be paid to asset value per share. It has been observed earlier in the chapter that the price of an asset is what it will earn. Balance-sheet values are

315

not necessarily a reliable indicator either of the current potential profitability of the assets in question or of the potential of those assets in the hands of another management. Management will inevitably look critically at balance-sheet values in any acquisition study. Nevertheless, if a bid or merger proposition is to be harmoniously agreed, due account must be taken of the balance-sheet asset value per share of the company under consideration.

THE MARKET AS A GUIDE

Finally, the stock-market itself contains an invaluable historical record of a company and its performance in relation to the economy and the market as a whole. In some senses the stock-market is a barometer of informed public opinion so far as the particular company's business is concerned. Relevant information concerning the company is received by the market from many different sources. The share price is constantly adjusted in response to such information. The record over a period of years will show whether or not an individual share price has kept in line with the market as a whole. Any marked divergence in performance will tell the analyst something about the characteristics of the company concerned. Since major trends change only gradually, it will be unlikely for an adverse relative performance in the last business cycle to be converted into a favourable relative performance in the next cycle. In this way the market can be used to glean information about the standing and status of individual firms.

Even so, it would be mistaken to believe that analysis can proceed with a fine degree of exactitude. Chart 40 gives an excellent illustration of market volatility. Earnings per share are plotted from 1965, with a tentative projection up to 1975. Share prices are also plotted from the same base year, with 1962 = 100, for both earnings and share prices. It will be seen that the market level swung sharply above trend and then fell dramatically to a point below trend. If the market as a whole is capable of such wild gyrations the analyst is well warned that individual price movements can be even more eccentric. Yet for most problems in business, stock-market analysis can be limited to the shorter-run considerations. Whether it is a question of determining the timing of a new issue or an acquisition, the horizon for the decision in question may well be limited to less

Chart 40

SHARE PRICES AND EARNINGS

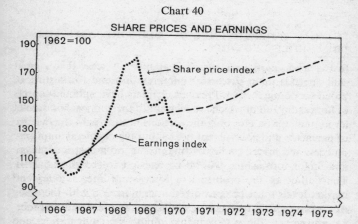

than two years. If this is so, the problem will best be approached by concentrating on the specific factors which will influence both the market and the individual company in the short-run.

It may be concluded, therefore, that the over-riding consideration is to have a thoroughgoing analysis of the factors of real importance to the business so far as government intervention in managing the economy is concerned. Not only will government policy determine the state of the money markets and have an over-riding influence on the interest rate levels, but other government actions will set the scene for business activity and influence the profit cycle. The analyst's task, therefore, in stock market problems, as with many other business-forecasting uncertainties, is to maintain as full an appreciation as possible of the way in which the economy is run by the political machine. In the British case, it is probably true to say that the over-riding consideration

317

for at least another decade will be the U.K. balance of payments.. Reasonable interpretation of the balance of payments changes and a sound assessment of the political reactions to the balance of payments problems will give good warnings of changes in the all-important factors bearing upon the security markets.

THE INTER-DEPENDENCE OF THE FORECASTS FOR THE WHOLE ECONOMY

In the stock-market analysis it is abundantly clear that a great deal depends upon successful interpretation and forecasting of broad economic factors. Previous chapters have outlined aspects of forecasting, all of which are relevant to the appraisal of market levels and stocks. Not only the sections dealing with the balance of payments and government policy, but the chapters on money, on costs and prices, on forecasting profits, on industrial analysis and sector forecasting, will all be relevant to security analysis. The outline of the problems of forecasting interest rates and market levels must be considered in conjunction with the study of the economic forecasts as a whole, and an observation of market and security price movements in both the United States and Britain over many years bears out the need to concentrate first and foremost on overall market movements. An investment policy based upon the successful reading of major cyclical movements will have beaten the average performance handsomely, for the plain fact is that most stocks move up and down in sympathy with the general direction of the market.

From this and the preceding chapters it will be seen that forecasting is far from being an exact science. Even if one major obstacle could be removed and we had exact and reliable statistics at hand describing the past, the need for judgement in forecasting would be as great as ever.

Nevertheless, a great deal can be done to minimize the uncertainty surrounding the future and, weak as much of the statistical material is, it is perfectly possible to construct forecasts which are positively helpful. Although it is not possible to provide an example of a forecast case study as comprehensive as the coverage of all the material contained in the individual chapters, an illustration is given in the following appendix of the forecasting stages for a single industry, working from the assumptions on which the forecast for the whole economy is based, to the relationships between the economy and the industry and then to the industry forecasts.

APPENDIX

A Forecast of Some Aspects of Consumers' Spending

Before forecasting the economy as a whole, it is necessary to adjust and reconcile the historical data. The following tables illustrate the corrections made to the official statistics published at that time.

Major Adjustments Applied to the Official Statistics

£ million

Current prices	1968		1969		1970	
	Basic	Actual	Basic	Actual	Basic	Actual
	3rd yr		2nd yr		1st yr	
Incomes from employment	+50	−20	+160	+179	+360	+354
Private consumption	+80	+100	+160	+217	+445	+456
Total incomes	+75	−13	+200	+225	+570	+547.
Total spending	+100	−20	+240	+374	+700	+715

1963 prices	1968	1969	1970
	Actual	Actual	Actual
Private consumption	+91	+179	+348
Total spending	−11	+312	+547

Spending and Incomes in Current Prices

£ million

	1964	1965	% change	1966	% change	1967	% change	1968	% change	1969	% change	1970	% change
Exports	6,110	6,550	+7.2	7,000	+6.9	7,150	+2.1	8,695	+21.6	9,750	+12.1	10,900	+11.8
Investment	5,860	6,325	+7.9	6,720	+6.2	7,250	+7.9	7,785	+7.4	8,140	+4.6	8,850	+8.7
Public consumption	5,550	6,090	+9.7	6,610	+8.5	7,280	+10.1	7,735	+6.3	8,160	+5.5	9,095	+11.5
Private consumption	21,510	22,965	+6.8	24,290	+5.8	25,370	+4.4	27,230	+7.3	28,900	+6.1	31,580	+9.3
Stocks	650	410		280		220		190		400		590	
Total final spending	39,680	42,340	+6.7	44,900	+6.0	47,270	+5.3	51,635	+9.2	55,350	+7.2	61,015	+10.2
Less: Imports	6,710	6,840	+1.9	7,095	+3.7	7,580	+6.8	9,050	+19.4	9,510	+5.1	10,540	+10.8
Less: Tax adjustment	3,950	4,420	+11.9	5,055	+14.4	5,210	+3.1	6,055	+16.2	7,015	+15.8	7,625	+8.7
TOTAL	29,020	31,080	+7.1	32,750	+5.4	34,480	+5.3	36,530	+5.9	38,825	+6.3	42,850	+10.4
Incomes from employment	19,695	21,200	+7.6	22,765	+7.4	23,765	+4.4	25,280	+6.4	27,320	+8.1	30,780	+12.7
Company profits	4,590	4,760	+3.7	4,440	-6.7	4,620	+4.1	4,995	+8.1	4,955	-0.8	5,065	+2.2
Public-sector profits	1,025	1,090	+6.3	1,140	+4.6	1,230	+7.9	1,480	+20.0	1,585	+7.1	1,550	-2.2
Self-employment and rent	4,010	4,360	+8.7	4,725	+8.4	5,060	+7.1	5,410	+6.9	5,780	+7.0	6,370	+10.2
Total domestic income	29,320	31,410	+7.1	33,070	+5.3	34,670	+4.8	37,165	+7.2	39,640	+6.7	43,765	+10.4
Less: Stock appreciation	-300	-330		-320		-185		-635		-815		-915	
TOTAL	29,020	31,080	+7.1	32,750	+5.4	34,480	+5.3	36,530	+5.9	38,825	+6.3	42,850	+10.4

Spending and Incomes in Current Prices: *not* seasonally adjusted

	1968				1969				1970			
	i	ii	iii	iv	i	ii	iii	iv	i	ii	iii	iv
Exports	2,090	2,125	2,210	2,270	2,225	2,470	2,505	2,550	2,590	2,775	2,625	2,910
Investment	1,950	1,860	1,935	2,040	2,065	1,935	2,015	2,125	2,170	2,085	2,230	2,365
Public consumption	1,950	1,900	1,925	1,960	2,030	1,980	2,030	2,120	2,170	2,235	2,315	2,375
Private consumption	6,520	6,700	6,785	7,225	6,780	7,180	7,260	7,680	7,225	7,810	8,030	8,515
Stocks	−125	140	130	45	120	145	85	50	−10	245	200	155
Total final spending	12,385	12,725	12,985	13,540	13,220	13,710	13,895	14,525	14,145	15,150	15,400	16,320
Less: Imports	2,235	2,230	2,325	2,260	2,325	2,380	2,415	2,390	2,435	2,715	2,670	2,720
Less: Tax adjustment	1,350	1,450	1,545	1,710	1,585	1,725	1,835	1,870	1,720	1,915	1,980	2,010
TOTAL	8,800	9,045	9,115	9,570	9,310	9,605	9,645	10,265	9,990	10,520	10,750	11,590
Employment incomes	6,100	6,220	6,385	6,575	6,495	6,750	6,840	7,235	7,155	7,525	7,795	8,305
Company profits	1,220	1,310	1,150	1,315	1,165	1,260	1,200	1,330	1,190	1,275	1,185	1,415
Public-sector profits	405	330	300	445	480	360	325	420	465	370	310	405
Self-employment and rent	1,300	1,330	1,375	1,405	1,370	1,425	1,470	1,515	1,495	1,550	1,630	1,695
Total domestic incomes	9,025	9,190	9,210	9,740	9,510	9,795	9,835	10,500	10,305	10,720	10,920	11,820
Less: Stock appreciation	−225	−145	−95	−170	−200	−190	−190	−235	−315	−200	−170	−230
TOTAL	8,800	9,045	9,115	9,570	9,310	9,605	9,645	10,265	9,990	10,520	10,750	11,590

Spending and Output in 1963 Prices

	1964	1965	1966	% change	1967	% change	1968	% change	1969	% change	1970	% change
Exports	6,020	6,315	6,575	+4·1	6,575	nil	7,380	+12·2	8,070	+9·3	8,395	+4·0
Investment	5,725	5,970	6,115	+2·4	6,515	+6·5	6,770	+3·9	6,780	+0·1	6,860	+1·2
Public consumption	5,310	5,460	5,595	+2·5	5,860	+4·7	5,890	+0·5	5,830	−1·0	5,930	+1·7
Private consumption	20,835	21,260	21,670	+1·9	22,080	+1·9	22,680	+2·7	22,860	+0·8	23,690	+3·6
Stocks	640	395	265		190		140		365		420	
Total final spending	38,530	39,400	40,220	+2·1	41,220	+2·5	42,860	+4·0	43,905	+2·4	45,295	+3·2
Less: Imports	6,500	6,545	6,715	+2·6	7,125	+6·1	7,635	+7·2	7,795	+2·1	8,255	+5·9
Less: Tax adjustment	3,745	3,745	3,860	+3·1	4,015	+4·0	4,205	+4·7	4,255	+1·2	4,470	+5·1
TOTAL	28,285	29,110	29,645	+1·8	30,080	+1·5	31,020	+3·1	31,855	+2·7	32,570	+2·2
1963 = 100												
Manufacturing	109·0	112·4	114·3	+1·7	114·3	nil	120·4	+5·3	125·1	+3·9	127·2	+1·7
Construction	111·6	114·3	115·4	+1·0	119·4	+3·5	120·8	+1·2	118·5	−1·9	115·0	−3·0
Industrial production	108·6	111·7	113·3	+1·4	113·9	+0·5	118·8	+4·3	122·4	+3·0	124·0	+1·3
Services	103·1	106·2	108·5	+2·2	110·9	+2·2	113·4	+2·3	116·1	+2·4	119·6	+3·0
TOTAL	105·54	108·62	110·62	+1·8	112·24	+1·5	115·75	+3·1	118·86	+2·7	121·55	+2·3

Spending and Output in 1963 Prices: seasonally adjusted

	1968				1969				1970			
	i	ii	iii	iv	i	ii	iii	iv	i	ii	iii	iv
Exports	1,825	1,775	1,870	1,910	1,895	2,005	2,080	2,090	2,100	2,100	2,010	2,185
Investment	1,675	1,695	1,695	1,705	1,715	1,700	1,690	1,675	1,705	1,710	1,725	1,720
Public consumption	1,490	1,480	1,470	1,450	1,465	1,450	1,460	1,455	1,475	1,490	1,495	1,470
Private consumption	5,790	5,585	5,620	5,685	5,665	5,715	5,730	5,750	5,775	5,920	5,985	6,010
Stocks	−110	+60	+75	+115	+115	+85	+45	+120	nil	+125	+120	+175
Total final spending	10,670	10,595	10,730	10,865	10,855	10,955	11,005	11,090	11,055	11,345	11,335	11,560
Less: Imports	1,915	1,875	1,920	1,925	1,940	1,940	1,935	1,980	1,995	2,075	2,030	2,155
Less: Tax adjustment	1,075	1,005	1,055	1,070	1,035	1,060	1,075	1,085	1,085	1,105	1,155	1,125
TOTAL	7,680	7,715	7,755	7,870	7,880	7,955	7,995	8,025	7,975	8,165	8,150	8,280

1963 = 100	i	ii	iii	iv	i	ii	iii	iv	i	ii	iii	iv
Manufacturing	117·6	119·5	121·1	123·4	123·2	125·1	125·9	126·3	125·1	127·1	126·8	129·3
Construction	120·3	121·5	120·2	121·3	117·9	121·2	117·8	116·8	115·0	116·3	116·0	112·5
Industrial production	116·7	118·2	119·2	121·8	121·3	122·7	122·8	123·1	122·5	124·2	123·7	125·3
Services	113·0	112·8	113·0	114·1	114·7	115·6	116·6	117·2	116·3	120·0	120·0	122·2
TOTAL	114·63	115·15	115·75	117·46	117·61	118·73	119·33	119·78	119·03	121·87	121·64	123·58

Price Factors: 1963 = 100

	1964	1965	1966	% change	1967	% change	1968	% change	1969	% change	1970	% change
Exports	101·5	103·6	106·5	+2·9	108·8	+2·1	117·8	+8·3	120·9	+2·6	129·9	+7·4*
Investment	102·4	106·0	109·9	+3·7	111·3	+1·3	115·0	+3·4	120·1	+4·4	129·0	+7·4
Public consumption	104·6	111·5	118·2	+5·9	124·3	+5·2	131·4	+5·8	140·0	+6·5	153·5	+9·7
Private consumption	103·3	108·0	112·1	+3·8	114·9	+2·5	120·1	+4·5	126·5	+5·3	133·3	+5·5
*Retail Price Index	107·0	112·1	116·5	+3·9	119·4	+2·5	125·0	+4·7	131·8	+5·4	140·2	+6·4
Imports	103·2	104·4	105·7	+1·2	106·4	+0·7	118·6	+11·5	122·0	+2·9	127·7	+4·6
Tax adjustment	105·4	118·0	130·9	+10·9	129·7	−0·9	144·0	+11·0	165·0	+14·6	170·5	+3·3
Total product	102·6	106·8	110·5	+3·5	114·7	+3·8	117·8	+2·7	121·9	+3·5	131·6	+7·9

	1968				1969				1970			
	i	ii	iii	iv	i	ii	iii	iv	i	ii	iii	iv
Exports	115·7	117·1	118·8	119·5	120·7	119·9	120·6	122·3	126·6	128·7	130·9	133·3
Investment	113·3	115·1	115·8	116·0	117·6	118·9	120·9	122·7	124·3	127·8	130·9	132·8
Public consumption	128·5	129·8	133·6	133·9	135·9	138·4	141·6	144·0	144·2	151·9	157·8	160·3
Private consumption	116·6	119·6	121·8	122·3	123·5	125·5	127·9	128·6	129·2	131·8	135·4	136·6
*Retail Price Index	122·1	125·0	125·7	127·2	129·7	131·8	132·0	133·7	136·2	139·5	141·1	144·0
Imports	117·0	117·7	120·0	119·7	120·3	121·6	122·9	123·3	125·1	127·8	128·8	128·7
Tax adjustment	128·4	145·7	148·8	152·6	156·8	163·7	174·8	164·5	165·2	172·5	173·1	170·7
Total product	116·4	117·2	118·9	118·6	120·1	120·8	122·0	124·5	126·6	129·3	133·6	136·4

* 16.1.62 = 100

The next stage is to establish the assumptions on which the overall forecasts are to be based. These are set out in the next two tables, first as a calendar and secondly as a set of rates of change and ratios.

THE ASSUMPTIONS

1971–6

   i) Minor, but no major wars
   ii) World inflation, but at declining rate
  iii) I.M.F. Drawing Rights $3 bn a year or more
  iv) 3 in 4 chance of effective E.E.C. entry 1973
   v) U.K. static labour supply
  vi) Gradual movement towards equal pay
 vii) Rising productivity trend 3–3½% p.a.
viii) Money supply rises at 7% p.a.
  ix) Switch from direct to indirect taxation

1971

   i) Resumption of 4% U.S. growth rate
  ii) Strong expansion of U.K. credit
 iii) Continuing government pressure on both public and private sector employers to reduce wage increases
 iv) Continued exchange rate uncertainties
  v) Exchange rates permitted to fluctuate more widely (3% either side of parity)
 vi) World trade acceleration at end year

1972

   i) Further acceleration of U.S. output
  ii) Purchase tax cut on luxury items
 iii) Reform of company taxation, effective 1973
 iv) Income tax and surtax on earned incomes merged
  v) Agricultural and housing subsidies reduced
 vi) Further increase in food import levies

vii) Odds on chance of increased price of gold and firming of exchange rates 1972 or 1973

1973

i) First adjustments towards E.E.C. systems
ii) V.A.T., probable rates: 20%, 12%, 6% and zero
iii) Income tax cut via higher allowances
iv) Reduction in net corporate taxation
v) Earnings-related Social Security contributions increased
vi) Pension increase

1974

i) Ending of Regional Employment Premium
ii) Social Security contributions increased
iii) General Election

1975

i) World trade slowdown
ii) Tighter money
iii) 3 in 4 chance of devaluation of the pound
iv) Social Security contributions increased
v) Pension increase
vi) Increased rates of V.A.T.

1976

Increased company taxation

The details of the forecast are constructed on the following assumptions and the resultant estimates are set out in tables showing labour factors, incomes, expenditure, costs and prices. Personal income and spending is derived from these estimates and shown separately, followed by a breakdown of consumers' spending by major categories.

The Assumptions

% Change on previous year	1971		1972		1970	1971	1972	1973	1974	1975	1976
	iii	iv	i	ii							
World output*	–	–	–	–	+2·5	+4·0	+6	+5·5	+4·5	+4	+4·5
World trade volume†	–	–	–	–	+10	+7	+8	+10	+9	+8	+8
World trade value†	–	–	–	–	+15	+12	+11·5	+12·5	+11	+10	+11
U.K. import prices	+4·7	+5·8	+5·8	+3·9	+4·7	+4·3	+4·0	+2·5	+2·4	+2·0	+9·2
U.K. export prices	+7·5	+6·7	+5·0	+3·8	+7·5	+7·6	+3·5	+2·7	+2·4	+2·5	+5·9
Wage rates	+12·0	+9·5	+7·5	+7·0	+10·3	+12·0	+7·4	+7·2	+7·2	+7·0	+6·8
Hourly earnings	+11·5	+10·2	+8·5	+8·5	+14·4	+13·0	+8·7	+8·4	+8·2	+8·0	+7·6
* O.E.C.D.											
† Manufactures											
Money supply	–	–	–	–	+9·4	+11·0	+10·5	+7·0	+6·0	+5·0	+4·5
Consumer credit	Relaxed	Relaxed	Relaxed	Relaxed	–	Relaxed	Relaxed	–	–	Tightened	–
Savings ratio – %	8·3	8·1	9·1	7·7	8·8	8·8	7·7	7·7	7·8	7·7	7·9
Personal tax rate – %‡	18·7	18·6	21·0	20·5	19·4	19·5	20·0	19·5	19·6	19·7	20·4
Indirect tax rate – %§	12·4	12·5	11·8	12·5	12·5	12·3	12·4	12·9	13·3	13·4	13·8
Social security taxes %‖	5·6	5·9	6·1	5·9	7·0	6·2	6·1	6·4	6·3	6·6	7·0
Govt. current spending ¶	+9·5	+9·0	+8·4	+9·8	+11·5	+10·8	+9·3	+9·1	+8·3	+8·7	+8·3
Public sector capital spending	+10·5	+10·9	+11·4	+12·2	+11·7	+10·7	+11·8	+11·7	+10·1	+7·6	+7·0
Net corporate taxation %**	35	35	35	33	37	35	33	31	30	30	31

‡ Income tax, surtax and employees' contributions as a % of total personal incomes, excluding grants
§ Indirect taxes, net of subsidies, import duties and import levies, as a % of final spending
‖ Including S.E.T. and R.E.P. on a % of wages and salaries bill
¶ Central and local government

Labour Productivity and incomes

% Change on previous year

YEARS	1965	1966	1967	1968	1969	1970	1971	1972	1973	1974	1975	1976
Total output	+2·9	+1·8	+1·5	+3·1	+2·7	+2·2	nil	+4·5	+3·9	+3·7	+2·6	+2·2
Total hours worked	−0·1	−1·2	−2·4	−0·3	−0·3	−1·7	−3·1	−0·6	−0·2	nil	nil	−0·2
Output per manhour	+3·0	+3·0	+4·0	+3·4	+3·0	+4·0	+3·2	+5·1	+4·1	+3·7	+2·6	+2·4
Labour incomes:												
Hourly wage rates	+6·3	+6·7	+4·0	+6·8	+5·4	+10·3	+12·0	+7·4	+7·2	+7·2	+7·0	+6·8
Income per manhour	+7·3	+8·3	+6·8	+6·2	+8·8	+14·4	+13·0	+8·7	+8·4	+8·2	+8·0	+7·6
Wages and salaries	+7·2	+7·0	+4·7	+5·9	+8·5	+12·5	+9·4	+8·0	+8·2	+8·2	+8·0	+7·4
Disposable incomes*	+6·7	+6·5	+4·6	+5·9	+6·8	+9·8	+9·0	+7·7	+8·0	+7·7	+7·1	+6·9

QUARTERS	1970 i	ii	iii	iv	1971 i	ii	iii	iv	1972 i	ii	iii	iv
Total output	+1·2	+2·6	+1·9	+3·2	−0·3	−0·7	+0·6	+0·2	+4·8	+4·2	+4·1	+4·8
Total hours worked	−1·2	−1·7	−1·8	−2·2	−2·3	−3·5	−3·3	−3·4	−1·9	−0·7	−0·3	+0·4
Output per manhour	+2·4	+4·4	+3·8	+5·5	+2·0	+2·9	+4·0	+5·9	+6·8	+4·9	+4·4	+4·4
Labour incomes:												
Hourly wage rates	+7·3	+9·4	+11·0	+13·2	+13·6	+13·2	+12·0	+9·5	+7·5	+7·0	+4·1	+7·6
Income per manhour	+11·6	+12·9	+15·6	+17·3	+15·8	+14·5	+11·5	+10·2	+8·5	+8·5	+8·7	+9·0
Wages and salaries	+10·3	+11·0	+13·5	+14·7	+13·1	+10·5	+7·8	+6·5	+6·4	+7·7	+8·4	+9·4
Disposable incomes*	+7·2	+8·8	+11·0	+11·9	+11·1	+9·1	+8·1	+8·0	+7·8	+8·3	+7·2	+6·9

* Total personal disposable incomes

Incomes

YEARS	1965	1966	1967	1968	1969	1970	1971	1972	1973	1974	1975	1976
No. at Work 1963 = 100	102·5	102·7	100·9	100·3	100·0	99·1	97·1	96·3	96·5	96·8	97·2	97·2
£ thousand million												
Employment incomes	21·20	22·77	23·76	25·28	27·32	30·78	33·63	36·43	39·59	42·82	46·44	50·15
Public-sector profits	1·09	1·14	1·23	1·48	1·58	1·54	1·51	1·54	1·58	1·61	1·64	1·64
Company profits	4·76	4·44	4·62	5·00	4·96	5·05	5·48	6·27	6·93	7·53	7·48	7·64
Other income*	4·36	4·72	5·06	5·41	5·78	6·35	6·86	7·29	7·78	8·10	8·58	9·06
Stock appreciation	−0·33	−0·32	−0·19	−0·64	−0·81	−0·92	−0·97	−0·72	−0·70	−0·71	−0·80	−1·41
TOTAL	31·08	32·75	34·48	36·53	38·83	42·80	46·51	50·81	55·18	59·35	63·34	67·08

QUARTERS†	1970				1971				1972			
	i	ii	iii	iv	i	ii	iii	iv	i	ii	iii	iv
£ thousand million												
Employment incomes	7·16	7·53	7·79	8·30	8·06	8·30	8·37	8·90	8·65	8·95	9·13	9·70
Public-sector profits	0·46	0·37	0·31	0·40	0·41	0·37	0·32	0·41	0·42	0·38	0·32	0·42
Company profits	1·19	1·26	1·18	1·42	1·23	1·36	1·36	1·53	1·55	1·60	1·48	1·64
Other income*	1·49	1·54	1·62	1·69	1·61	1·66	1·78	1·81	1·74	1·77	1·87	1·91
Stock appreciation	−0·31	−0·20	−0·17	−0·23	−0·33	−0·22	−0·16	−0·26	−0·20	−0·17	−0·15	−0·20
TOTAL	9·99	10·50	10·73	11·58	10·98	11·47	11·67	12·39	12·16	12·52	12·65	13·47

* Rent and self-employment
† Quarterly figures are not adjusted for seasonal variations

Total Expenditure: Current Prices, unadjusted

£ thousand million

YEARS	1965	1966	1967	1968	1969	1970	1971	1972	1973	1974	1975	1976
Exports	6·55	7·00	7·15	8·70	9·75	10·90	11·98	12·83	13·77	14·72	15·62	17·87
Investment	6·33	6·72	7·25	7·79	8·14	8·88	9·56	10·50	12·02	13·42	14·42	15·45
Public consumption	6·09	6·61	7·28	7·74	8·16	9·10	10·08	11·01	12·02	13·02	14·16	15·33
Private consumption	22·96	24·29	25·37	27·23	28·90	31·58	34·43	37·69	40·62	43·59	46·58	49·58
Change in stocks	0·41	0·28	0·22	0·19	0·40	0·51	0·24	0·51	0·73	0·99	0·77	0·51
Less: Imports	6·84	7·10	7·58	9·05	9·51	10·54	11·66	12·73	13·79	14·95	15·94	18·09
Less: Adjustments*	4·42	5·05	5·21	6·06	7·02	7·63	8·13	9·00	10·19	11·44	12·27	13·58
TOTAL	31·08	32·75	34·48	36·53	38·83	42·80	46·51	50·81	55·18	59·35	63·34	67·08

QUARTERS	1970				1971				1972			
	i	ii	iii	iv	i	ii	iii	iv	i	ii	iii	iv
Exports	2·59	2·78	2·63	2·91	2·76	3·07	3·06	3·09	3·08	3·26	3·22	3·27
Investment	2·17	2·09	2·26	2·36	2·37	2·28	2·38	2·54	2·57	2·48	2·62	2·82
Public consumption	2·17	2·24	2·32	2·37	2·44	2·51	2·53	2·59	2·65	2·75	2·78	2·83
Private consumption	7·23	7·81	8·03	8·51	7·88	8·53	8·73	9·29	8·82	9·31	9·49	10·07
Change in stocks	−0·01	0·22	0·15	0·15	0·08	0·10	0·06	nil	0·05	0·17	0·13	0·16
Less: Imports	2·44	2·72	2·67	2·72	2·73	2·97	3·02	2·93	2·99	3·21	3·29	3·24
Less: Adjustments*	1·72	1·92	1·98	2·01	1·81	2·05	2·08	2·19	2·02	2·24	2·29	2·45
TOTAL	9·99	10·50	10·73	11·59	10·98	11·47	11·67	12·39	12·16	12·52	12·65	13·47

* Less: taxes on expenditure, plus: subsidies, includes S.E.T. from 1966 to mid-1973

Total Expenditure: 1963 Prices, seasonally adjusted

£ thousand million

YEARS	1965	1966	1967	1968	1969	1970	1971	1972	1973	1974	1975	1976
Exports	6·32	6·57	6·57	7·38	8·07	8·40	8·58	8·87	9·27	9·68	10·02	10·82
Investment	5·97	6·12	6·51	6·77	6·78	6·88	6·90	7·17	7·57	7·80	8·28	8·46
Public consumption	5·46	5·60	5·86	5·89	5·83	5·93	6·02	6·20	6·33	6·50	6·68	6·86
Private consumption	21·26	21·67	22·08	22·68	22·86	23·69	24·13	25·34	26·35	27·32	28·24	28·66
Change in stocks	0·40	0·27	0·19	0·14	0·36	0·40	0·17	0·35	0·45	0·59	0·43	0·27
Less: Imports	6·55	6·71	7·13	7·64	7·79	8·26	8·75	9·19	9·71	10·29	10·75	11·17
Less: Adjustments*	3·75	3·86	4·02	4·21	4·25	4·47	4·50	4·72	4·92	5·13	5·30	5·46
TOTAL	29·11	29·65	30·08	31·02	31·86	32·57	32·56	34·01	35·35	36·65	37·61	38·45

QUARTERS	1970				1971				1972			
	i	ii	iii	iv	i	ii	iii	iv	i	ii	iii	iv
Exports	2·10	2·10	2·01	2·19	2·07	2·16	2·18	2·18	2·20	2·21	2·23	2·24
Investment	1·71	1·72	1·74	1·27	1·71	1·72	1·73	1·74	1·75	1·78	1·80	1·84
Public consumption	1·48	1·49	1·50	1·47	1·49	1·50	1·52	1·52	1·53	1·54	1·55	1·58
Private consumption	5·78	5·92	5·99	6·01	5·90	6·00	6·07	6·16	6·23	6·31	6·37	6·43
Change in stocks	nil	0·12	0·11	0·18	0·06	0·02	0·04	0·05	0·04	0·06	0·10	0·15
Less: Imports	2·00	2·08	2·03	2·16	2·17	2·19	2·19	2·20	2·24	2·28	2·32	2·35
Less: Adjustments*	1·09	1·11	1·16	1·13	1·10	1·12	1·13	1·15	1·16	1·17	1·19	1·20
TOTAL	7·98	8·17	8·15	8·28	7·96	8·10	8·20	8·30	8·34	8·44	8·54	8·69

* Less: taxes on expenditure, plus: subsidies, includes S.E.T. from end 1966 to mid-1973

Costs and Prices – Total

% Change on previous year

YEARS	1965	1966	1967	1968	1969	1970	1971	1972	1973	1974	1975	1976
Labour costs per unit	+4·6	+6·8	+2·5	+3·7	+5·8	+10·3	+8·6	+3·1	+4·2	+4·1	+5·6	+5·7
Import prices* (goods and services)	+1·3	+1·2	+0·7	+11·5	+2·9	+4·7	+4·3	+4·0	+2·5	+2·4	+2·0	+9·2
Total costs	+3·9	+5·7	+2·1	+5·3	+5·2	+9·2	+7·7	+3·3	+3·9	+3·8	+4·9	+6·4
Prices:												
Total output	+4·1	+3·5	+3·8	+2·7	+3·5	+7·8	+8·7	+4·6	+4·5	+3·7	+4·0	+3·6
Exports* (goods and services)	+2·2	+2·9	+2·1	+8·3	+2·5	+7·5	+7·6	+3·5	+2·7	+2·4	+2·5	+5·9
Consumer	+4·6	+3·8	+2·5	+4·5	+5·3	+5·5	+7·0	+4·3	+3·7	+3·5	+3·4	+4·8
Retail	+4·8	+3·9	+2·5	+4·7	+5·4	+6·4	+9·0	+4·7	+3·9	+3·7	+3·6	+5·1

QUARTERS	1970				1971				1972			
	i	ii	iii	iv	i	ii	iii	iv	i	ii	iii	iv
Labour cost per unit	+9·7	+9·1	+11·0	+10·9	+12·6	+10·8	+5·8	+5·8	+1·3	+2·3	+4·5	+3·9
Import prices* (goods and services)	+4·0	+5·1	+4·8	+4·4	+3·2	+3·7	+4·7	+5·8	+5·8	+3·9	+3·2	+3·1
Total costs	+8·6	+8·3	+9·7	+9·6	+10·7	+9·4	+5·6	+5·8	+1·3	+2·3	+4·5	+3·9
Prices												
Total output	+5·4	+6·8	+9·3	+9·5	+10·5	+9·9	+8·0	+6·8	+5·6	+4·8	+4·1	+3·9
Exports*	+4·9	+7·3	+8·5	+9·0	+8·0	+7·7	+7·5	+6·7	+5·0	+3·8	+3·0	+2·7
Consumer (goods and services)	+4·6	+5·0	+5·8	+6·2	+6·8	+7·6	+7·0	+6·6	+5·8	+3·8	+3·8	+3·9
Retail	+5·0	+5·9	+6·8	+7·7	+8·6	+9·8	+9·5	+8·3	+6·7	+4·2	+3·9	+3·9

* Effects of changes in tariffs and duties are *not* included

% *Change on previous year*

Costs and Prices in Manufacturing Industry

YEARS	1965	1966	1967	1968	1969	1970	1971	1972	1973	1974	1975	1976
Labour costs per unit	+6·4	+6·7	−2·7	+3·6	+5·4	+10·2	+8·1	+3·4	+4·5	+4·4	+6·0	+6·0
Material and fuel prices	+1·2	+2·5	−0·5	+9·1	+3·5	+3·9	+5·2	+3·1	+9·8	+5·8	+2·9	+7·0
Total costs	+3·8	+4·6	−1·6	+6·3	+4·4	+7·1	+6·6	+3·2	+7·2	+5·1	+4·4	+6·5
Prices:												
Home sales	+3·8	+2·6	+1·2	+4·0	+3·9	+6·6	+7·6	+4·1	+11·7	+6·9	+3·6	+5·7
Exports	+2·8	+4·6	+1·8	+8·6	+3·2	+7·7	+7·4	+3·5	+3·0	+2·6	+2·8	+6·2
Total sales	+3·6	+3·1	+1·4	+5·2	+3·7	+6·9	+7·6	+4·0	+9·5	+5·8	+3·4	+5·8

QUARTERS	1970				1971				1972			
	i	ii	iii	iv	i	ii	iii	iv	i	ii	iii	iv
Labour costs per unit	+7·9	+9·5	+12·7	+11·4	+10·4	+9·0	+6·1	+6·6	+2·7	+3·4	+3·9	+3·4
Material and fuel prices	+5·6	+4·8	+2·9	+2·6	+2·7	+5·5	+6·9	+5·7	+4·0	+2·4	+2·7	+2·8
Total costs	+6·7	+7·2	+7·8	+7·0	+6·6	+7·2	+6·5	+6·1	+3·4	+2·9	+3·3	+3·1
Prices:												
Home sales	+5·0	+6·2	+7·0	+8·0	+8·2	+8·3	+7·8	+6·2	+4·8	+3·9	+3·7	+3·9
Exports	+3·1	+5·4	+6·9	+8·3	+9·7	+9·3	+8·6	+6·6	+4·8	+3·5	+2·6	+3·0
Total sales	+4·5	+6·0	+7·0	+8·1	+8·5	+8·6	+8·0	+6·3	+4·8	+3·8	+3·4	+3·7

£ thousand million

YEARS	1965	1966	1967	1968	1969	1970	1971	1972	1973	1974	1975	1976
Incomes *	24·91	26·53	27·75	29·40	31·36	34·43	37·53	40·42	43·59	46·94	50·25	53·72
Credit changes	+0·01	−0·04	+0·12	+0·03	−0·15	+0·17	+0·22	+0·40	+0·39	+0·33	+0·20	+0·10
Less: Savings	1·96	2·10	2·50	2·20	2·31	3·02	3·32	3·13	3·36	3·68	3·87	4·24
Consumer spending:												
Current prices	22·96	24·29	25·37	27·23	28·90	31·58	34·43	37·69	40·62	43·59	46·58	49·58
Rate of change %	+6·8	+5·8	+4·4	+7·3	+6·1	+9·3	+9·0	+9·5	+7·8	+7·3	+6·9	+6·4
Constant prices†	21·26	21·67	22·08	22·68	22·86	23·69	24·13	25·34	26·35	27·32	28·24	28·66
Rate of change %	+2·0	+1·9	+1·9	+2·7	+0·8	+3·6	+1·9	+5·0	+4·0	+3·7	+3·4	+1·5
Consumer prices:												
Rate of change %	+4·6	+3·8	+2·5	+4·5	+5·3	+5·5	+7·0	+4·3	+3·7	+3·5	+3·4	+4·8

QUARTERS	1970				1971				1972			
	i	ii	iii	iv	i	ii	iii	iv	i	ii	iii	iv
Incomes *	8·01	8·41	8·76	9·25	8·90	9·18	9·47	9·99	9·60	9·96	10·16	10·70
Credit changes	−0·01	+0·06	+0·05	+0·07	−0·01	+0·06	+0·06	+0·11	+0·09	+0·12	+0·09	+0·10
Less: Savings	0·77	0·66	0·78	0·81	1·01	0·71	0·79	0·81	0·87	0·77	0·76	0·73
Consumer spending:												
Current prices	7·23	7·81	8·03	8·51	7·88	8·53	8·73	9·29	8·82	9·31	9·49	10·07
Rate of change %	+6·6	+8·8	+10·6	+10·9	+9·1	+9·2	+8·7	+9·1	+11·9	+9·1	+8·7	+8·4
Constant prices†	5·78	5·92	5·99	6·01	5·90	6·00	6·07	6·16	6·23	6·31	6·37	6·43
Rate of change %	+1·9	+3·6	+4·5	+4·5	+2·2	+1·4	+1·4	+2·5	+5·6	+5·2	+4·9	+4·4
Consumer prices:												
Rate of change %	+4·6	+5·0	+5·8	+6·2	+6·8	+7·6	+7·0	+6·6	+5·8	+3·8	+3·8	+3·9

* Personal disposable incomes † 1963 prices (seasonally adjusted)

Consumers' Spending: Current Prices, unadjusted

£ thousand million

YEARS	1965	1966	1967	1968	1969	1970	1971	1972	1973	1974	1975	1976
Food	5·065	5·321	5·483	5·672	5·988	6·363	6·835	7·199	7·560	7·960	8·398	8·870
Housing	2·592	2·848	3·077	3·321	3·625	4·040	4·597	5·042	5·604	6·097	6·597	7·151
Clothing	2·099	2·154	2·188	2·320	2·417	2·634	2·799	2·987	3·161	3·322	3·509	3·681
Durables	1·775	1·770	1·889	2·059	1·964	2·275	2·554	2·850	3·105	3·305	3·367	3·424
Alcoholic drink	1·432	1·534	1·623	1·739	1·873	2·112	2·325	2·462	2·637	2·804	2·989	3·150
Tobacco	1·428	1·504	1·512	1·578	1·694	1·720	1·671	1·833	1·975	2·094	2·217	2·330
Fuel and light	1·087	1·161	1·208	1·340	1·421	1·495	1·601	1·698	1·817	1·973	2·122	2·256
Non-essentials*	10·694	11·302	11·902	12·999	13·755	15·328	16·927	18·931	20·503	22·144	23·737	25·272

	1971				1972			
QUARTERS	i	ii	iii	iv	i	ii	iii	iv
Food	1·654	1·691	1·694	1·796	1·743	1·781	1·787	1·888
Housing	1·066	1·163	1·174	1·194	1·211	1·279	1·269	1·283
Clothing	0·547	0·684	0·670	0·898	0·608	0·725	0·709	0·945
Durables	0·607	0·652	0·628	0·667	0·692	0·728	0·695	0·735
Alcoholic drink	0·452	0·556	0·609	0·708	0·486	0·583	0·643	0·750
Tobacco	0·383	0·423	0·434	0·431	0·426	0·472	0·475	0·460
Fuel and light	0·497	0·370	0·306	0·428	0·533	0·386	0·336	0·443
Non-essentials*	3·733	4·199	4·452	4·543	4·299	4·667	4·914	5·051

	1970				1971
QUARTERS	i	ii	iii	iv	i
Food	1·521	1·569	1·579	1·694	1·654
Housing	0·952	1·018	1·030	1·040	1·066
Clothing	0·515	0·643	0·622	0·854	0·547
Durables	0·526	0·585	0·570	0·594	0·607
Alcoholic drink	0·400	0·489	0·573	0·650	0·452
Tobacco	0·388	0·450	0·450	0·432	0·383
Fuel and light	0·491	0·347	0·268	0·389	0·497
Non-essentials*	3·358	3·783	4·081	4·106	3·733

* Durables, alcoholic drink, services, etc.

Consumers' Spending: Current Prices, unadjusted

% Change on previous year

YEARS	1965	1966	1967	1968	1969	1970	1971	1972	1973	1974	1975	1976
Food	+3·5	+5·1	+3·0	+3·4	+5·6	+6·3	+7·4	+5·3	+5·0	+5·3	+5·5	+5·6
Housing	+10·6	+9·9	+8·0	+7·9	+9·2	+11·4	+13·8	+9·7	+11·1	+8·8	+8·2	+8·4
Clothing	+6·5	+2·6	+1·6	+6·0	+4·2	+9·0	+6·3	+6·7	+5·8	+5·1	+5·6	+4·9
Durables	+1·7	−0·3	+6·7	+9·0	−4·6	+15·8	+12·3	+11·6	+8·9	+6·4	+1·9	+1·7
Alcoholic drink	+7·8	+7·1	+5·8	+7·1	+7·7	+12·8	+8·0	+10·1	+7·1	+6·3	+6·6	+5·4
Tobacco	+6·3	+5·3	+0·5	+4·4	+7·4	+1·5	−2·8	+9·7	+7·7	+6·0	+5·9	+5·1
Fuel and light	+8·7	+6·8	+4·0	+10·9	+6·0	+5·2	+7·1	+6·3	+7·0	+8·6	+7·6	+6·3
Non-essentials*	+7·4	+5·7	+5·3	+9·2	+5·8	+11·4	+10·4	+11·8	+8·3	+8·0	+7·2	+6·5

QUARTERS	1970				1971				1972			
	i	ii	iii	iv	i	ii	iii	iv	i	ii	iii	iv
Food	+5·3	+5·5	+6·7	+7·4	+8·7	+7·8	+7·3	+6·0	+5·4	+5·3	+5·5	+5·1
Housing	+11·0	+10·9	+11·7	+12·2	+12·0	+14·2	+14·0	+14·8	+13·6	+10·0	+8·1	+7·5
Clothing	+6·8	+7·3	+8·7	+11·8	+6·2	+6·4	+7·7	+5·2	+11·2	+6·0	+5·8	+5·2
Durables	+12·2	+13·6	+15·4	+22·2	+15·4	+11·5	+10·2	+12·3	+14·0	+11·7	+10·7	+10·2
Alcoholic drink	+10·5	+12·4	+16·2	+11·5	+13·0	+13·7	+6·3	+8·9	+7·5	+4·9	+5·6	+5·9
Tobacco	−1·0	+2·3	+3·2	+1·4	−1·3	−6·0	−3·6	−0·2	+11·2	+11·6	+9·4	+6·7
Fuel and light	+4·9	+4·2	+7·2	+5·1	+1·2	+6·6	+14·2	+10·0	+7·9	+4·3	+9·8	+3·5
Non-essentials*	+7·1	+11·2	+13·4	+13·6	+11·2	+11·0	+9·1	+10·6	+15·2	+11·1	+10·4	+11·2

* Durables, alcoholic drink, services, etc.

Consumers' Spending: 1963 Prices, seasonally adjusted

£ thousand million

YEARS	1965	1966	1967	1968	1969	1970	1971	1972	1973	1974	1975	1976
Food	4·770	4·854	4·903	4·926	4·930	4·984	5·022	5·072	5·111	5·163	5·209	5·240
Housing	2·279	2·337	2·457	2·555	2·633	2·724	2·824	2·961	3·107	3·247	3·390	3·516
Clothing	2·026	2·025	2·027	2·117	2·123	2·195	2·203	2·287	2·377	2·434	2·512	2·560
Durables	1·724	1·699	1·779	1·851	1·701	1·851	1·949	2·136	2·277	2·378	2·368	2·310
Alcoholic drink	1·246	1·284	1·323	1·377	1·407	1·501	1·567	1·617	1·678	1·728	1·775	1·810
Tobacco	1·224	1·264	1·271	1·265	1·250	1·248	1·168	1·211	1·220	1·220	1·220	1·215
Fuel and light	1·035	1·068	1·097	1·151	1·224	1·277	1·309	1·350	1·413	1·473	1·536	1·600
Non-essentials*	9·926	10·122	10·325	10·666	10·700	11·262	11·604	12·454	13·122	13·783	14·373	14·529

QUARTERS	1970				1971				1972			
	i	ii	iii	iv	i	ii	iii	iv	i	ii	iii	iv
Food	1·237	1·242	1·250	1·255	1·263	1·246	1·252	1·261	1·266	1·266	1·269	1·271
Housing	0·672	0·676	0·685	0·691	0·695	0·702	0·708	0·719	0·725	0·735	0·745	0·756
Clothing	0·531	0·554	0·549	0·561	0·531	0·553	0·556	0·563	0·563	0·568	0·575	0·581
Durables	0·429	0·454	0·479	0·489	0·451	0·466	0·502	0·530	0·519	0·522	0·538	0·557
Alcoholic drink	0·363	0·363	0·395	0·380	0·386	0·391	0·394	0·396	0·399	0·401	0·407	0·410
Tobacco	0·295	0·319	0·322	0·312	0·284	0·290	0·297	0·297	0·299	0·302	0·305	0·305
Fuel and light	0·327	0·326	0·310	0·314	0·320	0·330	0·328	0·331	0·333	0·336	0·339	0·342
Non-essentials*	2·713	2·803	2·869	2·877	2·807	2·879	2·929	2·989	3·044	3·103	3·132	3·175

* Durables, alcoholic drink, services, etc.

Consumers' Spending: 1963 Prices, seasonally adjusted

% Change on previous year

YEARS	1965	1966	1967	1968	1969	1970	1971	1972	1973	1974	1975	1976
Food	nil	+1·8	+1·0	+0·5	nil	+1·1	+0·8	+1·0	+0·8	+1·0	+0·9	+0·6
Housing	+3·8	+2·6	+5·1	+4·0	+3·1	+3·5	+3·7	+4·9	+4·9	+4·5	+4·4	+3·7
Clothing	+4·3	nil	+0·1	+4·4	+0·3	+3·4	+0·4	+3·8	+3·9	+2·4	+3·2	+1·9
Durables	nil	−1·5	+4·7	+4·1	−8·1	+8·8	+5·3	+9·6	+6·6	+4·4	−0·4	−2·4
Alcoholic drink	−1·4	+3·0	+3·0	+4·1	+2·2	+6·7	+4·4	+3·2	+3·8	+3·0	+2·7	+2·0
Tobacco	−3·6	+3·3	+0·6	−0·5	−1·2	−0·2	−6·4	+3·7	+0·7	nil	nil	−0·4
Fuel and light	+6·4	+3·2	+2·7	+4·9	+6·3	+4·3	+2·5	+3·1	+4·7	+4·2	+4·3	+4·2
Non-essentials*	+2·5	+2·0	+2·0	+3·3	+0·3	+5·3	+3·0	+7·3	+5·4	+5·0	+4·0	+1·1

QUARTERS	1970				1971				1972			
	i	ii	iii	iv	i	ii	iii	iv	i	ii	iii	iv
Food	+0·4	+1·2	+1·5	+1·2	+2·1	+0·3	+0·2	+0·5	+0·2	+1·4	+1·4	+0·8
Housing	+3·5	+3·0	+3·5	+3·8	+3·4	+3·8	+3·4	+4·1	+4·3	+4·7	+5·2	+5·1
Clothing	+1·9	+2·4	+3·4	+5·8	nil	−0·2	+1·3	+0·4	+6·0	+2·7	+3·4	+3·2
Durables	+8·1	+6·8	+6·9	+13·5	+5·1	+2·6	+4·8	+8·4	+15·1	+12·0	+7·2	+5·1
Alcoholic drink	+4·3	+6·1	+10·6	+5·6	+6·3	+7·7	−0·3	+4·2	+3·4	+2·6	+3·3	+3·5
Tobacco	−2·3	nil	+2·5	−1·0	−3·7	−9·1	−7·8	−4·8	+5·3	+4·1	+2·7	+2·7
Fuel and light	+4·8	+4·5	+4·4	+3·6	−2·1	+1·2	+5·8	+5·4	+6·7	+1·8	+3·4	+3·3
Non-essentials*	+2·4	+5·4	+6·1	+6·7	+3·5	+2·7	+2·1	+3·9	+8·4	+7·8	+6·9	+6·2

* Durables, alcoholic drink, services, etc.

The method by which consumers' spending in aggregate is broken down into forecasts for individual sectors of consumers' spending is illustrated in the following tables, in which the rate of growth over the past ten years and five years are shown for separate categories. The estimates are given in current and constant prices and the price factors are shown separately.

The growth rates for each category are also shown as a ratio to growth in consumers' spending as a whole, and the experience over the past ten and five year periods are used as a guide to forecasting the average growth rates for the forecast period. The fact that this has to be done for current and constant values as well as prices, and the three sets of figures reconciled, ensures a fair degree of consistency.

Growth end Relative Growth Rates
% p.a. (ratio to total spending)

	1959–69		1964–9		1969–75	
Bread and cereals:						
current	3·5	(57)	3·5	(56)	4·8	(60)
constant	−0·2	(−107)	−0·8	(−140)	−0·8	(−123)
price	3·7	(109)	4·3	(105)	5·6	(130)
Sugar preserves and	3·6	(59)	3·8	(61)	4·9	(61)
confectionery	0·1	(4)	0·1	(5)	–	(–)
	3·5	(103)	3·7	(90)	4·9	(115)
Dairy products	3·6	(59)	4·2	(68)	5·8	(73)
	1·4	(54)	0·7	(35)	1·4	(40)
	2·2	(65)	3·5	(85)	4·3	(100)
Beverages	2·9	(48)	3·2	(52)	3·8	(48)
	1·9	(73)	1·9	(95)	2·4	(69)
	1·0	(29)	1·3	(32)	1·4	(32)
Footwear	4·5	(74)	3·8	(61)	5·4	(68)
	2·0	(77)	1·2	(60)	2·2	(63)
	2·5	(74)	2·6	(63)	3·1	(72)

Growth and Relative Growth Rates – *continued*

	1959–69		1964–9		1969–75	
Menswear	4·5	(74)	3·7	(60)	5·8	(73)
	2·0	(77)	0·9	(45)	2·3	(66)
	2·5	(74)	2·8	(68)	3·4	(78)
Women's and infant's	4·8	(79)	4·5	(73)	6·5	(81)
wear	3·1	(119)	2·4	(120)	3·2	(91)
	1·6	(47)	2·1	(51)	3·2	(75)
Beer	6·8	(111)	6·8	(110)	7·4	(93)
	2·6	(100)	3·7	(165)	2·6	(103)
	4·1	(121)	3·0	(73)	4·7	(110)
Wines and spirits	7·5	(123)	6·2	(100)	8·3	(104)
	3·4	(131)	0·6	(30)	3·6	(103)
	4·0	(118)	5·6	(137)	4·5	(105)
Books, newspapers	6·4	(105)	7·2	(116)	8·6	(108)
and magazines	–	–	−0·4	(−120)	0·5	(14)
	6·4	(188)	7·6	(185)	8·1	(188)
Chemists' goods	6·4	(105)	6·1	(98)	7·1	(89)
	3·2	(123)	1·8	(90)	2·7	(77)
	3·1	(91)	4·2	(102)	4·3	(100)
Vehicle running costs	14·2	(233)	14·5	(244)	12·3	(154)
	10·1	(388)	8·3	(415)	7·7	(220)
	3·7	(109)	5·7	(139)	4·3	(100)
Cinema	−1·9	(−131)	−1·3	(−120)	−0·3	(−104)
	−8·2	(−415)	−8·6	(−530)	−8·2	(−334)
	6·9	(203)	8·0	(195)	8·6	(200)
Other entertainments	7·9	(130)	7·7	(124)	9·2	(115)
	5·7	(219)	2·7	(135)	4·7	(134)
	2·1	(62)	4·9	(120)	4·3	(100)

Finally, this kind of generalized forecast is used as a guideline to construct more detailed forecasts. In the case of a forecast for multiple stores (given below), key ratios are calculated relating the sector to consumers' spending and the economy. Taking into account the main assumptions for the sector and the latest information on the industry, forecasts are constructed for both the short term and long term, drawing out sales, price, cost and profit series.

Key Ratios

The forecast to 1975 is derived from the following key demand factors and ratios:

	1968–75 % per annum increase	
Volume		
Gross Domestic Product	2·9	same as previous five years
Consumers' spending	3·1	above previous five years
Value		
Gross Domestic Product	7·1	above previous five years
Consumers' spending	7·3	above previous five years
Prices		
All goods and services	4·1	above previous five years
Retail	4·3	above previous five years

Ratios of growth rates	1958–68 %	1963–8 %	1968–75 %
Value			
Retail sales/Consumers' spending	69	76	75
Multiple stores/Retail sales	179	170	148

These result in the following forecasts:

	1968–75 % per annum increase	
Total value of retail sales	5·4	above previous five years
Value of sales of multiple stores	8·0	same as previous five years

Long-Term Prospects

1 Further reductions in income tax and reductions in the higher rates of purchase tax will reverse a slower sales trend and produce high rates of growth in 1973–4.

2 U.K. entry into the Common Market in 1973 will lead to higher food prices and changes in the pattern of spending.

3 Prices of durable goods will rise faster but with little change in volume.

Multiple Stores Sales

Type of shop

	1969 £m.	1975 £m.	Change %
Food and supermarkets	2,145	3,330	+55
Clothing and footwear	1,025	1,490	+45
Durable goods	605	1,070	+77
All other	960	1,630	+70
TOTAL	4,735	7,520	+59

4 Competition will remain keen. In some sectors increased profits will arise from faster turnover and smaller margins.

5 On average profit margins will recover in 1973 and then flatten out, below levels obtained in the mid-sixties.

Mutiple Stores

£ million	1964	1965	1966	1967	1968	1969	1970	1971	1972	1973	1974	1975
Sales	3,250	3,560	3,815	4,025	4,405	4,735	5,145	5,570	5,980	6,500	7,020	7,520
Less: Purchases	2,280	2,485	2,630	2,775	3,025	3,252	3,495	3,775	4,065	4,380	4,685	5,005
Less: Labour	465	510	575	615	680	738	815	880	935	1,010	1,095	1,185
Less: Rent, etc.	155	180	215	235	265	285	315	360	410	460	515	570
Total costs	2,900	3,175	3,420	3,625	3,970	4,275	4,625	5,015	5,410	5,850	6,295	6,760
Equals Gross trading profits	350	385	395	400	435	460	520	555	570	650	725	760
Profit margins %	10·8	10·8	10·4	9·9	9·9	9·7	10·1	10·0	9·5	10·0	10·3	10·1
change on previous year %												
Sales	+8·1	+9·5	+7·1	+5·5	+9·4	+7·5	+8·7	+8·3	+7·4	+8·7	+8·0	+7·1
Purchases	+7·5	+9·0	+5·8	+5·5	+9·0	+7·5	+7·5	+8·0	+7·7	+7·7	+7·0	+7·0
Labour	+8·1	+9·6	+12·7	+7·0	+10·6	+8·5	+10·4	+8·0	+6·3	+8·0	+8·4	+8·2
Rent, etc.	+7·7	+16·1	+19·4	+9·3	+12·8	+7·5	+10·5	+14·3	+13·9	+12·2	+12·0	+10·7
Total costs	+7·2	+9·5	+7·7	+6·0	+9·5	+7·7	+8·2	+8·4	+7·9	+8·1	+7·6	+7·4
Gross trading profits	+17	+10	+3	+1	+9	+6	+13	+7	+3	+14	+12	+5

Conclusions

1 Over the next five years the most rapid sales growth is expected in durable goods shops.

2 Multiples will increase their share of total retail trade, at the expense of independents and co-operative societies, from 36% in 1969 to 37% in 1970 and 42% in 1975.

Bibliography

Aldcroft, Derek, and Fearon, Peter, *Economic Growth in Twentieth Century Britain*, Macmillan, 1969.

Ashton, D., and Simister, L., *The Role of Forecasting in Planning*, Staples Press, 1970.

Bagley, William A., *Facts and How to Find Them*, Pitman, 1962.

Bain, A. D., *The Control of the Money Supply*, Penguin Books, 1970.

Ball, J., and Burns, T., 'The Prospect for Faster Growth in Britain', *National Westminster Bank Review*, November 1968.

Bank of England, *The Operation of Monetary Policy since the Radcliffe Report*, December 1969.

Beckerman and Associates, *The British Economy in 1975*, N.I.E.S.R., Cambridge University Press, 1965.

Bratt, E. C., *Business Forecasting*, John Wiley, New York, 1956.

Brittan, Samuel, *Steering the Economy, The Role of the Treasury*, Secker & Warburg, 1969.

Brown, R. G., *Exponential Smoothing for Predicting Demand*, Operations Research Society of America, November 1956.

Butler, W. F., and Kavesh, R. A., *How Business Economists Forecast*, Prentice Hall, Englewood Cliffs, New Jersey, 1966.

Cairncross, Sir Alec, 'Economic Forecasting', *Economic Journal*, December 1969.

Cambridge University Department of Applied Economics, *A Programme for Growth*, Chapman & Hall, 1962. (And subsequent issues in a series.)

Cave, Richard E., and Associates, *Britain's Economic Prospects*, The Brookings Institution, Allen & Unwin, 1968.

Clarke, W. M., *Britain's Invisible Earnings*, BNEC, 1967.

Denison, E. F., *Why Growth Rates Differ*, The Brookings Institution, Washington, 1967.

Dorfman, R., Samuelson, P. A., and Solow, R. M., *Linear Programming and Economic Analysis*, McGraw Hill, New York, 1958.

Economic Trends, 'Short-Term Economic Forecasting in the U.K.', August 1964.

Economic Trends, 'Short-term Forecasts of Income, Expenditure and Saving', February 1968.

Edwards, R., *Economic Planning and Electricity Forecasting*, The Electricity Council, 1966.

Fourth Report from the Estimates Committee, *Government Statistical Services*, H.M.S.O., 1966.

Geary, R. C., *Europe's Future in Figures*, North-Holland Publishing Coy, Amsterdam, 1962.

Institute of Costs and Works Accountants, *Introduction to Business Forecasting*, 1959.

Jones, E. O., and Morrell, J. G., 'Environmental Forecasting in British Industry', *Journal of Management Studies*, Vol. 3, 1966.

Jouvenel, B. de, *The Art of Conjecture*, Weidenfeld & Nicolson, 1967.

Kahn, H., and Wiener, A. J., *The Year 2000*, Macmillan, New York, 1967.

Kaldor, N., *The Causes of the Slow Rate of Growth of the United Kingdom*, Cambridge University Press, 1966.

Kaldor, N., 'The New Monetarism', *Lloyds Bank Review*, July 1970.

Leontief, W., *Input–Output Economics*, Oxford University Press, New York, 1966.

Mason, R. D., *Statistical Techniques in Business and Economics*, Irwin, Homewood, Illinois, 1967.

Maddison, Angus, *Economic Growth in the West*, Allen & Unwin, 1964.

Morrell, James, *Business Forecasting for Finance and Industry*, Gower Press, London, 1969.

National Plan, The, Cmnd 2764, 1965.

National Accounts Statistics: Sources and Methods, H.M.S.O., 1968.

N.I.E.S.R. Review, 'The Change in the Relationship Between Unemployment and Earnings Increases: A Review of Some Possible Explanations', November 1970.

N.I.E.S.R. Review, 'A Long-Term View of Housing', November 1961.

N.I.E.S.R., 'Short-Term Forecasting of Housing Development', August 1967.

Nicholson, J. L., 'The Measurement of Quality Changes', *Economic Journal*, September 1967.

O.E.C.D., *Techniques of Economic Forecasting*, 1965.

Paish, F. W., 'Business Cycles in Britain', *Lloyds Bank Review*, October 1970.

Paish, F. W., 'How the Economy Works', *Lloyds Bank Review*, July 1968.

Paish, F. W., *Long-Term and Short-Term Interest Rates in the United Kingdom*, Manchester University Press, 1962.

Prest, A. R., *Public Finance*, Ebenezer Baylis, London, 1960.

Schwarz, A. J., 'Why Money Matters', *Lloyds Bank Review*, October 1969.

United Nations, *Studies in Long-Term Economic Projections for the World Economy*, New York, 1964.

Wilson, Aubrey, *The Assessment of Industrial Markets*, Hutchinson, 1968.

Wolfe, H. D., *Business Forecasting Methods*, Holt, Rinehart and Winston, New York, 1966.

Walters, A. A., *Money in Boom and Slump*, I.E.A. Hobart Paper, 44.

Statistical Sources

All table and chart material has been taken from the following sources. Publishers are shown in parentheses.

Annual Abstract of Statistics (Central Statistical Office – C.S.O.)

British Economy: Key Statistics 1900–66 (*The Times* on behalf of the London and Cambridge Economic Service)

National Income and Expenditure (Blue Book) (C.S.O.)

Census of Population (Registrars General, H.M.S.O.)

Census of Production (Department of Trade and Industry – D.T.I.)

Census of Distribution (D.T.I.)

Family Expenditure Survey (H.M.S.O.)

Household Food Consumption and Expenditure (H.M.S.O.)

Commissioners of Inland Revenue Annual Report (H.M.S.O.)

Report of the Commissioners of H.M. Customs and Excise (H.M.S.O.)

Monthly Digest of Statistics (C.S.O.)

Trade and Industry (D.T.I.)

Business Monitor (D.T.I.)

Department of Employment Gazette (H.M.S.O.)

Financial Statistics (C.S.O.)

Bank of England Quarterly (Bank of England)

Economic Trends (C.S.O.)

National Institute Economic Review (*N.I.E.S.R.*) (N.I.E.S.R.)

Abstract of Regional Statistics (C.S.O.)

Framework Forecasts, a private subscription service issued by James Morrell and Associates. Data shown in *Framework Forecasts* differs from the official sources, since the official figures are 'corrected' for analytical purposes before incorporation to the historical series shown in *Framework Forecasts*.

Notes on Contributors

JAMES MORRELL. Chairman of James Morrell & Associates Ltd, economic advisers and forecasting specialists. He has spent most of his working career in business forecasting.

Born in 1923, he was educated at Christ's Hospital and, after war service in the R.A.F., at Ruskin College and Wadham College, Oxford, where he graduated in philosophy, politics and economics. After working for the Ford Motor Company on project analysis he joined a leading firm of stockbrokers as an investment analyst, and spent ten years in the City before forming his own company. Since 1960 he has headed a team of forecasters drawn from different firms in industry and commerce and has developed its forecasting work to the point where the firm's monthly service 'Framework Forecasts' is widely circulated in business and government circles.

He is Economic Editor of the journal *Management Today*, writes and lectures widely on various business subjects, is responsible for the *Sunday Telegraph* 'Business Forecast' and is economic adviser to a number of leading industrial companies, stockbrokers and merchant banks. He is a Fellow of the Royal Statistical Society, and a member of the Society of Investment Analysts, the Long-Range Planning Society and the Business Economists Group. He is the author of *Business Forecasting for Finance and Industry*, and is Visiting Professor of Business Finance at the University of Bradford.

L. S. STANILAND. Director of James Morrell & Associates and economic adviser to a number of leading companies. He has been engaged for the past fifteen years as a business economist, first in the steel industry and then as Economic Research Officer with the British Railways Board.

D. F. V. ASHBY. Economist with Bankers Trust and formerly with James Morrell & Associates. He was previously with the Bank of London & South America, the Government Economic Service and the Economist Intelligence Unit.

C. C. DAVIS. Economist with National & Grindlays Bank engaged in assessing economic trends and their impact on the monetary system of the countries in which the Bank operates. He previously worked as an investment analyst with a London firm of stockbrokers.

C. D. BARNARD. Economist of the British Tourist Authority since 1966. He was previously head of the forecasting unit at British Insulated Callender's Cables, after spending several years forecasting for E.M.I. and Morphy-Richards. He has also had experience in banking both at home and overseas.

T. LAUGHARNE. Economist with James Morrell & Associates. He was previously with the Corporate Planning and Economics Department of Esso Europe and Esso Petroleum, and formerly an economist with Kodak.

R. J. HALL. Director of James Morrell & Associates and economic adviser to a number of leading businesses. He was previously Economic Adviser to the Post Office Central Headquarters, and formerly head of the Market Analysis Section, British Iron and Steel Federation.

SANDRA MASON. A senior research officer at London Graduate School of Business Studies. She was previously a free-lance financial consultant, and for eight years with a leading merchant bank as economist and senior financial analyst.

B. ASHER. Company economist with Standard Telephones – part of I. T. & T. He has had previous experience as an economist with Elliott Automation and English Electric. He worked as research assistant for the Royal Commission on the Monetary System, and is a part-time Director of James Morrell & Associates.

R. B. MCDANIEL. Economist with Thomas Tilling, an industrial holding company with wide interests, including manufacture and distribution of building materials. He specializes in investigations into new industries and acquisitions.

ALLAN F. HODGSON. Economist with Ivory & Sime, investment managers in Edinburgh. Previously with a Scottish investment trust, he has had considerable experience in working with industry models based on input–output data in collaboration with James Morrell & Associates.

MELVYN ROWE. Investment analyst with leading Scottish investment trust. He has specialized in industrial forecasting in collaboration with James Morrell & Associates.

Index

Acquisitions, role of financial forecasts, 27; assessing relative share prices, 315–16

Actuaries/Stock Exchange 'Classification of Quoted Securities', 284

Administration, constraint on economic changes, 83, 152

Agriculture, financing subsidies, 146; price support and R.P.I. forecasting, 171; income from self-employment, 189

Alcoholic drinks and tobacco, 149, 150; weighting in R.P.I. and R.R.P.I., 172, 173

Annual Abstract of Statistics, 282, 294

Assumptions, place in forecasting, 78, 136, 265, 266, 286–7, 289; internal and external, 78; influence of Government policy, 79; 'firm' and 'future', 79–81; on economic growth, 239

Australia, British interests, 220

Aviation, earnings from, 92; price deflators, 94

Balance of payments, 39; and swings in profitability, 22; ante-dated statistics, 32; influence on economic policy, 33, 44, 85–6, 231, 306; factors involved in forecasting, 50, 85 ff.; measured in actual money terms, 89; composition of 'other services', 92–3; influence of military spending abroad, 96; current account (1964–9), 97; capital and other investment flows, 98; new presentation of statistics, 98; and I.M.F., 102; and individual firms, 102–3; recurrent crises, 106, 133, 233, 234, 243, 304; counterpart to deficiencies, 111, 112; emergence of a surplus (1970), 122; and Bank Rate, 127; and the Budget, 139; and interest rates, 307, 309; over-riding importance in business analysis, 317–18

Balance sheets, in acquisition studies, 315–16

Bank credits, and consumer demand, 22; an addition to personal incomes, 46, 193–4; influence on supply of money, 108; variation in rise and fall, 120–21; ratio to deposits, 122, 123; adoption of more flexible policy, 127–8

Bank deposits, by U.K. residents, 109, 110, 111, 118, 119; elements affecting

MORE ABOUT PENGUINS
AND PELICANS

Penguinews, which appears every month, contains details of all the new books issued by Penguins as they are published. From time to time it is supplemented by *Penguins in Print*, which is a complete list of all available books published by Penguins. (There are well over three thousand of these.)

A specimen of *Penguinews* will be sent to you free on request, and you can become a subscriber for the price of the postage. For a year's issues (including the complete lists) please send 30p if you live in the United Kingdom, or 60p if you live elsewhere. Just write to Dept EP, Penguin Books Ltd, Harmondsworth, Middlesex, enclosing a cheque or postal order, and your name will be added to the mailing list.

Note: *Penguinews* and *Penguins in Print* are not available in the U.S.A. or Canada

Pelican Library of Business and Management

COMPUTERS, MANAGERS AND SOCIETY

Michael Rose

'Here is a book on computers and computer technology written by a sociologist, and it is one of the very few which sets out clearly, simply and, even more important, objectively what computers are all about. It is also amusing . . .' – *New Society*

After a general survey of the development of computer-controlled data processing, Michael Rose examines the complex effects of the computer upon the clerical worker – the new opportunities, the dangers of alienation, the threat of technological unemployment. He then focuses upon the fast-developing problems of managers. Many of the standard managerial functions can already be programmed. But should executives delegate qualitative decisions to a machine? And if so, how far can and should these changes go?

'Computerization' presents managers with new opportunities on a structural scale unmatched since the Industrial Revolution. Do they really understand the new situation? Can they, when it is transforming itself so rapidly? And are we enough aware of the effects of the computer upon an even larger social group – society itself – now faced with the need to clarify its whole attitude to technological change?

'Knowledgeable, intelligent and clearly written' – *The Times Literary Supplement*

Pelican Library of Business and Management

MANAGEMENT THINKERS

Edited by A. Tillett, T. Kempner and G. Wills

'British management was backward by the end of the nineteenth century and, with notable exceptions, has never caught up.'

'The Ford Co. from October 1912 to October 1913 hired 54,000 men to maintain an average working force of 13,000. This was a labour turnover of 416 per cent for the year.

With observations like these this book vividly recalls and presents the problems of industry from the industrial revolution to the present day.

   Management Thinkers contains reading from the pioneers of management thought – Frederick Taylor, Henri Fayol, Seebohm Rowntree, Mary Parker Follett, Elton Mayo and C. I. Barnard.

   The problems of industry are the problems of today. This is a history of how these problems have been tackled in the past, together with a careful assessment of the contribution the management thinkers have made to the world we live in now.

Pelican Library of Business and Management

PROGRESS OF MANAGEMENT
RESEARCH

Edited by Nigel Farrow

'Management research', writes Nigel Farrow, 'is science's Oliver Twist: a delicate and neglected infant of obscure parentage, it has been suddenly claimed by various competing godfathers for reasons ranging from disinterested charity to commercial exploitation.'

This volume in the Pelican Library of Business and Management contains ten articles which originally appeared as a series in *Business Management*. It is a sign of the fluid state of management studies that the contributors include professors of marketing, business administration, industrial psychology, operational research, and industrial and management engineering, as well as economists and consultants. Covering the functional areas of production, personnel, finance, and marketing, they indicate the debt owed by business research to economics, mathematics, psychology, and sociology.

It remains a question whether management research does better to be wide, general, and abstract (a pursuit for academic cloisters); or specific, local, and concrete (an exercise for the oil-grimed shop). But in any case the recent research outlined in these essays is constructive and practical and never loses sight of the manager on the spot.

MATHEMATICS IN MANAGEMENT

Albert Battersby

Sophisticated methods of planning, control, and decision-making, together with the advent of the electronic computer, have already brought mathematics well to the fore in modern industry and commerce. At the present rate of advance, mathematics will soon be an indispensable tool of the intelligent manager.

Mathematics in Management has been specially written, for managers and others, to provide a sound basis of knowledge about the methods of operational research now being applied in public industries and services, to save resources and prune expenditure. Some such account is urgently needed, since general education has not kept pace with advances in this field, and mathematicians have difficulty in 'talking' to managers.

Among the particular topics covered by Albert Battersby in this Pelican are network analysis, simple functions, linear programming, simulation, and electronic computers. The author employs a minimum of mathematical notation in his text and, wherever possible, makes his points with the help of drawings. He has also included a set of exercises with full solutions.

Also available

SALES FORECASTING

(*Not for sale in the U.S.A.*)